Making Choices for Multicultural Education

Five Approaches to Race, Class, and Gender

Christine E. Sleeter
California State University, Monterey Bay

Carl A. Grant
University of Wisconsin–Madison

WILEY

JOHN WILEY & SONS, INC.

To Roberta, Ellen, and Ron
and Carl and Alicia

VICE PRESIDENT & PUBLISHER	Jay O'Callaghan
EXECUTIVE EDITOR	Christopher Johnson
AQUISITION EDITOR	Robert Johnston
SENIOR PRODUCTION EDITOR	Sandra Dumas
EXECUTIVE MARKETING MANAGER	Jeffrey Rucker
CREATIVE DIRECTOR	Harry Nolan
DESIGNER	Hope Miller
COVER PHOTO	©George B. Diebold/Corbis Images
MEDIA EDITOR	Sasha Giacoppo
EDITORIAL ASSISTANT	Katie Melega
PRODUCTION MANAGEMENT SERVICES	Hermitage Publishing Services

This book was set in 10/12 Palatino by Hermitage Publishing Services and printed and bound by R. R. Donnelley/Crawfordsville. The cover was printed by Phoenix Color Corporation.

This book is printed on acid-free paper. ∞

Library of Congress Cataloging in Publication Data:

Sleeter, Christine, E. Grant, Carl A.
Making Choices for Multicultural Education: Five Approaches to Race, Class, and Gender

ISBN-13 978-0-471-74658-4
ISBN-10 0-471-74658-4

Printed in the United States of America

10 9 8 7 6 5 4 3 2 1

Preface

Our primary reason for writing *Making Choices for Multicultural Education: Five Approaches to Race, Class, and Gender* was to offer the educational community a way of thinking about race, language, culture, class, gender, and disability in teaching. Editions subsequent to the first were also written to serve as a major voice, a repository of references and resources, in the multicultural debates that have ensued since the publication of the first edition in 1988. This fifth edition incorporates recent literature relevant to ongoing struggles and offers continued reflection on and insight into this evolving field of study and practice. More specifically, this edition includes recent demographics, discussion of equity issues in the context of the accountability movement and particularly *No Child Left Behind*, a recasting of the deficit ideology, some inclusion of religion, and research that connects culturally situated teaching and learning with student achievement.

For the first edition we reviewed over 200 articles and 60 books about multicultural education.[1] We have continued our review since then. This investigation is thorough, though not exhaustive, since publications about multicultural education are being released daily. The publications are in many disciplines and are aimed at students and educators at different levels of learning.

WHAT DO WE MEAN BY MULTICULTURAL EDUCATION?

People mean different things by the term *multicultural education*. For one thing, they do not always agree on what forms of diversity it addresses. Some people think only about racial or cultural diversity, whereas others conceptualize gender, social class, and additional forms of diversity. At the same time, many people who discuss gender equity, for example, share concerns similar to those of multicultural education advocates but virtually ignore race and culture. Still others

---

[1] C. A. Grant & C. E. Sleeter. The literature on multicultural education: Review and analysis, *Educational Review, 37* (1985), 97–118; C. A. Grant, C. E. Sleeter, & J. E. Anderson. The literature on multicultural education: Review and analysis, Part II, *Educational Studies, 12* (1986), 47–71; C. E. Sleeter & C. A. Grant, An analysis of multicultural education in the U.S.A., *Harvard Educational Review, 57* (1987), 421–444.

conceptualize multicultural education in relationship to issues of public policy, such as immigration (e.g., California's Taxpayers' Protection Act) and bilingualism (e.g., English Only legislation).

In this book we focus on multiple forms of difference that also define unequal positions of power in the United States. These include race, language, social class, gender, disability, and sexual orientation. We take the position that schools generally operate in ways that favor the "haves." In Chapter 1, we synthesize data about schooling and the wider social context to support this position. In subsequent chapters, we ask how schooling could work differently to treat diverse groups more equally. We synthesize research and theory underlying five approaches to what multicultural education could mean, and we illustrate these approaches with examples and vignettes, applying each approach to various forms of diversity.

Chapter 2 explores "Teaching the Exceptional and Culturally Different." Teachers who advocate this approach are concerned mainly about helping low-achieving students catch up and succeed in school so that they can "make it" in the mainstream of society. Teachers are not so concerned with criticizing or trying to change the mainstream itself, but rather with building bridges between children and that mainstream.

Chapter 3 examines the "Human Relations" approach, which focuses on improving affective dimensions of the classroom: how students relate to each other, how they feel about themselves, and how they feel about diverse groups in the community and society.

Chapter 4 concentrates on the "Single-Group Studies" approach. Teachers who use this approach teach about one specific group, or one group at a time, such as African Americans, Native Americans, women, or people with disabilities. The approach rests on a great deal of research and theorizing being done in departments of ethnic studies as well as gay and lesbian studies in higher education, making it more complex than many classroom teachers realize at first.

The "Multicultural Education" approach is the focus of Chapter 5. This is the approach long-time advocates of multicultural education have most discussed. It involves complete reform of the entire education process to reflect and support diversity, addressing dimensions of schooling such as curriculum, tracking and grouping, staffing, and testing. It also focuses on improving student achievement, but unlike Chapter 2, it supports the development of a culturally pluralistic mainstream that does not require assimilation for success.

Chapter 6 discusses "Multicultural Social Justice Education," which calls attention to equity issues and empowering young people to make social changes. Like the "Multicultural Education" approach, this one also involves reform of the entire education process, but it focuses much more explicitly on social critique and democratic citizen participation.

We believe that educators need to be very clear about what multicultural education means to them. What goals do they actually have in mind? What are their target student populations? What is their vision of society? What ideas do they have about how to achieve a better society? What assumptions do they make about learning? It is important for you, the reader, to be clear about your own beliefs so that you can achieve what you are attempting.

In Chapter 7, after sharing what we have learned about each of the other approaches, we explain the one we advocate. As objective as we tried to be in writing the first six chapters, we know that what people say and how they see the world are shaped by their ideology, background, and vision of the world. Our students want to know which approach we favor, and our readers probably will as well. Also, we know that the colleagues and students with whom we work are thoughtful people who are not easily persuaded, and most are capable of making up their own minds.

HOW TO USE THIS BOOK

We have found two different uses for *Making Choices for Multicultural Education*. Some people read it to gain an overview of the history and thinking behind multicultural education. Such readers often read the book quickly, pausing to reflect mainly on differences among the approaches. This text may be used in a course that includes one or two other books on issues related to multicultural education, providing students with a comprehensive overview of the field.

A second way to use the book is to spend time examining how to use each approach to multicultural education in the classroom. The companion text, *Turning on Learning* (published by John Wiley & Sons), can be very helpful and was intended to be used with this one. It is organized according to the same chapter plan as this text, but it provides examples of lesson plans using each approach. When using the books together, a student or teacher can read, for example, the theory behind the "Single-Group Studies" approach in Chapter 4 of *Making Choices*, then examine several lesson plans that illustrate the same approach in Chapter 4 of *Turning on Learning*. In addition to lesson plans, each chapter of *Turning on Learning* contains one or two action research activities, such as a textbook analysis instrument and a stereotyping quiz.

A teacher educator can structure an entire course around *Making Choices for Multicultural Education*. The book can be used alone, or it can be supplemented with other readings or texts. For example, you could spend several weeks in the semester examining various teaching strategies that help improve the achievement of low-income students and/or students of color, using Chapter 2 as a base and supplementing it with material about bilingual education or culture and cognitive style. Similarly, you could pair Chapter 6 ("Multicultural Social Justice Education") with readings on critical pedagogy and antiracist education.

We believe that *Making Choices for Multicultural Education: Five Approaches to Race, Class, and Gender* makes a vital contribution to the fields of multicultural education, gender studies, inclusive education, and critical teaching at an important time in the development of these concepts. Enjoy the fruit of our labor, and if you are inclined, please let us know what you think, for we enjoyed and learned from your comments regarding the previous editions, and we know that your thoughts will continue to help us to grow.

ACKNOWLEDGMENTS

We are grateful to the wide audiences that gave our first four editions of *Making Choices for Multicultural Education* a warm reception, making this fifth edition possible. This edition reflects events and our own growth, but it is largely similar to the earlier editions. Readers of earlier editions generally affirmed for us the validity of the ideas we developed; some also offered us critiques, compliments, and suggestions.

We would like to thank the students in our courses at the University of Wisconsin–Parkside, California State University Monterey Bay, and the University of Wisconsin–Madison in which we have used this book, for their helpful feedback. Their questions, reactions, and even difficulties with portions of the text helped us to make this edition stronger. Sincere appreciation is extended to Lisa Loutzenheiser for her excellent ideas about gay, lesbian, and bisexual issues. Super thanks go to Anthony Brown, Keffrelyn Brown, Peggy Morrison, and Kim Wieczorek for library research—accessing more recent resources—and insightful comments and contributions to the overall process. Great appreciation is extended to Kristen Buras for her illuminating ideas, patience, scholarship, and excellence throughout this revision, and much gratitude is offered to Jennifer Austin for the many ways she helped.

The following reviewers are acknowledged for their helpful suggestions and enthusiastic reception of this book: Alan Crawford, California State University–Los Angeles; Kathleen Sernak, Purdue University; and Frank Gulbrandsen, University of Minnesota–Duluth.

Brief Contents

Contents

CHAPTER ONE

Illusions of Progress: Business as Usual

Picture the following class: Of its 30 students (15 girls and 15 boys), 18 are White, 5 are African American, 5 are Latino (3 Mexican Americans, 1 Puerto Rican, and 1 Cuban American), 1 is American Indian, and 1 is second-generation Asian American. Two of the African American students, 2 Latino students, and 3 White students come from families that live below the poverty line, while another 3 White students are from upper-income homes. About three-quarters are from homes that identify as Christian; one is Jewish; and the remaining are from homes that are either nonreligious or members of another religion such as Islam or Buddhism. These distinctions are not readily visible, however, because most of the students are wearing jeans and cotton shirts or T-shirts. Nevertheless, a glance at home addresses and at the free-lunch roster indicates the students' socioeconomic status.

The students' families vary widely: Only 4 students come from families in which the father but not the mother works outside the home, 6 are from single-parent families (2 of which live below the poverty line), and both parents of the remaining 20 students hold or have recently held jobs at least part time. Most of the students grew up speaking English, but 3 of the Latino students speak Spanish at home and 1 White student speaks French at home. The students' academic skills vary widely: Two spend part of the day in a class for children with learning disabilities, another spends part of the day in a program for special needs students, 1 is in a program for gifted students, and 1 is in a speech therapy program.

How does a teacher teach such a wide variety of students? What sort of curriculum should be taught? Should all students be taught the same curriculum? What role do standards and annual exams play? What teaching strategies are used? How are students grouped for instruction, or are they grouped at all? How are they seated? You may find conflicting images forming in your head. Of these images, one may depict how you believe a teacher should teach these students, another may depict how you have seen a teacher whose class you observed teach these students, and yet another may depict how most teachers really do teach them.

We based our hypothetical class on statistics describing the composition of public schools in the United States in the first decade of the twenty-first century

(Hardy, 2003; Orfield & Lee, 2005; U.S. Department of Commerce, Bureau of the Census, 2004a; U.S. Department of Education. National Center for Educational Statistics, 2005; World Christian Encyclopedia, 2001). Actually, student composition varies widely across the country, even within the same city or the same school. But given the diversity of U.S. students, schools, and classrooms, the same questions persist. How do teachers actually teach their students, and how might students be taught better?

This book addresses these central questions. We recognize, however, that schools do not exist in a vacuum but are closely connected to the society they serve. Therefore, when considering what kind of education would best serve the United States' increasingly diverse student population, we need to consider the nature of the society in which schools exist. This chapter will first discuss briefly the nature of equity and diversity in society in the 2000s in relation to race, language, culture, sexuality, gender, social class, and disability. Then it will synthesize recent research to demonstrate how teachers actually teach America's diverse student population, and how education reform efforts are influencing teaching efforts. Finally, it will provide the framework used in subsequent chapters to address alternative approaches to teaching.

SOCIETY TODAY

It would seem that in some cases racism, sexism, and bias against people with disabilities may no longer be serious societal problems. Increasingly, White women and African American men and women are being elected mayors of large cities. Latino men and women are rising in the political structure; many Native Americans own businesses. In the 2004 elections, eight women took gubernatorial seats, a record of 69 women took seats in the U.S. House of Representatives, and 14 of the 100 senators were women. Latino, Asian American, and Native American political clout is growing as well.

In addition, African Americans have leading roles in television entertainment, and it is becoming rather commonplace to see people of color and both sexes reporting the news or hosting television programs in large urban television markets. One can think of additional illustrations of progress in the past decade. Women and people of color as astronauts are no longer big news; the U.S. Supreme Court has an active female member and its second African American justice, and the United States has its second African American Secretary of State.

These indications of progress obscure the larger picture, however. In this section, we will offer a statistical portrait of continued patterns of inequality and discrimination based on race, ethnicity, gender, sexual orientation, social class, and disability to complicate the depiction of continued progress that many people take for granted. There is considerable evidence that U.S. society is still very stratified on the basis of race, gender, sexuality, and disability. In fact, stratification based on socioeconomic status is a prominent feature of U.S. society, and social policy in the last four decades has had minimal impact on changing it.

Race and Ethnicity

Americans have been reminded repeatedly that the population of the United States is rapidly becoming more racially and ethnically diverse. In 2003, the U.S. population was 12.1% African American; 13.9% Latino; 4.3% Asian or Pacific Islander; 0.8% American Indian or Alaska Native, and 76.2% non-Latino White (U.S. Department of Commerce, Bureau of the Census, 2003). Between 2000 and 2003, over 3.6 million immigrants joined the U.S. population. These immigrants came from every part of the world. About a half million came from Europe, 0.2 million from Africa, and 1.2 million from Asia. The largest portion (about 45%) of immigrants, about 1.6 million, came from Latin America and the Caribbean, contributing to a social phenomenon being called "the hispanization of America" (U.S. Department of Homeland Security, 2003).

In addition to the official figures, population experts estimate that there were also approximately 10 million undocumented immigrants in the United States as of 2004. Roughly 60% are believed to have come from Mexico and another 20% from the rest of Latin America, bringing the Latino share of that total to 80%, or 8 million (Passell, 2005). Latino immigrants, most of them young adults in their prime child-bearing years, have birth rates twice as high as those of non-Latinos. Consequently, Latino population growth is driven both by immigration and by increases in the second generation. Historically, the vast majority of Latino immigrants lived in concentrated areas in the traditional Latino states of California, Texas, Illinois, New York, New Jersey, Florida, and New Mexico. Although Latino populations continue to grow in these states, since 1980 Latinos have increasingly dispersed throughout the United States, entering the workforce in a variety of industries, mainly agriculture, construction, manufacturing, and service. About half of the Latino population in 2004 lived in neighborhoods in which they were not the majority, and in "new settlement" states such as Arizona, Nevada, Georgia, North Carolina, Oregon, Virginia, Washington, and Massachusetts, where Latino population growth had been 130% from 1990 to 2000. States with an emerging Latino population, such as Nebraska and Kansas, produced smaller absolute numbers (increases of fewer than 200,000 between 1980 and 2000) but very high rates of growth (more than 200%) (Suro & Tafoya, 2004). It is estimated that Latinos will compose about 25% of the U.S. population by 2050.

With increased racial and ethnic diversity comes greater cultural, linguistic, and religious diversity. Eck (2002) points out that "The United States is the most religiously diverse nation in the world." Although Christianity is by far the largest religion, increasingly one finds "Islamic centers and mosques, Hindu and Buddhist temples," in addition to Jewish temples and more traditional churches. Furthermore, religious diversity is not limited to urban areas but increasingly is found in small towns throughout the United States.

This diversity enlarges the pool of cultural resources existing in the United States, while at the same time engendering misunderstanding and resentment. In addition, the growing racial and ethnic diversity of the United States underscores the urgent need for our nation to come to grips with racism. Whereas European immigrants had been able to blend in with the dominant population after a generation or two, non-Europeans continue to be visibly distinct from Euro-Americans and thus experience racism, a situation that causes disillusionment even among those who came to the United States full of hope and optimism.

Americans often cite improved racial attitudes as a sign of racial progress. According to 2004 Gallup polls, most Americans of all races say that they have close personal friends from other racial groups. Seventy-eight percent of Blacks and 61% of Latinos said that they would prefer to live in racially mixed neighborhoods, while only 57% of Whites agreed. Indeed, perceptions of racial equality in the United States vary significantly depending on the ethnicity of the respondent. The Gallup polls found that, although 61% of Whites are "satisfied with the position of Blacks and other minorities," only 44% of non-Whites are "satisfied." Seventy-seven percent of Whites felt that Blacks had equal job opportunities, while only 41% of Blacks felt that equal opportunities were available to their racial group. Similarly, 86% of Whites perceived that Blacks had equal opportunities for education and housing, while only 51% of Blacks perceived that equal education and housing opportunities were available (Carlson, 2004; Jones, 2004; Mazzuca, 2004).

Although the laws mandate equal opportunities for all, African Americans, Latinos, and Native Americans are still distinctly subordinate educationally, economically, and politically. While high school completion for African Americans in 2003 was 80%, only 17% completed a four-year college degree. High school completion rates for Latino students had only achieved 57% as of 2003, and 11% of Latino students graduated from four-year colleges. For White students, the rates were 85% and 28%, respectively (U.S. Department of Commerce, Bureau of the Census, 2004a). African Americans and Latinos earn consistently less than their White counterparts with the same level of education. White high school graduates earn a median annual income of $30,700, compared to $25,580 for Blacks and $25,500 for Latinos, a gap of 22%. White professionals with advanced degrees earn a median annual income of $60,320, whereas Blacks with the same educational level earn $51,220, and Hispanics $51,740 (U.S. Department of Labor, 2005a). These disparities extend to teachers. Latino teachers' average income is around $41,000 per year, compared with White teachers' $43,000 income (U.S. Department of Commerce, Bureau of the Census, 2004a). As Table 1-1 shows, education does not pay off equally for members of different racial groups; being White has measurable economic and employment advantages.

TABLE 1-1.
Earnings of Full-rime, Year-Round Workers, Age 25 and Older (2002)

Education Attained	Four Years High School	1–3 Years College	Bachelor's Degree
	Income Earned		
White	$28,145	$30,570	$52,470
Black	$22,823	$26,711	$42,285
Latino	$24,163	$26,459	$40,848

Source: U.S. Department of Commerce, Bureau of the Census (2004a), Table 215.

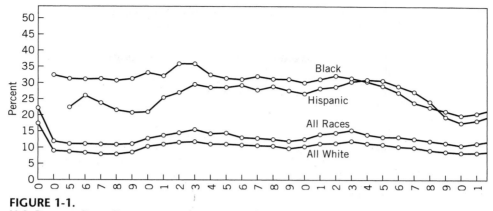

FIGURE 1-1.
U.S. Poverty Rate: Percentage of Persons Below Poverty Line
Source: U.S. Department of Commerce, Bureau of the Census. (2004a). Statistical abstract of the United States: 2004-2005. Washington, D.C.: U.S. Government Printing Office, Table 683.

People of color continue to experience poverty and unemployment dispro-portionately. Figure 1-1 shows the poverty rate from 1960 to 2002 for persons based on race. The trends it shows continue: In 2004, for example, Whites suffered poverty rates of 8.2%, Latinos, 22.5%, and Blacks, 24.4% (U.S. Department of Com-merce, Bureau of the Census, 2004a). Data on Native Americans are not reported as systematically as they are for other groups, but many tribes experience devas-tating poverty and unemployment. Native American household median income was $30,599 in 2000, compared to $44,687 for White American households (U.S. Department of Commerce, Bureau of the Census, 2004a). In 2000, the poverty rate for Native Americans was 25.7%, and Native American unemployment rates were estimated as high as 46% in 2004 (Center for Community Change, 2005).

Children are particularly hard hit by poverty (see Table 1-2). In 2002, 13% of White children were identified as living in poverty, compared with 32% of African American children and 28% of Latino children. Of those children living with female heads of household, 35% of White children, 48% of Black children, 30% of Asian American children, and 50% of Hispanic children lived in poverty (National Center for Health Statistics, 2004). Concentrated poverty matters, not only for the quality of life of children, but also for their school achievement. As Orfield and Lee (2005) point out, racial segregation and concentrated poverty tend to occur together. In the process, students who attend high-poverty schools have consider-ably less access to conditions that are part of a high-quality education (such as well-qualified teachers and a challenging academic curriculum) than students who attend affluent schools. We desperately need policies aimed at substantially reducing poverty and meeting basic human needs.

The gap in employment has not improved either. Whites continue to have the greatest access to available jobs. In 2005, the unemployment rate was 4.4% for Whites, 6.6% for Latinos, and 10.4% for Blacks (U.S. Department of Labor, Bureau

TABLE 1-2.
Children under 18 Living in Poverty: 1960–2002

| Year | Percentage of Children in Poverty | | | |
	White	Black	Hispanic	Total
1960	20.0	65.5	—	26.5
1965	14.4	47.4	—	20.7
1970	10.5	41.5	—	14.9
1975	12.5	41.4	34.5	16.8
1980	13.4	42.1	33.0	17.9
1981	14.7	44.2	35.4	19.5
1982	16.5	47.3	38.9	21.3
1983	17.0	46.2	37.7	21.8
1984	16.1	46.2	38.7	21.0
1985	15.6	43.1	39.6	20.1
1986	15.3	42.6	37.1	19.8
1987	15.0	45.1	39.3	20.0
1988	14.1	43.5	37.6	19.2
1989	14.1	43.2	35.5	19.0
1990	15.1	44.2	37.7	19.9
1991	16.1	45.6	39.8	21.1
1992	16.5	46.3	39.0	21.6
1993	17.0	45.9	39.9	22.0
1994	16.3	43.3	41.1	21.2
1995	16.2	41.9	40.0	20.8
1996	16.3	39.9	40.3	20.5
1997	16.1	37.2	36.8	19.9
1998	15.1	36.7	34.4	18.9
1999	13.5	33.1	30.3	16.9
2000	12.4	30.9	27.6	15.6
2001	12.8	30.0	27.4	15.6
2002	13.1	52.1	28.2	16.3

| Year | Percentage of Children in Poverty Living with Female Householder | | | |
	White	Black	Hispanic	Total
1960	21.0	29.4	—	23.7
1965	27.0	49.7	—	31.7
1970	36.6	60.8	—	45.8
1975	41.7	70.1	42.9	51.4
1980	41.3	75.4	47.1	52.8
1981	42.0	74.3	48.5	52.2
1982	—	—	—	—
1983	39.3	74.5	42.5	50.0
1984	41.8	74.9	47.2	52.4
1985	43.0	78.4	49.6	53.8
1986	45.7	80.5	49.5	56.6
1987	46.0	79.0	47.2	56.9
1988	49.7	78.4	48.7	58.7
1989	46.3	78.1	46.4	56.7
1990	46.9	80.3	47.8	57.9
1991	47.4	83.1	47.0	59.0
1992	43.2	79.1	37.5	55.3
1993	45.0	81.6	45.6	56.8
1994	46.4	82.2	45.6	57.7
1995	38.0	55.5	59.3	44.8
1996	38.9	52.8	61.2	44.3
1997	39.7	49.0	56.7	43.5
1998	35.7	48.9	53.2	40.9
1999	31.6	47.2	46.4	37.4
2002	22.6	35.8	35.3	26.5

Source: U.S. Department of Commerce, Bureau of the Census. (2004a). *Statistical, Abstract of the United States: 2004–2005*. Washington, DC: U.S. Government Printing Office, Tables 684 and 690.

of Labor Statistics, 2005b). In 2003, only about 72% of all recent African American high school graduates were employed, compared to about 89% of White recent high school graduates and 83% of White high school dropouts (U.S. Department of Commerce, Bureau of the Census, 2004a). There are several reasons for this phenomenon. Racial discrimination in hiring is one of them. Another reason for the employment gap is that, increasingly, jobs are not located where people of color live. After World War II, millions of people of color moved to urban areas to take manufacturing jobs, which over the past two decades have been exported by the thousands to Third World countries. This has left many people in inner-city areas with reduced access to jobs except for service jobs that pay minimum wage. Even the export of technology jobs, which hurts technically trained workers in the United States, has hit well-educated workers of color. As the Coalition for Fair Employment in Technology (2004) points out, "When high technology jobs are shifted from the United States, it robs the fastest growing segment of highly-skilled black workers and entrepreneurs from the opportunity to grow."

Job openings increasingly are located in suburban areas, which are populated more by White families than by families of color. Housing in the United States is still very segregated by both race and class (Orfield & Lee, 2005). People of color find it more difficult than Whites to relocate because of housing discrimination. When people of color are matched with White home-seekers on factors such as income and family size, over half the time the White home-seekers are given more options and better chances to locate housing. In the 2000s, housing discrimination practices are subtle but pervasive. Researchers in several cities have documented the practice of denying the availability of rental housing to callers with accents that can be identified as Black English Vernacular or Chicano English (Purnell, Idsardi, and Baugh, 1999).

As a result of differential access to jobs, housing, and health institutions, other estimates of quality of life vary according to race. For example, in 2002, 85% of White Americans were covered by health insurance, while 83% of Asian Americans, 81% of African Americans, 66%, of Latino Americans, and 61% of American Indians and Alaska Natives were similarly insured. The percentage of all Americans without health insurance rose from 16.3% in 1998 to 17% in 2002. Moreover, as Figure 1-2 shows, Whites enjoy a longer life expectancy than Americans of color. In 2002, for instance, the life expectancy of the Black male at birth was age 69, compared to 75 years for the White male (National Center for Health Statistics, 2004). Native Americans are especially short-changed on life span, the average life expectancy being 2.5 years less than that of other groups of color (U.S. Department of Health and Human Services, 2001). As life expectancy for the general population increases, a racial gap persists.

People of color are also more likely than Whites to be imprisoned. Research on incarceration rates through the 1990s indicates that an estimated 28% of Black males will enter state or federal prison during their lifetime, as compared to 16% of Latino males and 4.4% of White males (U.S. Department of Justice, 2002). In 2004, jail inmates were 43.2% Black, 18.9% Latino, and 2.2% other races, while only 35.7% were non-Latino White (Harrison & Beck, 2005). Furthermore, as of January

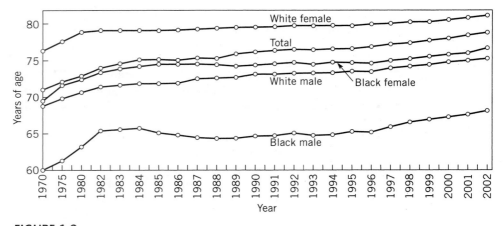

FIGURE 1-2.
Life Expectancy at Birth

Source: Data from U.S. Center for Health Statistics, U.S. Department of Health and Human Services, *Vital Statistics of the United States, Annual, and Monthly Vital Statistics Reports.* Washington, DC: U.S. Government Printing Office; National Center for Health Statistics (2004).

1, 2005, of the 3,455 prisoners under sentence of death, 1,444 (or 42%) were Black, 356 (or 10%) were Hispanic, 39 (or 1%) were American Indian, 40 (or 1 %) were Asian, and 1,576 (46%) were White (with 1 listed as "other") (Fins, 2005). These prison statistics are especially alarming when contrasted with the percentages of each race in the overall U.S. population: Black 12%, Hispanic 14%, American Indian 1%, Asian 4%, and White 76%.

People of color are also still locked out of much of the political system, even though increasing numbers of them are now big-city mayors. Although the political representation of particular gender and racial groups in the House of Representatives and Senate has increased over time, such increases are minimal. Only five African Americans have ever been elected to the U.S. Senate. Through 2004 there have been only five African American, five Asian American, five Hispanic, and three Native American senators in the history of the U.S. Senate. The rest of the U.S. senators throughout history have been White Americans. In the 109th Congress there were one African American and two Latino Senators (U.S. Senate Historical Office, 2005). Out of 435 members of the House of Representatives, 40 (9%) were African American, 22 were Latino (5%), 4 were Asian American (0.9%), and 2 (0.5%) were Native American, though these groups represent significantly larger percentages of the overall U.S. population (Ethnic Majority, 2004).

In sum, by every major indicator discussed above, in terms of education, economic status, jobs, health care, housing, and political power, privilege for people of European descent continues to be institutionalized in United States society.

Gender

Women, too, are still distinctly subordinate, both economically and politically, in spite of recent gains. Women are participating in the labor market in ever-growing

TABLE 1-3.
The Wage Gap over Time: Earnings of Full-time Female Workers Compared to Each Dollar Earned by Full-time Mate Workers (1955–2003)

Year	Female Earnings per Dollar of Male Earnings	Year	Female Earnings per Dollar of Male Earnings
1955	63.9¢	1985	68.2¢
1959	61.3¢1	1986	69.2¢
1960	60.8¢	1989	68.0¢
1962	59.5¢	1990	71.0¢
1965	60.0¢	1991	74.3¢
1967	57.8¢	1992	75.8¢
1970	59.4¢	1993	77.1¢
1972	57.9¢	1994	76.4¢
1973	56.6¢	1995	75.4¢
1975	58.8¢	1996	75.0¢
1977	58.9¢	1997	74.5¢
1979	59.6¢	1998	76.3¢
1980	60.2¢	1999	73.1¢
1981	59.2¢	2000	74.9¢
1982	61.7¢	2001	75.8¢
1983	63.8¢	2002	76.4¢
1984	67.8¢	2003	76.3¢

Source: U.S. Department of Commerce, Bureau of the Census (2005).

numbers. However, the earnings of full-time working women are only about 80% the earnings of full-time working men (U.S. Department of Labor, 2004a). This wage gap has fluctuated over the last three decades and appears to be shrinking as women enter male-dominated fields (Table 1-3). As Table 1-4 shows, this gap exists between men and women who have attained the same levels of education.

One major institutional factor perpetuating this situation is that, in both managerial and professional occupational groups, women and men tend to work

TABLE 1-4.
Average Earnings of Full-time Workers, by Educational Attainment and Sex (2002)

Education	Average Earnings	
	Men	Women
Not high school graduate	$22,092	$13,459
High school graduate	32,673	21,141
Some college, no degree	36,869	22,292
Associate's degree	42,392	27,341
Bachelor's degree	63,503	37,909
Master's degree	73,629	47,368
Professional	138,827	61,583
Doctorate	99,607	66,426

Source: U.S. Department of Commerce, Bureau of the Census (2004a), Table 215.

TABLE 1-5.
The Wage Gap between Full-time, Year-Round Working Men and Women (2002)

	Men's Earnings	Women's Earnings	Women's Earnings as % of Men's
Management, business, and financial occupations	$59,716	$41,276	69%
Professional and related occupations	56,438	40,080	62%
Service occupations	26,105	20,008	71%
Sales and office occupations	37,400	26,950	66%
Natural resources, construction, and maintenance	32,618	25,901	59%
Production, transportation, and material moving occupations	31,144	21,907	69%

Source: U.S. Department of Commerce, Bureau of the Census (2004a), Table 624.

in different specific occupations and women are concentrated in low-paying occupations. Women are making substantial inroads into some high-paying, traditionally male occupations, such as law. Nevertheless, as recently as 2003, most female workers were still concentrated in low-paying "pink-collar" ghettos. In professional and related occupations, women were much less likely than men to be employed in some of the highest paying fields, such as engineering and computer and mathematical occupations. Instead, women were more likely to work in lower paying professions, such as education, training, and library occupations (U.S. Department of Labor, 2004a). For example, in 2003, only 27% of lawyers were women, but 84% of paralegals and office clerks were women. In management, only 23% of chief executives and 28% of general and operations managers were women, while 65% of education administrators and 71% of health service managers were women. Eighty percent of social workers, 82% of K–12 teachers, and 92% of nurses were women, while 90% of engineers, 55% of college professors, and 70% of physicians were men. In food service, 80% of head chefs were men, and 72% of food preparation and service workers were women. In sales, men held most of the management positions, and women held most of the positions as cashiers and clerks (U.S. Department of Commerce, Bureau of the Census, 2004a). In addition, the median weekly earnings of women in these occupations and others were less than those of men (Table 1-5).

As women increasingly become heads of households, this persistent wage gap contributes heavily to the pauperization of women and children. In 2002, 26.5% of single-parent female-headed households were in poverty, compared with 12.1% of single-parent male-headed households. In 2002, while the average married-couple family earned $61,254, and the average single male parent earned $41.711, the average single female head of household earned only $29,001. In 2002, 26.5% of all female-headed households lived below the poverty line, with higher percentages of 35% in Black and Hispanic female-headed households (U.S. Department of Commerce, Bureau of the Census, 2004a).

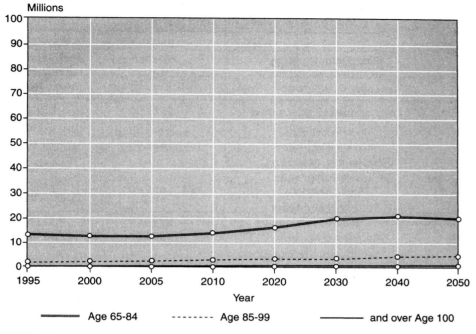

FIGURE 1-3.
Growth in the Elderly Population
Source: U.S. Department of Commerce, Bureau of the Census, *Statistical Abstracts of the United States* (2000). Resident population by age and sex, 1980 to 1999. Washington, DC: U.S. Government Printing Office, 2000, Table 12, p. 13.

This situation heavily affects children. Women are given custody of children in about 84% of divorce cases and often must attempt to support the family on a low-wage budget. In 2002, 16% of all children, 32% of Black children, and 28% of Hispanic lived in poverty. In addition, children represent a declining proportion of the population, whereas the elderly represent a rising proportion (Figure 1-3). U.S. Census Bureau population projections estimate that while the proportion of the population under 18 in 2005 is 18% and the population of those over 65 is 12%, by 2050 the proportion of children will remain approximately constant, while the proportion of elderly will rise to 21% (U.S. Department of Commerce, Bureau of the Census, 2004a). One implication of this demographic shift, according to the National Commission on Children (1991), is that "each worker will bear a greater burden of support for the nation's retirees" (p. 5).

The influx of women into the labor market is taking another toll on women as well. Because housework and childcare continue to be regarded as women's responsibilities, most husbands do not yet assume an equal share of these roles, although they share more now than they did 20 years ago. Consequently, married women who hold jobs are finding themselves with less and less leisure time. So, professional women have fewer opportunities to move up than men. Isn't it also true that because of increasing poverty and decreasing middle-class status, few women have the luxury of being homemakers or choosing to work shorter hours? One of the quality-of-life privileges denied to poor families is being with their children.

Violence against women is another manifestation of women's devalued status in society. The National Violence Against Women Survey of 2000 found that 25% of all women reported physical abuse by an intimate partner and that only about one-fourth of these incidents are reported to the police (Tjaden & Thoennes, 2000). Many women regard violence against women as a power issue, the act of beating representing an attempt to reaffirm women's subordinate status.

The political position of women has improved somewhat but is still no better than their economic position. Although greatly increasing numbers of women have been elected to local and state offices, women still constitute only a small minority of officeholders at the state level and an even smaller minority at the national level. There have been only 25 women governors in U.S. history. In 2005, only eight (16%) governors were women. No women of color have ever been governor of a U.S. state. Of the 7,382 people serving in state legislatures in 2005, 1,647 (22.3%) were women; 298 (4%) were women of color. Just 14 of the mayors of America's largest 100 cities were women. Although 37 (15.2%) of the 243 cities with populations over 100,000 had women mayors in 2005, only 8 were women of color.

In 2005, women held 14 Senate seats (14%) and 59 seats in the House of Representatives (13.6%). In total, 73 of the 535 members of Congress (both houses) were women (13.6% overall). All 14 women senators were White, with only one woman of color ever elected to the Senate, Carol Moseley Braun from Illinois. Women of color constitute 3.4% of the total 535 members of Congress, remaining woefully underrepresented politically.

As of December 2003, the United States ranked sixtieth in the world in terms of women's representation in national legislatures or parliaments out of over 180 directly electing countries. There has been limited growth in women's participation in politics in the United States since the press proclaimed "the year of the woman" in 1992, while other countries seek ideas and implement democratic change nationally and through political parties to increase the number of women in politics (The White House Project, 2005).

As women gained ground in both the political sphere and the job market during the late 1970s and 1980s, a backlash grew—one that many women regard as a move to keep women in their place domestically and to protect male access to better-paying jobs. Observing this reaction, Wolf (1991) analyzed the growth of the beauty industry, arguing that the media were projecting an increasingly thin and "perfect" beauty image to women, who were responding by becoming increasingly obsessed with losing weight and changing how they looked. She reported, for example, that 90% of young American women believed they weighed too much, 5% to 10% were anorexic, and most would rather lose 10 to 15 pounds than achieve any other goal in life.

Anorexia nervosa was not officially classified as a psychiatric disorder until 1980. It is, however, a growing problem among adolescent females. Its incidence in the United States doubled between 1970 and 2000. Estimates of the incidence of anorexia range between 0.5 and 1% of female adolescents. Over 90% of patients diagnosed with the disorder as of 1998 were female. Recent studies indicate that anorexia is increasingly common among women of all races and social classes in the United States. Anorexia nervosa is a serious public health problem not only because of its rising incidence, but also because it has one of the highest mortality rates of any psychiatric disorder. The rising incidence of anorexia is thought to reflect the idealization of thinness as a badge of upper-class status as well as of female beauty (Frey, 2002). The American Anorexia/Bulimia Association estimated 1,000 deaths a year from anorexia nervosa (National Mental Illness Screening Project, 1996). Wolf traces this obsession with beauty to profit-making beauty industries, beauty requirements for some careers (such as television reporting), and media images that are sold to women.

Sexual Orientation

As the political and social climates have improved for women, there has also been some improvement for gay men, lesbians, and bisexual men and women. Issues surrounding sexual orientation have been brought into the public eye, particularly since the 1969 Stonewall Riots in New York City. Stonewall is considered a turning point in the modern fight for gay, lesbian, and bisexual rights because it was one of the first incidents in which gay men, transsexuals, and lesbians fought back when harassed by the police. In the ensuing years, gay, lesbian, bisexual, and transgendered people worked to frame sexual orientation not as an illness, but rather as a struggle for civil rights.

In many ways, it has grown easier for the estimated 10% of the population who is gay, lesbian, or bisexual to be "out," yet prejudice and discrimination still exist. A major debate in the 2004 presidential election focused on gay marriage. Right-wing politicians proposed a constitutional amendment to "outlaw" gay marriage at the same time that some states took steps toward legalizing it. "Gay marriage" became a symbol for dividing our society between the "moral" and "immoral" as religion played an increasing role in politics. The United States has no federal law protecting the rights of gay men, lesbians, and bisexual men and women, and many states still have laws on their books outlawing "homosexual conduct." This lingering prejudice has a profound effect on children who come from homes and families headed by homosexual caretakers. In school, these students often feel threatened or reluctant to discuss their home life with friends and the teacher.

Although many gay, lesbian, bisexual, and transgendered (GLBT) youth find little conflict in terms of their own sexual orientation, others are not so fortunate. Overall, gay, lesbian, and bisexual youth compare favorably with heterosexually identified adolescents in regard to resilience, reactions to distress, or insecurities (Herdt & Boxer, 1993). However, a national study of suicide risk among gay and lesbian youth confirms previous reports that gay and lesbian youth are more likely to attempt suicide as compared to other adolescents (Russell & Joyner,

2001). The study found that gay and lesbian youth were twice as likely to attempt suicide, 1.7 times as likely to abuse alcohol, and also more likely to be affected by depression and a family member or friend's suicide attempt, and more likely to have been victimized.

GLBT youth have a greater incidence of homelessness than heterosexual youth. Several studies have indicated the severity of this problem. Kruks (1991) indicated that the Los Angeles County Task Force on Runaway and Homeless Youth reported that approximately 25 to 35% of their youth were GLB. Similarly, he reported that the Seattle Commission on Children and Youth estimated that 40% of their homeless youth were GLB. These figures are much higher than the estimated population of homosexuality in the United States, probably about 2 to 5% (Diamond, 1993). Such youth suffer from health issues of poor living conditions, malnutrition, lack of medical care, and increased rates of violence.

Social Class

The United States is distinctly stratified by social class and appears to be becoming more so. Although debates about racism and sexism have always existed, and in the last three decades have been quite plentiful, Americans have devoted much less attention to social class stratification. Yet there are tremendous inequities in the distribution of wealth. According to the U.S. Department of Congress, Census Bureau (2004a), while the wealthiest fifth of the U.S. population's share of income rose from 44% of the total in 1973 to 50% in 2002, everyone else's share fell. According to Ulrich (2004), "One percent of Americans now own not quite 50 percent of the national wealth."

In other words, more and more Americans have been downwardly mobile over the past three decades, and the gap between the wealthiest Americans and the majority has widened. Part of this downward mobility has taken the form of workers losing a job, and then either not finding another one or finding another job that pays less or that is not full time. For example, between 2001 and 2003 a total of 11.4 million workers were displaced, over a million more than in the previous two years. Two-thirds of displaced workers had found new jobs by January 2004; 20% were unemployed, and 13% had left the labor force. Of those who were reemployed, only 43% were earning as much as they had previously (U.S. Department of Labor, Bureau of Labor Statistics, 2004b).

As a result, the proportion of people lacking access to basics such as health care, food, and housing has been increasing. In 2003, the official poverty rate was 12.5%, or 35.9 million people, a steady increase over the past three years (U.S. Department of Commerce, Bureau of the Census, 2004b). Although people of color are disproportionately impoverished, about half of those below the poverty line are White. In 2003, 15.6%, or 45 million people, lacked health insurance. This proportion has been inching upward, partly because minimum wage jobs do not offer health insurance and because increasingly better-paying jobs are also cutting health insurance (U.S. Department of Commerce, Bureau of the Census, 2004b).

As poverty is increasing, so are requests for food assistance. In 2000, officials in major cities reported that requests for food assistance had increased by

17% over the previous year, with families including children representing about two-thirds of those seeking assistance. Officials attributed the growing inability to pay for food to the increase of low-paying jobs, soaring housing costs, and unemployment. They also reported increased demand for emergency shelter, attributing the growing homelessness largely to lack of affordable housing (Headley & Lowe, 2000).

Although the United States is a relatively wealthy nation, it has not been able to rid itself of poverty. Many find it tempting to blame the poor themselves for poverty, arguing that the unemployed do not want to work. However, our economy sustains an unemployment rate that rarely falls below 7%. This statistic means that there are not enough jobs to go around and that 7% of Americans actively seeking work are unable to find it; this figure does not include those who have given up and have stopped looking. We speculate that as wealthy Americans live further and further away from those who are poor, and as those who are poor become increasingly diverse, those with wealth are increasingly less aware of those in poverty and feel increasingly less responsibility to do anything about it. Ironically, however, it is not those who are poor who are outsourcing jobs or cutting benefits, but rather those who have enough money to invest in businesses, who demand an increase in profits.

Three decades ago, Harrington (1984) argued that there was a growing gap between rich and poor in the United States and that the middle class was shrinking as a result of changes in the economic structure:

> People who, twenty or even ten years ago, were secure in their jobs and communities now live somewhere between poverty and semiaffluence, walking the edge of an economic precipice. Their problems will be ameliorated, but far from ended, by economic recovery, if this really does come. For they, or people like them, are likely to face downward social mobility for twenty or thirty years, unless this country turns around. These are not, then, the instant "new poor" that the media discovered in that winter of American discontent, 1982–83. (p. 64)

Almost a decade later, with the U.S. economy still operating at a subpar level, Hacker (1992) pointed out in *Two Nations* that the economic situation for many was still very dismal. He observed that many who had jobs were employed for less than a full day's work or for only part of the year. He also disclosed that in addition to the number of men and women who were officially recorded as unemployed, at least an equal number had given up the search for a job. Because of the inability of these people to find work, the Bureau of Labor Statistics has created a category called "discouraged worker" (p. 105). Rather than facing this growing polarization of U.S. society, we have allowed it to continue to grow.

Disability

People with disabilities, who total about 55 million Americans, constitute a subordinate group. Historically, public concern for their welfare has risen and fallen. With the passage in 1990 of the Americans with Disabilities Act, it is hoped that public concern will remain active, but if history is an accurate guide, this concern may wane. Federal and state laws for disabled people do make a difference in that they offer greater protection for the rights of people with disabilities and they demand that support services be expanded. However, laws and services on behalf of people with disabilities are usually made by nondisabled people and often are not as comprehensive as people with disabilities would recommend. Furthermore, disabled people as a group are overrepresented in the ranks of the poor, and they are somewhat invisible as an impoverished group because statistics on their employment and income are not widely kept and published.

Most disabled adults are either unemployed or employed part time, and their earnings are often below the poverty level. In 1998, only 31.2% of disabled high school graduates were employed—only a 2% increase since 1972 (U.S. Department of Labor, Bureau of Labor Statistics, 1998). While about 79% of nondisabled people work full time, only about 29% of people with disabilities do so. Furthermore, the average income of people with disabilities is substantially lower than it is for nondisabled people (Bergstrom, 1999). Unemployment and poverty are particularly severe among disabled people of color, who face double discrimination in the job market.

People with disability lack access to facilities and the opportunities that those without disabilities enjoy. For example, zoning laws restrict locations of homes for deinstitutionalized people with mental retardation. Blind, deaf, and physically impaired people have legal rights to public facilities, but in practice they find it difficult or impossible to get around in many buildings, communicate with public service workers, or use certain public channels of communication. The *Americans with Disabilities Act* (1990) is supposed to remove these barriers, and it helps to the extent that it is followed and people are aware of it. An article in *The Disability Rag*, a disability activist publication, pointed out that the act "drew national attention to the fact that the problems disabled people face are primarily discrimination—not health—problems" (The Americans with Disabilities Act, 1991, p. 11). However, many people working on the act's implementation still treat those with disabilities as incapable persons rather than as intelligent collaborators.

Moreover, opposition to the act is mounting because of the costs it will incur. For example, Johnson (2005) reviewed two pieces of legislation in California that were backed by business groups that would make it more difficult for people with disabilities to sue for access violations. She pointed out that "Instead of obeying access laws, businesses have chosen the curiously mean-spirited approach of ignoring calls for access, ignoring informative seminars, ignoring laws on the books," and then taken measures to stop people with disabilities when they sue.

In addition, the Americans with Disabilities Act does not resolve certain issues. For example, it specifies that housing is to be accessible, but many builders are not familiar with or interested in accessibility (Johnson, 1991), and the legislation does not address the scarcity of low-cost housing. Chicago's Access Living, for example, referred people with disabilities to housing but ran out of low-cost housing to which they could refer them, partly because the federal funds for low-income housing have been slashed drastically ("No housing," 1990). In addition, people with disabilities are often targets of violence and hate crimes. "Data about rape, child sexual abuse, incest, sexual harassment, battery, neglect, defamation, and other forms of violence directed at disabled people indicate that they are much more likely to be targeted for violence than their nondisabled cohorts" ("Hate," 1992, p. 5).

BUSINESS AS USUAL

Before we discuss approaches that teachers can take to deal constructively with diversity and inequities, it is important to describe what often occurs in classrooms and schools. Schools are a reflection of the society to which they belong. Just as a few improvements in society may give an incomplete or inaccurate view of progress in reducing racism, sexism, class bias, and bias against disabilities, a few improvements in our schools are similarly misleading. In many schools, one can readily observe students of color and White students socializing; girls in classes such as woodshop and autoshop, once considered the exclusive domain of the boys; boys in family/consumer studies classes, once considered no-man's land; teachers and students speaking Spanish in mathematics classes; and students in wheelchairs attending proms and participating in many other school events. Also, in some schools the cheering squad, band, and sports teams reflect the diversity of the student body. Moreover, in integrated schools it is not unusual for a person of color to be the president of the student council, a class officer, or a member of the homecoming queen's court.

Furthermore, most teachers and school administrators support equal opportunity and access to all courses and activities for all students enrolled in the school. They support events that recognize the contributions of people of color and women; many welcome mainstreamed special education students into their classes; most will not tolerate sexist behavior in the classroom; and virtually all support having students from different socioeconomic strata attend the same school. Also, many teachers examine their curriculum materials for bias, are willing to attend workshops dealing with multicultural education, and try to avoid using any instructional materials that are obviously biased.

These examples suggest that success for all students is the order of business in classrooms and schools. To the discerning observer, however, much has been left out. Like the society we described earlier, schools are beset with equity problems.

Our description of "business as usual" is based on studies published during the 1990s and 2000s in which researchers observed what actually takes place in the schools. We will describe major patterns that emerge. We acknowledge that schools and classrooms vary, although those that vary significantly are usually few and far between. We invite you to compare this description with schools that may be familiar to you. The description is organized into five categories: what teachers teach, how student learning is assessed, how teachers teach, how students are grouped, and student culture.

What Teachers Teach

What teachers teach is driven currently by the curriculum standards—textbook–test trilogy, the beginnings of which are often traced to *A Nation at Risk*

(National Commission on Excellence in Education, 1983), which framed the main purpose of schools as regaining U.S. economic competitive advantage internationally. Many reports published during the 1980s argued that U.S. students were increasingly failing to learn skills and knowledge the United States needs for international economic competition and that workers of tomorrow would need to master skill sets such as "technological visualization; abstract reasoning, mathematical, scientific, and computer expertise; knowledge of specific technologies and production techniques; [and] individual initiative" (Berliner & Biddle, 1995, p. 141). The 1980s also saw a wave of conservative critiques that charged multicultural curricula as being intellectually weak and as addressing minority student achievement by appealing mainly to self-esteem rather than hard work (e.g., Bloom, 1989; Ravitch, 1990; Schlesinger, 1992).

In response, in the 1980s states began to develop disciplinary content standards and testing programs. Because of philosophical disagreements over what all students should know within the disciplines, attempts to establish national content standards were not successful, although the National Council of Teachers of Mathematics (NCTM) established a set of mathematics standards that have subsequently been used by most states. Drafts of national standards documents informed states as they wrote their own content standards for the various subject areas. By the mid-1990s, most states had content standards in place. As a result, what students learn is similar from school to school and state to state.

Based on a study of 1,289 elementary teachers in various parts of the country, Moon, Brighton, and Callahan (2003) found a highly prevalent "belief that the standards, as operationalized by the state assessment, are the gospel, and most teachers feel unable to deviate from them. In many cases, this belief is validated by school and/or district policies, strictly monitored pacing guides, and/or administrative mandates." Glickman (2000/2001) characterized standardized curriculum as the institutionalization of a "single definition" of a well-educated person: rather than fostering a variety of perspectives and areas of expertise, increasingly students in the United States are being taught the same things, regardless of student or teacher interest.

States and school districts strive to match textbooks to standards so that students will be taught what they are tested on. Although 20 years ago discussions of diversity in textbooks were fairly common, many educators today assume that curricula are now sufficiently multicultural and that this is no longer an important issue. One has only to thumb through a text today to see people of different ethnic backgrounds and both sexes. Yet, based on a historical analysis of textbook controversies, Zimmerman (2002) observed that we now have "a history of many colors but one idea, culturally diverse yet intellectually static" (p. 15). Texts vary in their quality of representation of diverse group, but one still finds common patterns.

Whites receive the most attention and appear in the widest variety of roles, dominating story lines and lists of accomplishments. African Americans, the next most represented racial group, occupy a more limited range of roles and less attention historically. Asian Americans and Latinos appear mainly in the background with virtually no history or contemporary ethnic experience. Native Americans appear mainly in the past, and Arab Americans are not only generally absent (Jacobs, 1981), but also are ignored in textbook analyses. Texts say very little about contemporary race relations or racial issues, usually sanitizing greatly what they mention (Byrne, 2001; Clawson, 2002; Foster, 1999; Loewen, 1995; Marquez, 1994; Sleeter & Grant, 1991).

Most texts have successfully eliminated most sexist language. However, males are usually represented more than females. Females appear in both traditional and nontraditional roles, although some texts develop nontraditional roles much more than others. Topics in texts, particularly in social studies, come from male more than female experiences, and texts generally ignore sexism issues of both today and historically (Foley & Boulware, 1996; Humphreys, 1997; Jones et al., 1997; Koza, 1994; Sleeter, & Grant 1991). Gay and lesbian people are virtually invisible (Hogben & Waterman, 1997). Many texts use gender-neutral language to refer to marriage partners, but because several state propositions now define marriage as only between a man and a woman, some publishers are changing the gender-neutral language to heterosexual language (e.g., from "marriage partners" to "husband and wife").

In general, texts suggest that the United States is not class stratified, that almost everyone is middle class, and that people have not struggled over distribution of wealth. Furthermore, texts often link poverty with people of color, particularly in illustrations (Clawson, 2002; Loewen, 1995; Sleeter & Grant, 1991). Disability is addressed in only a few textbook analyses (Sleeter & Grant, 1991; Taub & Fanflik, 2000), which have found people with disabilities very underrepresented and information about disability scarce.

Appropriate curriculum for linguistic minority students has been an ongoing issue. Since the U.S. Supreme Court decision in *Lau v. Nichols* (1974), schools have been required to provide help in learning English as well as instruction in the student's language while the student is learning English. Under business as usual, this has meant providing bilingual or English as a Second Language (ESL) instruction for as short a time as possible until the student achieves minimal English proficiency. While a significant bilingual education movement developed programs and strategies to meet the needs of linguistic minority students, particularly in the Southwest and Northeast, debates at the federal level between 1980 and 2000 revolved around how to teach English most effectively rather than how to promote bilingualism.

Federal policy for language-minority students learning English changed dramatically with passage of *No Child Left Behind* (NCLB) in 2001. Federal law requiring access to native language instruction was eliminated. In its place, Title III, which focuses exclusively on English acquisition, eliminated recognition of the benefits of bilingual education and bilingualism, issues of cultural differences and the needs for multicultural understanding, and acknowledgment of factors that have negatively impacted the education of students learning English (e.g., segregation, improper placement in special education, underrepresentation in gifted and talented education, and shortages of bilingual teachers). Federal policy is now aimed at ensuring that linguistic minority students "enter all-English instruction settings" (Wright, 2002, p. 80).

In sum, what teachers teach is increasingly being driven by federal and state policies that prescribe content and that are aimed toward cultural and linguistic assimilation, with some recognition of diversity but not necessarily diverse viewpoints.

How Student Learning Is Assessed

Student learning can be assessed in a variety of ways. Standardized assessment compares individual student scores either with those of other students of their same grade or age level (norm-referenced), or with prespecified levels of mastery (criterion referenced). High-stakes testing means that important decisions affecting students, such as whether they graduate or whether their school is considered effective, are made on the basis of one or a handful of standardized tests.

Authentic assessment, on the other hand, involves judging students' learning on the basis of the quality of their performance on real (authentic) learning tasks. Ryan (1994) explained, "Authentic assessment is the process of gathering evidence and documenting a student's learning and growth in an authentic context" (p. 1). Generally, "The student's work is compared to his or her previous work rather than compared to the work of others, in order to measure growth and progress" (p. 1).

Currently, assessment of student learning is being driven primarily by *No Child Left Behind*, which mandates that states receiving federal funding

> implement statewide accountability systems covering all public schools and students. These systems must be based on challenging State standards in reading and mathematics [science was added in 2005], annual testing for all students in grades 3–8, and annual statewide progress objectives ensuring that all groups of students reach proficiency within 12 years. Assessment results and State progress objectives must be broken out by poverty, race, ethnicity, disability, and limited English proficiency to ensure that no group is left behind. (U.S. Department of Education, 2001)

By school year 2013–2014, all students are to score at or above the proficient level established by their state. This requirement has pressed schools to use more standardized assessment and less authentic assessment.

States have responded somewhat differently, although most have put into place extensive state-mandated standardized testing systems. For example, California requires an extensive test battery be given to all students in grades 2–11, which includes criterion-referenced tests in English/language arts, math, science, and (at the secondary level only) history–social science. In addition, students in grades 2–8 are to take a norm-referenced test in reading, language, spelling, mathematics, and science. Furthermore, all tenth graders are required to take the criterion-referenced California High School Exit Examination in language arts and math, required for graduation beginning with the class of 2006. In Nebraska, by contrast, curriculum and assessment are controlled at the district level. The state monitors student assessment; most assessments are chosen and some are developed at the district level, with teacher participation. Standardized tests are part of the package but do not necessarily dominate.

According to the American Psychological Association (2005), the potential problem with the current increased emphasis on testing is not necessarily the tests per se but the instances when tests have unintended and potentially negative consequences for individual students, groups of students, or the educational system more broadly. Racial and ethnic minority students or students with a disability or limited English proficiency may be systematically excluded or disadvantaged by the test or the test-taking conditions, especially under NCLB, where schools whose students do not score well are stigmatized and sanctioned. The National Assessment of Educational Progress (NAEP) has consistently documented correlations between race, ethnicity, and parent income level and scores on standardized tests (U.S. Department of Education, 2003). White and higher income students have consistently scored higher than Hispanic, Black, and lower income students. For linguistic minority students who are learning English and are forced to take a test in a language in which they are not yet proficient, consequences are severe. In many schools that are under immense pressure to raise test scores and narrowly focus instruction on the test, instruction emphasizing the true needs of linguistically diverse and culturally diverse students is discouraged (Lipman, 2004; Wright, 2002).

Pressure on schools and educators to meet testing requirements mandated by NCLB has focused effort and attention on test preparation to the exclusion of other curriculum areas, and on test scores to the exclusion of multiple measures and definitions of intelligence and achievement. This is particularly the case in schools where student achievement is low, which tend to be high-poverty schools. There is growing concern that test-driven reforms are having a detrimental effect on students who historically have not been well served by schools in many school districts. For example, school administrators are reporting concern that minimum competency graduation exams, especially if imposed without additional resources, will lead students with disabilities to leave school without graduating (Manset-Williamson & Washburn, 2002). Use of exit exams for graduation tends to reduce graduation rates and increase the dropout rates of students of color, language-minority students, and students from poverty communities (Haney, 2000; Madaus & Clarke, 2001; Natriello & Pallas, 2001; Ruiz de Velasco, 2005).

Although tests are supposed to measure general achievement and learning, critics point out that scores on state content tests do not necessarily correlate with other established measures of student learning, such as advanced placement testing (Linn, Baker, & Betebenner, 2002; Shepard, 2000). For example, a study of data from 28 states found scant evidence to support the proposition that high-stakes tests—including graduation exams—increased student learning on measures other than the state achievement test (Amrein & Berliner, 2002). On the contrary, a comparison of student achievement on multiple independent measures of academic growth in states where high-stakes tests were used and those where such tests were not used suggests that high-stakes tests may actually inhibit the academic achievement of students rather than foster their academic growth.

Teachers cannot, by themselves, change testing policies that they believe are detrimental to their students. However, it is important for teachers to speak out about the effects of testing, whether those effects are positive or negative, and to learn to use classroom-based assessment processes to guide instruction, rather than becoming turned off to assessment altogether.

How Teachers Teach

One can distinguish between two quite different models of what it means to teach: teaching as telling and teaching as engaging students in making sense of academic concepts. In the first model, emphasis is on what the teacher does and students tend to be in a passive role; in the second, emphasis is on what the students do.

Historically, the first model has tended to dominate, although less so in elementary than secondary classrooms (Cuban, 1984; Goodlad, 1984). The pressure on teachers to teach tests appears to be intensifying the pattern of enacting teaching as telling. The accountability movement, driven top-down by political forces, increasingly has taken educational decisions out of the hands of educators, with the result being an increasing deprofessionalization of teachers. Johnson and Johnson (2002) found that as classrooms are caught up in the accountability craze, teachers are ordered to get students ready for the tests. Consequently, instruction concentrates on passing the test, often at the expense of the "total" child. In a study of 1,289 elementary teachers, Moon, Brighton, and Callahan (2003) found that teachers reduced their use of projects and other creative teaching strategies, and closely followed strictly monitored pacing guides, not because this results in better instruction but because it is what they are pressured to do.

Ironically, pressing schools into a testing mold pushes teachers away from offering the kind of active, engaged teaching that prompts the greatest learning. For example, Cohen and Lotan (2004) concluded that research shows that "the more students talk and work together, the greater their learning gains" (p. 739). Active, constructivist teaching is used much less in U.S. classrooms than in the nations that outscored U.S. students in the Third International Mathematics and Science Study (TIMMS). Wiggins and McTighe (2001) noted that U.S. teachers tend to present ideas, whereas teachers in Germany and Japan, two countries that outscore the United States, involve students in working with ideas.

Teaching to the test (and teaching how to take tests)—teaching as telling—is becoming a substitute for deeper intellectual inquiry, particularly in schools serving low-income students and students of color (Hillocks, 2002; Jones, Jones, & Hargrove, 2003; Kornhaber, 2004; Lipman, 2004; Madaus & Clarke, 2001; McNeil & Valenzuela, 2001; Meier, 2002). For example, in a comparison of four Chicago schools following test-driven accountability reform, Lipman (2003) found that only a minority of students were actually being prepared to become professionals and knowledge workers. "The majority, overwhelmingly students of color, are being prepared for skilled and unskilled low-wage sectors or pushed out of school altogether" (p. 342). The new accountability policies had not, in fact, improved the quality of teaching in poverty schools but had only altered the terms under which unequal education was being delivered.

The amount teachers are expected to do has a detrimental effect on teaching. During the school year 1993–1994, for example, the average hours worked by full-time teachers per week before and after school and on weekends ranged from 11 to 13 hours, depending on the nature of the school setting (U.S. Department of Education, 1996, p. 27, Table 48-1). Unfortunately, the overtaxing of teachers, lack of teaching and planning time, and classroom interruptions most directly impact students who are marginalized and can least afford it.

Another instructional problem that occurs in some classrooms is favoritism. Many teachers interact with, call on, praise, and intellectually challenge students who are White or Asian, male, and middle class more than other students in the same classroom. Teachers often reprimand Black male students the most. Some teachers give female students far less attention than male students, a pattern more prevalent with parent volunteers in the classroom than with teachers themselves. Observations of classrooms where gay students are present note that teachers more readily deal with racist and sexist name calling than with homophobic comments.

Antiracist educator Lee (2002) connects teachers' use of limited recall questions with who participates and who does not, and describes the resulting frustration of students who would like to participate if only interaction were structured to enable more to do so meaningfully:

> I cannot tell you the number of times that I have sat in classrooms where kids keep putting their hands up and, because the questioning stops as soon as the first person demonstrates the ability to recall, do not have the opportunity to participate. One time a student who was sitting next to me, after putting her hand up for every question, stamped in frustration and said, 'They never ask me!' Unfortunately the teacher heard only the stamping but not the statement that accompanied it. The student was reprimanded. (p. 30)

Many teachers resist these patterns (Berger, 2003; Sleeter, 2005), although they depend on administrative support to do so. But much of the usual classroom instruction discourages some students, turns off others, and fails to engage the minds of many. Moreover, students who tend to become turned off, disengaged, or frustrated are disproportionately lower-class students and students of color.

How Students Are Grouped

Within school districts, students are grouped in various ways that tend to reproduce unequal access to quality education. Many people today think that schooling is no longer segregated, but in fact, schools are becoming more and more so through a combination of race, class, and language. According to Orfield and Lee (2005), "Segregation has never just been by race: segregation by race is systematically linked to other forms of segregation, including segregation by socioeconomic status, by residential location, and increasingly by language" (p. 14). They go on to point out that "From an educational perspective, perhaps the most important of those linkages is with the level of concentrated poverty in a school" (p. 5).

White students are the most racially isolated or most likely to attend schools that are overwhelmingly populated by members of their own racial group. Furthermore, White and Asian students are far less likely than African American and Latino students to attend schools in which the majority of students live in poverty, although White rural poverty is also a stark reality. As Orfield and Lee (2005) point out, as a consequence of both residential and school segregation, "Black and Latino students are more than three times as likely as whites to be in high poverty schools and 12 times as likely to be in schools where almost everyone is poor" (p. 18). Furthermore, increased segregation of Latino students interferes with their acquisition of English language competence (Garcia, 2001). These patterns of segregation have significance for the resources accessible to students.

Teachers in high-poverty schools are much more likely to be undercredentialed or new than teachers in more affluent schools. Consequently, students are much less likely to have access to strong teachers who have learned to teach and are interesting and demanding as well. Two studies in California also found that schools attended by students of color, language-minority students, and poor students are also less likely to have access to teachers with professional training for teaching English learners; forms of assessment that capture what language minority students can do and that help guide classroom instruction; meaningful instructional time when students are in school; sufficient textbooks, computers, and other materials for students; materials that English learners can understand; and functional school facilities (Gándara, Rumberger, Maxwell-Jolley, & Callahan, 2003; Oakes, Blasi & Rogers, 2004). Moreover, schools serving mainly low-income students and students of color are more likely than are schools serving mainly affluent and White students to adopt highly scripted curriculum packages in order to teach to tests and to socialize new teachers into using teaching processes that emphasize memory work at the expense of thinking (Achinstein, Ogawa, & Speiglman, 2004).

Ability grouping, found extensively in elementary schools, corresponds to tracking, a pervasive feature of high schools in the major academic areas. The pros and cons of ability grouping and tracking are a continuous focus of debate among teachers, as demonstrated on the "Speak Out" page of the American Federation of Teachers' publication *On Campus* (Lucas, 1992; Mitchell, 1992). Here, two teachers argued their positions on ability grouping, one basically arguing that ability grouping can create a label that lasts a lifetime and the other arguing that talented students must not be ignored.

But tracking continues to perpetuate race and class inequities by sorting students into different classes that are then taught differently. Oakes's (1985) investigation of 25 secondary schools across the country in the late 1970s found considerable use of tracking. In multiracial schools, upper-track classes were disproportionately White, whereas lower-track classes were disproportionately minority and lower class. Upper-track students tended to receive the following: at least 80% of class time spent on instruction, considerable homework, more varied teaching activities, clear instruction, emphasis on higher-level thinking skills, and exposure to content that would gain them access to college. Lower-track students, on the other hand, received about 67% of class time spent on instruction, half (or less) the homework of upper-track students, varied materials but very routinized instructional activities, less clarity in instruction, emphasis on rote memory, and content oriented around everyday-life skills (which may seem practical but also may block access to college). Most upper-track students reported enthusiasm for school and feelings of personal competence, whereas lower-track students were often turned off to school and felt academically incompetent.

Tracking is still pervasive, still following the same patterns that Oakes described (Lucas & Berends, 2002). Although people often say that tracking and grouping meet students' instructional needs and provide opportunity for advancement, for the most part lower groups are being turned off to school and are not being pushed to catch up, causing them to grow increasingly different from other groups as they proceed through school. Lower-ability group and lower-track class work is also often boring. Contrary to the conventional wisdom, a study found that both high-achieving and low-achieving students were more likely to *fail* lower-level than upper-level courses and to do better in upper-level courses (A New Core Curriculum for All, 2003) because the lower-level courses were more boring, and the upper-level courses more interesting and challenging. Also contrary to conventional wisdom, we can raise expectations and student achievement by eliminating lower-level courses. In a New York high school in which this has been done, all students are served in heterogeneous upper-track classes, and test results show increases in achievement among both traditionally low- and high-achievers, and a marked closing of the racial achievement gap (Burris, Heubert, & Levin, 2004).

Special education fits into the tracking system in many ways, though less so for the physically, visually, and hearing impaired than for other categories. Summarizing recent research, the Education Commission of the States (2003) reported that

> disparities are consistently found in the special education categories that carry the greatest stigma, including mental retardation, emotional disturbance and, to a lesser degree, learning disabilities (LD). For instance, American Indian students are consistently represented in disproportionately large numbers in the LD category. And more than twice the number of black students (2.6%) are identified as mentally retarded when compared with white students (1.2%). In fact, some studies show that African-American children are almost three times more likely to be labeled "mentally retarded" than their white counterparts.

Classes for gifted students are still disproportionately White. In some schools, Latino students are overrepresented in special education; in others, they are placed in bilingual education whether or not this is appropriate. Learning disability classes of the 1970s and 1980s have shifted from protective areas for White, middle-class, failing children to remedial classes for students previously classified as retarded or slow.

Like tracking and grouping, placement in special education has consequences for students' access to high expectations and quality education. For some students, special education offers needed academic help and support; for others it becomes a trap and a label. The *Individuals with Disabilities Act,* passed by Congress and signed into law in 1997, mandates that overrepresentation of students of color be examined and addressed, leaving it up to the states to determine how to do this.

For linguistic minority students, a variety of placement options exist, at least conceptually (Crawford, 2004). Submersion is placement in an all-English environment with no language support. Although *Lau v. Nichols* rendered this option illegal in 1974, it persists in the form of benign neglect. English as a Second Language (ESL) pullout entails offering instruction in English outside the mainstream class, usually for 30 to 45 minutes per day. Structured English Immersion involves placement in an English-only class in which the teacher makes instructional adjustments designed to help students understand content and learn English. In a Transitional Bilingual Education placement, students are taught part of the day in their first language for a period of time lasting up to three years, while they learn to function in English. In a Developmental Bilingual Education placement, students learn in both languages, with the goal being development of full academic competence in both languages. Dual Immersion programs teach two languages to both English Language Learners and native English speakers, gradually integrating them and alternating the language of instruction. Their goal is to promote full academic competence in two languages among both immigrant and native-English speaking students. Dual Immersion programs are producing encouraging research on achievement but are still relatively uncommon. Given the press toward achievement testing in English, most English Language Learners are in either submersion programs (when alternatives are not available), Structured English Immersion classrooms, or ESL pullout programs. In addition, some schools offer Newcomer programs for recent immigrants, to help ease transition into the United States and its schools.

An important question about language placements is the extent to which they offer challenging academic learning while supporting students' language and identity. Advocates of bilingual education argue that programs should strive toward both goals. We have seen where the pressure to move students into English-only classrooms, however, sometimes turns bilingual education or ESL classes into low-level remedial classes, thereby creating a new lower track in a school. As we will discuss later in this book, this kind of situation reflects problems not with bilingual education itself, but rather with its implementation when coupled with low expectations of language-minority students.

Title IX (an education amendment of 1972) forbids schools from restricting access to courses and school activities based on sex. Although classes are integrated by gender much more now than they were 20 or 30 years ago, one can still find some gender differences in access, particularly at the high school and college level, where male students often dominate computer and upper-level science courses. It is worth noting, however, that the tremendous progress schools have made in opening up access to equal opportunities to both sexes still needs to be replicated with respect to other forms of diversity.

Student Culture

Students do not respond to schools in a mechanical fashion. Researchers are increasingly aware that student cultures develop in ways that often help to reproduce existing social patterns, make it difficult to change student behavior, and reaffirm to teachers that their own behavior toward students is correct. Often, great gaps exist between how teachers and students perceive each other and how they perceive themselves.

Student culture can be thought of as a complex set of collective narratives that children and youth construct about themselves, in relationship to other people, social situations, and social locations. Although children and youth share a common generation with others of their age group, as well as exposure to dominant media imagery, their worlds and their access to society's resources also vary widely by race, gender, social class, geographic location, and so forth. Thus, one cannot very helpfully describe a general student culture.

For example, Steinberg and Kincheloe (1998) found that youth who grow up in affluent communities tended to construct a collective sense of themselves as entitled to have and consume material goods and to lie and cheat while getting away with it. Youth create this sense of self through being recipients of expensive items routinely, being constantly marketed to by companies trying to cultivate them as consumers, viewing films that portray youth partying and destroying, and growing up in fragmented families. Urban hip-hop youth, on the other hand, construct a culture that attempts to define possibilities in the context of poverty and relatively powerlessness. Rap, for example, often draws attention to the problems of urban communities and to youth local empowerment strategies. Hip-hop culture can be understood as a struggle for self-determination in a context of societal attempts to contain and control urban youth (Ginwright, 2004).

Performance is a part of displaying cultural identity. Markers of cultural identity include hairstyle, clothing, jewelry, speech patterns, and style of walking. Often teachers battle with youth over identity markers, without awareness that these markers represent young people's attempts to define and control their own emerging identities.

Student culture has relevance to "business as usual" because it helps shape many of the decisions students make about school and because it develops as much from within the school as from outside it. Many teachers believe that all or most of their students' values and beliefs are generated only from outside; students who fail, turn off, drop out, or choose low-ability classes are doing so in spite of the school's attempt to give all an equal chance. These teachers often blame the students' home culture or society in general.

Although society and home cannot be discounted, they do not determine student behavior. In a very real sense, students determine it as they make sense of the school experience they confront every day. All the patterns described here as business as usual present students with experiences that vary according to student race, social class, and gender, among other factors; the experiences that students have outside the school give them frameworks that also vary by race, social class, and gender, and students use these frameworks to interpret school life.

A gap has always existed between teachers and students, resulting at least from age and role and often compounded by differences in cultural background. This gap has recently been widened, as an increasing number of students come from homes that have alternative lifestyles and family arrangements. Some teachers bridge this gap and grasp the differences in student culture and lifestyle fairly well; many do not, interpreting student behavior as part of the natural order of things that teachers need to control and to discourage from being reproduced. As the teaching staff in the United States becomes increasingly older and remains predominantly White, it is quite possible that the gap between teachers and students, and especially low socioeconomic-status students and students of color, will widen to become a chasm in many schools.

APPROACHES TO MULTICULTURAL EDUCATION

The problems we have just described have existed for a long time and have been recognized and contested by many educators. In fact, the progress that we have noted has come about largely through the efforts of educators, working in conjunction with community and social movements, to make schools, along with other social institutions, fairer and more responsive to the needs of the students.

The reforms that educators have advocated bear different names but are directed toward common practices. Some of the more common names for these reforms are multicultural education, nonsexist education, human relations, gender fair education, multiethnic education, ethnic studies, sex equity, bilingual/bicultural education, antiracist teaching, and inclusion. Multicultural education has emerged as an umbrella concept that deals with race, culture, language, social class, gender, and disability. Although many educators still apply it only to race, it is the term most frequently extended to include additional forms of diversity. For this reason, we will use the term *multicultural education* to refer to educational practices directed toward race, culture, language, social class, gender, sexuality, and disability, although in selecting the term we do not imply that race is the primary form of social inequality that needs to be addressed.

Educators have not advocated a single, unified plan for multicultural education. Responding to somewhat different issues in different schools, employing different conceptual views of school and society, and holding somewhat different visions of the good society, educators over the years have constructed different approaches to multicultural education. For example, based on a review of advocacy literature in multicultural education, Gibson (1976) identified five approaches: (1) education of the culturally different, or benevolent multiculturalism, which seeks to incorporate culturally different students more effectively into mainstream culture and society; (2) education about cultural differences, which teaches all students about cultural differences in an effort to promote better cross-cultural understanding; (3) education for cultural pluralism, which seeks to preserve ethnic cultures and increase the power of ethnic minority groups; (4) bicultural education, which seeks to prepare students to operate successfully in two different cultures; and (5) "multicultural education as the normal human experience," which teaches students to function in multiple cultural contexts, ethnic or otherwise.

Writing about antioppressive education, Kumashiro (2002) identified four approaches: (1) education for the other, which focused on improving educational experiences for students who face discrimination and oppression; (2) education about the other, which entails reworking the curriculum so that it reflects historically oppressed peoples; (3) "education that is critical of privileging and othering," which focuses on engaging students in changing institutional systems of oppression; and (4) education that changes students and society, which involves changing the complex and subtle everyday processes in schools that enact oppression.

In this book, we develop our own typology, which overlaps somewhat with those by Gibson and Kumashiro. Based on our work as teachers, administrators, college professors, and ethnographic researchers, as well as on extensive reviews of the literature on multicultural education (Grant, 1992; Grant & Sleeter, 1985; Grant, Sleeter, & Anderson, 1986; Sleeter & Grant, 1987), we constructed this typology of approaches to multicultural education as a way of attempting to clarify what people actually mean when they talk about or say they "do" multicultural education. We have found that educators often assume a meaning of multicultural education, without having considered alternatives. So, we wrote this book to help elucidate some of the major alternatives.

During the 1960s, in efforts to desegregate schools, many White educators "discovered" students of color and saw them as culturally deprived. This view was contested vigorously by those who argued that these students were different, not deficient, and that the school should accept their cultural differences. Similarly, many special educators argued that students with disabilities bring differences that should be accepted and built on. The approach that emerged—*Teaching the Exceptional and the Culturally Different*—focuses on adapting instruction to student differences for the purpose of helping these students succeed more effectively in the mainstream.

During about the same period, but building on the post–World War II Intercultural Education Movement, other educators argued that love, respect, and more effective communication should be developed in schools to bring people who differ closer together. This developed into the *Human Relations* approach.

The 1960s also saw the emergence of more assertive approaches to change the mainstream of America rather than try to fit people into it. Ethnic studies, women's studies, and, to a lesser extent, labor studies were developed in an effort to deepen scholarship on specific groups, raise consciousness regarding that group's oppression, rethink the group's identity, and mobilize for social action. In the 1970s and 1980s, additional groups, such as gays and lesbians, engaged in similar work. We termed this work *Single-Group Studies.*

The *Multicultural Education* approach emerged during the early 1970s and has continued to develop as some educators have grown disenchanted with earlier approaches and as others have begun conceptualizing more complete and complex plans for reforming education. This approach links race, language, culture, gender, disability, and, to a lesser extent, social class, working toward making the entire school celebrate human diversity and equal opportunity.

Finally, the 1970s and 1980s saw the development of a fifth approach, which we are calling *Multicultural Social Justice Education.* Throughout the 1990s and into the twenty-first century, this approach has been gaining in recognition and credibility, in part because it extends the Multicultural Education approach into the realm of social action and focuses at least as much on challenging social stratification as on celebrating human diversity and equal opportunity.

PLAN OF SUBSEQUENT CHAPTERS

The existing literature on these various approaches, though more analytical now than when we did the first edition in 1988, is nevertheless still somewhat fragmented and conceptually weak. Much of it simply prescribes what teachers should do, offering short and sometimes simplistic reasons. Some of the literature ignores previous writings on multicultural education and discusses the concept as if it has no history. In addition, other writings selectively choose the approach to multicultural education that authors wish to discuss and ignore the other approaches. Similarly, the authors of some books and articles that are well conceptualized and well researched in a specific area of multicultural education tend to present their approaches as if they were the only approaches.

The chapters that follow offer two major features that are designed to correct these shortcomings. First, they explicate the five approaches and allow the reader to compare them. A critique of each approach is offered to help with this comparison. The reader is invited to think through the goals, assumptions, and practices of each approach to determine which makes the most sense.

Second, each approach is developed in some depth. The first part of each chapter discusses each approach's goals, assumptions, and theoretical base. This material provides a clearer picture of what the approach is attempting to do and why, as well as guidance for developing strategies to implement it. Next, recommended practices are summarized, followed by one or two vignettes that illustrate the approach in action. Then the approach is critiqued from the vantage points of other approaches. Finally, a table summarizing the main goals, target audience, and recommended practices is presented, enabling the reader to see the main ideas of the approach at a glance. Readers who are interested in seeing more direct classroom applications are encouraged to pair this text with its companion, *Turning on Learning* (Grant & Sleeter, 2006).

We invite the reader to think through carefully which approach makes the most sense. We are not without our own opinion on this issue. After presenting each approach in what we hope is an unbiased manner, we will argue (in our last chapter) why we feel that one approach is preferable to the other four.

REFERENCES

Achinstein, B., Ogawa, R. T., & Speiglman, A. (2004). Are we creating separate and unequal tracks of teachers? The effects of state policy, local conditions, and teacher characteristics on new teacher socialization. *American Educational Research Journal, 41(3),* 557–603.

American Psychological Association. (2005). *Appropriate use of high-stakes testing in our nation's schools.* Washington, DC: APA Office of Public Affairs.

The Americans with Disabilities Act: Where we are now. (1991, January/February). *The Disability Rag,* 11–19.

Amrein, A. L., & Berliner, D. C. (2002). High-stakes testing, uncertainty, and student learning. *Education Policy Analysis Archives, 10(18).* Retrieved January 15, 2003, from http://epaa.asu.edu/epaa/v10n18/.

A New Core Curriculum for All. (2003). *Thinking K-16, a publication of the Education Trust, 7(1).*

Berger, R. (2003). *An ethic of excellence.* Portsmouth, NH: Heinemann.

Bergstrom, M. S. (1999). The disability equation: Does disability = poverty? Horizon: People and possibilities. Retrieved June 3, 2005 at http://www.horizonmag.com/poverty/disabilitytnt.asp.

Berliner, D. C., & Biddle, B. J. (1995). *The manufactured crisis: Myths, fraud and the attack on America's public schools.* Cambridge: Perseus Books.

Bloom, A. C. (1989). *The closing of the American mind.* New York: Simon & Schuster.

Burris, C. C., Heubert, J., & Levin, H. (2004). Math acceleration for all. *Educational Leadership, 61(5),* 68–71.

Byrne, M. M. (2001). Uncovering racial bias in nursing fundamentals textbooks. *Nursing and Health Care Perspectives, 22(6),* 299–303.

Carlson, D. K. (2004). As Blacks mark history, satisfaction gap persists. Gallup Poll News Service. Retrieved April 4, 2005 from http://www.gallup.com/poll/content/

Center for Community Change. (2005). Native American background information. Retrieved May 30, 2005 from http://www.communitychange.org/issues/nativeamerican/background/.

Clawson, R. A. (2002). Poor people, Black faces: The portrayal of poverty in economics textbooks. *Journal of Black Studies, 32(3),* 352–361.

Coalition for Fair Employment in Technology. (2004). Outsourcing is cost-shifting. Retrieved June 2, 2005 at http://www.blackmoney.com/coalition.html

Cohen, E. G., & Lotan, R. A. (2004). Equity in heterogeneous classrooms. In J. A. Banks & C. A. M. Banks (Eds.). *Handbook of research on multicultural education* (pp. 736–750). San Francisco: Jossey-Bass.

Crawford, J. (2004). *Educating English learners,* 5th ed. Los Angeles: Bilingual Educational Services.

Cuban, L. (1984). *How teachers taught.* New York: Longman.

Diamond, M. (1993). Homosexuality and bisexuality in different populations. *Archives of Sexual Behavior, 22(4),* 291–310.

Eck, D. L. (2002). *A new religious America.* San Francisco: HarperCollins.

Education Commission of the States. (2003). Addressing the disproportionate number of minority students in special education. *ECS StateNotes.* Retrieved February 22, 2005 at http://www.ecs.org/clearinghouse/48/90/4890.htm.

Ethnic Majority. (2004). African, Hispanic (Latino), and Asian Americans in politics. Retrieved June 2, 2005 from http://www.ethnicmajority.com/POLITICAL.HTM.

Fins, D. (2005). *Death row U.S.A.* Washington, DC: NAACP Legal Defense and Educational Fund.

Foley, C. L., & Boulware, B. J. (1996). Gender equity in 1990 middle school basal readers. *Reading Improvement, 33(4),* 220–223.

Foster, S. J. (1999). The struggle for American identity: Treatment of ethnic groups in United States history textbooks. *History of Education, 28(3),* 251–278

Frey, D. (2002). Anorexia nervosa. Medical Network, Inc. Retrieved June 1, 2005 from http://www.healthatoz.com/healthatoz/Atoz/ency/anorexia_nervosa.jsp.

Gándara, P., Rumberger, R., Maxwell-Jolly, J., & Callahan, R. (2003, October 7). English learners in California schools: Unequal resources, unequal outcomes. *Education Policy*

Analysis Archives, 11(36). Retrieved October 8, 2003 from http://epaa.asu.edu/epaa/v11n36/.

Garcia, E. E. (2001). *Latino education in the United States.* Lanham, MD: Rowman and Littlefield.

Gibson, M. A. (1976). Approaches to multicultural education in the United States: Some concepts and assumptions. *Anthropology and Education Quarterly, 7,* 7–18.

Ginwright, S. A. (2004). *Black in school: Afrocentric reform, urban youth, and the promise of hip-hop culture.* New York: Teachers College Press.

Glickman, C. D. (2000/2001, December/January). Holding sacred ground: The impact of standardization. *Educational Leadership, 46–9.*

Goodlad, J. I. (1984). *A place called school.* New York: McGraw-Hill.

Grant, C. A. (Ed.). (1992). *Research and multicultural education.* London: Falmer Press.

Grant, C. A., & Sleeter, C. E. (1985). The literature on multicultural education: Review and analysis. *Educational Review, 37,* 97–118.

Grant, C. A., & Sleeter, C. E. (2006). *Turning on learning.* New York: Wiley.

Grant, C. A., Sleeter, C. E., & Anderson, J. E. (1986). The literature on multicultural education: Review and analysis, Part II. *Educational Studies, 12,* 47–71.

Hacker, A. (1992). *Two nations: Black and white, separate, hostile, and unequal.* New York: Charles Scribner's Sons.

Haney, W. (2000). The myth of the Texas miracle in education. *Educational Policy Analysis Archives, 8(4).* Retrieved August 15, 2004 at http://epaa.asu.edu/epaa/v8n41.

Hardy, L. (2003). The politics of gifted education. *American School Board Journal, 190(8),* 26.

Harrington, M. (1984). *The new American poverty.* New York: Holt, Rinehart & Winston.

Harrison, P. M., & Beck, A. J. (2005). *Prison and jail inmates at midyear 2004.* Washington, DC: U.S. Department of Justice Office of Justice Programs.

Hate. (1992, May/June). *The Disability Rag,* 4–7.

Headley, J., & Lowe, E. (2000). Mayors' 16th annual survey on "hunger and homelessness in America's cities" finds increased levels of hunger, increased capacity to meet demand. Retrieved June 3, 2005 from http://www.usmayors.org/uscm/news/pree_releases/documents/hunger_rel ease.htm

Herdt, G., & Boxer, A. (1993). *Children of horizons: How gay and lesbian teens are leading a new way out of the closet.* Boston: Beacon Press.

Hillocks, G. (2002). *The testing trap; How state writing assessments control learning.* New York: TC Press.

Hogben, M., & Waterman, C. K. (1997). Are all of your students represented in their textbooks? A content analysis of coverage of diversity issues in introductory psychology textbooks. *Teaching of Psychology, 24(2),* 95–100.

Humphreys, J. T. (1997). Sex and geographic representation in two music education history books. *Bulletin of the Council for Research in Music Education, 131,* 67–86.

Jacobs, D. (1981). Teaching the Arab world: Evaluating textbooks. *Social Studies 72(4),* 150–153.

Johnson, D., & Johnson B. (2002). *High stakes: Children, testing and failure and American schools: A year in the life of a rural school.* Lanham, MD: Rowman & Littlefield Publishers.

Johnson, M. (1991, March/April). What builders don't know. *The Disability Rag,* 12–17.

Johnson, M. (2005). Business strikes back: California firms press state bills to stop access lawsuits. Ragged Edge Online. Retrieved June 3, 2005 from http://www.ragged-edgemagazine.com/focus/notifact0505.html.

Jones, J. (2004). Blacks more pessimistic than Whites about economic opportunities. Gallup Poll News Service. Retrieved April 4, 2005 from http://www.gallup.com/poll/content/

Jones, M. A., Kitetu, C., & Sunderland, J. (1997). Discourse roles, gender and language text-book dialogues: Who learns what from John and Sally? *Gender and Education, 9(4)*, 469–490.

Jones, M. G., Jones, B. D., & Hargrove, T. Y. (2003). *The unintended consequences of high-stakes testing.* Lanham, MD: Rowman & Littlefield.

Kornhaber, M. L. (2004). Assessment, standards and equity. In J. A. Banks & C. A. M. Banks (Eds.). *Handbook of research on multicultural education* (pp. 91–109). San Francisco: Jossey-Bass.

Koza, J. E. (1994). Females in 1988 middle school music textbooks: An analysis of illustra-tions. *Journal of Research in Music Education 42(2)*, 145–171.

Kruks, G. (1991). Gay and lesbian homeless youth. *Journal of Adolescent Health, 12(7)*, 515–518.

Kumashiro, K. K. (2002). *Troubling education: Queer activism and antioppressive pedagogy.* New York: RoutledgeFalmer.

Lee, E. (2002). Anti-racist education: Pulling together to close the gaps. In E. Lee, D. Menkart, & M. Okazawa-Rey (Eds.). *Beyond heroes and holidays* (pp. 26–35). Washington, DC: Teaching for Change.

Linn, R. L., Baker, E. L., & Betebenner, D. W. (2002). Accountability systems: Implications of requirements of the No Child Left Behind Act of 2001. *Educational Researcher, 31(6)*, 3–16.

Lipman, P. (2003). Chicago school policy: Regulating Black and Latino youth in the global city. *Race Ethnicity and Education, 6(4)*, 331–356.

Lipman, P. (2004). *High stakes education.* New York: RoutledgeFalmer.

Loewen, J. W. (1995). *Lies my teacher told me.* New York: The New Press.

Lucas, L. (1992). Does ability grouping do more harm than good? Don't ignore the potential of talented students. *On Campus, 11(6)*, 6.

Lucas, S. R., & Berends, M. (2002). Sociodemographic diversity, correlated achievement, and de facto tracking. *Sociology of Education, 75(4)*, 328–348.

Madaus, G., & Clarke, M. (2001). The adverse impact of high-stakes testing on minority stu-dents: Evidence from one hundred years of test data. In G. Orfield & M. L. Kornhaber (Eds.). *Raising standards or raising barriers: Inequality and high-stakes testing in public educa-tion* (pp. 85–106). New York: Century Foundation Press.

Manset-Williamson, G., & Washburn, S. (2002). Administrators' perspectives of the impact of mandatory graduation qualifying examinations for students with learning disabilities. *Journal of Special Education Leadership, 15(2)*, 49–59.

Marquez, S. A. (1994). Distorting the image of "Hispanic" women in sociology: Problematic strategies of presentation in the introductory text. *Teaching Sociology, 22(3)*, 231–236.

Mazzuca, J. (2004). For most Americans, friendship is colorblind. Gallup Poll News Service. Retrieved April 4, 2005 from http://www.gallup.com/poll/content/

McNeil, L., & Valenzuela, A. (2001). The harmful impact of the TAAS system of testing in Texas: Beneath the accountability rhetoric. In G. Orfield & M. L. Kornhaber (Eds.). *Raising standards or raising barriers: Inequality and high-stakes testing in public education* (pp. 127–150). New York: Century Foundation Press.

Meier, D. (2002). *In schools we trust.* Boston: Beacon Press.

Mitchell, B. L. (1992). Does ability grouping do more harm than good? It creates labels that last a life time. *On Campus, 11(6)*, 6–9.

Moon, T. R., Brighton, C. M., & Callahan, C. M. (2003). State standardized testing programs: Friend or foe of gifted education? *Roeper Review, 25(2)*, 49–60.

National Center for Health Statistics. (2004). *Health, United States, 2004 with chartbook on trends in the health of Americans.* Hyattsville, MD: National Center for Health Statistics.

National Commission on Children. (1991). *Beyond rhetoric.* Washington, DC: U.S. Government Printing Office.

National Commission on Excellence in Education. (1983). *A nation at risk.* Washington, DC: U.S. Government Printing Office.

National Mental Illness Screening Project. (1996). *Who suffers from eating disorders?* Washington, DC.

Natriello, G., & Pallas, A. (2001). The development and impact of high-stakes testing. In G. Orfield & M. L. Kornhaber, (Eds.). *Raising standards or raising barriers: Inequality and high-stakes testing in public education* (pp. 19–38). New York: Century Foundation Press.

No Housing to Refer People To. (1990, May/June). *The Disability Rag, 7.*

Oakes, J. (1985). *Keeping track: How schools structure inequality.* New Haven, CT: Yale University Press.

Oakes, J., Blasi, G., & Rogers, J. (2004). Accountability for adequate and equitable opportunities to learn. In K. Sirtonik (Ed.). *Holding accountability accountable: What ought to matter in public education.* New York: Teachers College Press.

Orfield, G., & Lee, C. (2005). *Why segregation matters: Poverty and educational inequality.* Cambridge, MA: Harvard University Civil Rights Project.

Passell, J. S. (2005). *Estimates of the size and characteristics of the undocumented population.* Washington, DC: Pew Hispanic Center.

Purnell, T., W. Idsardi, & Baugh, J. (1999). Perceptual and phonetic experiments on American English Dialect identification. *Journal of Language and Social Psychology, 18,* 10–30.

Ravitch, D. (1990). Diversity and democracy: Multicultural education in America. *American Educator, 14(1),* 16–20, 46–68.

Ruiz de Velasco, J. (2005). Performance-based school reforms and the federal role in helping students that serve language-minority students. In A. Valenzuela (Ed.). *Leaving children behind* (pp. 33–56). Albany, NY: SUNY Press.

Russell, S. T., & Joyner, K. (2001). Adolescent sexual orientation and suicide risk: Evidence from a natural study. *American Journal of Public Health, 91(8),* 1276.

Ryan, D. C. (1994). *Authentic assessment.* Westminster, CA: Teacher Created Materials.

Scheslinger, A. M., Jr. (1992). *The disuniting of America.* New York: Norton.

Shepard, L. A. (2000). The role of assessment in a learning culture. *Educational Researcher, 29(7),* 4–14.

Sleeter, C. E. (2005). *Un-standardizing curriculum: Multicultural teaching in standards-based classrooms.* New York: Teachers College Press.

Sleeter, C. E., & Grant, C. A. (1987). An analysis of multicultural education in the U.S.A. *Harvard Educational Review, 57,* 421–444.

Sleeter, C. E., & Grant, C. (1991). Race, class, gender, and disability in current textbooks. In M. W. Apple & L. K. Christian-Smith (Eds.). *The politics of the textbook* (pp. 78–110). New York: Routledge.

Steinberg, S. R., & Kincheloe, J. L. (1998). Privileged and getting away with it: The cultural studies of white, middle-class youth. *Studies in the Literary Imagination, 31(1).*

Suro, R., & Tafoya, S. (2004). *Dispersal and concentration: Patterns of Latino residential settlement.* Washington, DC: Pew Hispanic Center.

Taub, D. E., & Fanflik, P. L. (2000). The inclusion of disability in introductory sociology textbooks. *Teaching Sociology, 28(1),* 12–23.

Tjaden P., & Thoennes, N. (2000). *Full report of the prevalence, incidence, and consequences of violence against women: findings from the national violence against women survey* (Report NCJ 183781). Washington, DC: National Institute of Justice.

Ulrich, R. (2004). Taxing proposals. TomPaine. Commonsense. Retrieved June 3, 2005 at http://www.tompaine.com/articles.

U.S. Department of Commerce, Bureau of the Census. (2003). American community survey. Retrieved March 1, 2005 from http://factfinder.census.gov.

U.S. Department of Commerce, Bureau of the Census. (2004a). *Statistical Abstract of the United States: 2004–2005.* Washington, DC: U.S. Government Printing Office.

U.S. Department of Commerce, Bureau of the Census. (2004b). *Income, poverty, and health insurance coverage in the U.S., 2003.* Washington, DC: U.S. Government Printing Office.

U.S. Department of Commerce, Bureau of the Census. (2005). Housing and Household Economic Statistics Division. Retrieved June 3, 2005 from http://www.census.gov/hhes/www/income/histinc/p36ar.html

U.S. Department of Education. (2001). No Child Left Behind. Retrieved September 18, 2003 at http://www.ed.gov/nclb/overview/intro/execsumm.html.

U.S. Department of Education, National Center for Education Statistics. (1996). *The Condition of Education 1996.* Washington, DC: U.S. Government Printing Office.

U.S. Department of Education, National Center for Education Statistics. (2003). Nations Report Card. Retrieved March 29, 2005 from http://nces.ed.gov/nationsreportcard/naepdata/getdata.asp.

U.S. Department of Education, National Center for Educational Statistics. (2005). The condition of education, 2000–2005. Retrieved June 2, 2005 from http://nces.ed.gov/programs/coe/.

U.S. Department of Health and Human Services. (2001). Health disparities trends. Health and heritage brochure, Indian health service. Retrieved April 28, 2005 from http://info.ihs.gov/Health/Health1.pdf.

U.S. Department of Homeland Security. (2003). Yearbook of immigration statistics 2003. Retrieved June 2, 2005 from http://uscis.gov/graphics/shared/statistics/yearbook/YrBk03Im.htm

U.S. Department of Justice. (2002). Demographic trends in correctional population by race. Retrieved June 2, 2005 from http://www.ojp.usdoj.gov/bjs/glance/tables/cpracetab.htm

U.S. Department of Labor, Bureau of Labor Statistics. (1998). *Monthly Labor Review Online.* Washington, DC: U.S. Government Printing Office.

U.S. Department of Labor, Bureau of Labor Statistics. (2004a). Highlights of women's earnings in 2003. Retrieved May 25, 2005 from http://www.bls.gov/cps/cpswom2003.pdf

U.S. Department of Labor, Bureau of Labor Statistics. (2004b). Displaced workers summary. Retrieved June 3, 2005 from http://www.bls.gov/news.release/disp.nr0.htm

U.S. Department of Labor, Bureau of Labor Statistics. (2005a). Usual weekly earnings of wage and salary workers: Fourth quarter 2004. Retrieved April 5, 2005, from http://www.bls.gov/cps/

U.S. Department of Labor, Bureau of Labor Statistics, (2005b). Adjustments to household survey population estimates in January 2005. Retrieved March 25, 2005 from http://www.bls.gov/cps/.

U.S. Senate Historical Office. (2005). Minorities in the Senate. Retrieved June 2, 2005 from http://www.senate.gov/artandhistory/history/common/briefing/minority_senators.htm.

The White House Project. (2005). Snapshots of current political leadership. Retrieved June 1, 2005 from http://www.thewhitehouseproject.org/know_facts/snapshots_women.html.

Wiggins, G., & McTighe, J. (2001). *Understanding by design,* 2nd ed. Alexandria, VA: Association for Supervision and Curriculum Development.

Wolf, N. (1991). *The beauty myth: How images of beauty are used against women.* New York: William Morrow.

World Christian Encyclopedia. (2001). *A comparative survey of churches and religions in the modern world,* 2nd ed. New York: Oxford University Press.

Wright, W. E. (2002). The effects of high stakes testing in an inner-city elementary school: The curriculum, the teachers, and the English language learners. Current Issues in Education [On-line], 5(5). Retrieved April 6, 2004 at http://cie.ed.asu.edu/volume5/number5/

Zimmerman, J. (2002). *Whose America? Culture wars in the public schools.* Cambridge, MA: Harvard University Press.

CHAPTER TWO

Teaching the Exceptional and the Culturally Different

Classrooms are diverse. Students differ from each other in numerous ways, including academic achievement, learning ability, gender, ethnic and racial background, and family background. As teachers, what do we make of these differences? Particularly as schools today are pressured to raise student achievement test scores, how can teachers work constructively with the differences in their classrooms? This approach to multicultural education focuses on adapting classroom processes to help a variety of students learn the standard curriculum, in order to be prepared for the work world and other demands of the future.

GOALS

Teachers are responsible for helping students achieve. Many teachers also see themselves as responsible for helping students fit into the mainstream of American society. They believe that students who do not readily fit in or test well because of cultural background, language, learning style, or learning ability require teaching strategies that remediate deficiencies or build bridges between the student and the school. To these teachers, multicultural education might mean adapting how one teaches exceptional or culturally different students to enable them to achieve in school and better meet the traditional demands of American life.

Proponents of this approach regard U.S. society as basically good and just, and believe that the main goal of schooling is to assimilate the young into that society, as shown in Table 2-1. The goal of this approach is to equip students with the cognitive skills, concepts, information, language, and values required by American society in order to hold a job and function within the society's existing institutions and culture. Most proponents regard immigrants, the poor, the unemployed, people with disabilities, and alienated members of society as lacking primarily the right skills, values, and knowledge.

TABLE 2-1.
Teaching the Exceptional and the Culturally Different

Societal goals:	Help fit people Into the existing social structure.
School goals:	Teach dominant traditional educational aims more effectively by building bridges between the student and the demands of the school.
Target students:	Lower-class, special education, limited English proficiency, female students who need to pass standard tests, or students of color who are behind in achievement in main school subjects.
Practices:	
Curriculum	Make relevant to students' experiential background; fill in gaps in basic skills and knowledge; teach to pass tests, teach content in language students can understand; use first language as basis for teaching standard English.
Instruction	Build on students' learning styles; adapt to students' skill levels; teach as effectively and efficiently as possible to enable students to catch up.
Other aspects of classroom	Use decorations showing group members integrated into mainstream society.
Support services	Use transitional bilingual education, ESL, remedial classes, special education as temporary and intensive aids to fill gaps in knowledge.
Other schoolwide concerns	Involve lower-class and parents of color in supporting work of the school.

According to this approach, modifications are made in schooling to facilitate these students' academic achievement and their transition to the mainstream culture that White, middle-class children are learning. This approach is based on the human capital theory of society. After presenting it, we will discuss two quite different orientations that teachers use to interpret student differences: one that views differences as deficiencies and the other that views differences simply as differences.

THE HUMAN CAPITAL THEORY OF EDUCATION AND SOCIETY

The human capital theory holds that education is a form of investment in that the individual acquires skills and knowledge that can be converted into income when used to get a job. You probably have been told that you should go to school so that you can get a good job and that the more time and energy you invest in school, the better the job you will get. For example, California Business for Education Excellence (2002) explains:

> The world is changing in sweeping ways, and schools must adapt to reflect these changes. In earlier generations, well-paid assembly-line workers didn't need advance mathematics or problem-solving skills. But those jobs are a thing of the past, and so are assembly-line schools—where some students learn and many more do not. Tech-

nological innovation, highspeed communication, and creative problem solving characterize today's society. Schools must prepare students for this new economy. (p. 6)

This approach assumes that opportunities open up to individuals at a level commensurate with the level of education they have acquired and that the more individuals develop their human capital through education, the better their life circumstances, our economy, and society in general will be. It assumes that the poor are poor mainly because they have not developed their human capital. Theoretically, then, poverty and inequality result largely from insufficient opportunity for people of color, the poor, people with disabilities, and women to acquire the knowledge and skills society needs.

U.S. citizens frequently look to the schools to solve social problems. People who subscribe to the human capital theory often call for school reforms when they perceive the United States experiencing a national crisis. During the late 1950s, when the Soviet Union launched Sputnik (the first space vehicle), many Americans became concerned that the United States was falling behind in the Cold War and called on schools to upgrade science, math, and foreign-language instruction. Similarly, in the 1980s, as the United States experienced loss of previously undisputed economic supremacy in the world market, many people again called on the schools to supply the "human capital" necessary to develop the American competitive edge. Beginning with *A Nation at Risk,* published in 1983 (National Commission on Excellence in Education), reports made recommendations such as lengthening the school day and school year, instituting more testing, raising standards for achievement, getting back to basics, and upgrading science and math instruction. Passage of *No Child Left Behind* in 2001 represents the federal government's most recent attempt to reform schools in order to develop human capital for national or business needs. Each of these efforts symbolizes an increasing national preoccupation with accountability, the efficient and successful production of human capital, and economic, global competition.

Some groups of students have tended to lag behind in school achievement as well as in the broader mainstream society. They include children of color, children from low-income homes, children with disabilities, children whose native language is not English, and, in some areas such as math, girls. Even though school achievement gaps based on race and gender had been steadily closing through the 1970s and 1980s (as measured, for example, by the National Assessment of Educational Progress and the Scholastic Assessment Test [SAT]), gaps still remain, started to widen again during the past decade, and have become even more worrisome as standards for achievement have been raised.

Educators who view multicultural education as Teaching the Exceptional and the Culturally Different share a common goal: to help children who are "different" become as "mainstream" as possible through education so that they can invest themselves in work that will bring them society's rewards. The approach assumes that, ultimately, assimilation has the best chance for eradicating poverty, unemployment, racism, sexism, and general social tensions because it helps everybody develop sufficiently to play a productive role in society and share a common culture.

But educators who adopt this approach to multicultural education fall into two quite different camps. Those who subscribe to the *deficiency orientation* see prevailing standards for "American culture" and "normal" human development as universally correct, and they trace failures to achieve those standards to supposed deficiencies in children's home environments, physiological and mental endowments, or in both. Those who subscribe to the *difference orientation* see prevailing standards as relative to the demands of a particular culture and hold that different cultural contexts produce equally healthy but different patterns of normal development. Individuals can learn to function productively in mainstream culture as well as in their own community culture. We will present and critique the deficiency orientation, and then discuss promise in the difference orientation.

DEFICIENCY ORIENTATION

Think of a person who is successful in today's society, such as a lawyer or a businessperson. That person probably has developed a high level of literacy, a respect for time schedules, competitive skills, an ability to act independently of other people, certain interpersonal skills, excellence in the use of Standard English, and so forth. Now think of a person who seems unsuccessful. How would you compare the successful person with the unsuccessful one? In making such a comparison—which we do all the time—we frequently think of the less successful adult or student in terms of what we believe she or he lacks: reading ability, motivation, exposure to knowledge, discipline, language skills, and so forth.

The deficiency orientation focuses on what one believes members of another group lack, usually based on a comparison to the abilities and cultural resources one has and with which one is familiar. Adherents to the deficiency orientation regard people who exemplify the values, skills, and abilities that mainstream society requires as the standard for normal development. Psychological theories of normal development have been based on this standard and have codified it in the form of various intelligence and personality tests. People who subscribe to the deficiency orientation focus primarily on either presumed cultural deficiencies or physiological and mental deficiencies.

Cultural "Deficiency"

In our education classes, we hear students refer to poor children as disadvantaged, socially deprived, low socioeconomic, culturally deprived, and culturally deficient. Over the past 20 years, *children-at-risk* has become another popular label. Although different labels highlight different images—some stressing socioeconomic disadvantage, others educational disadvantage—they all trace problems back to the child's living environment.

You may hear similar analyses in teachers' lounges, but descriptions of at-risk students in the education literature are more careful. For example, according to Ralph (1989) the at-risk factors today vary "from all-encompassing background factors—low income, low achievement, handicapping condition, minority status, inner-city household, and limited proficiency in English—to concrete, specific measures, such as dropping out of high school" (p. 396).

In the 2000s, attention to the "achievement gap" (the average difference in test scores between different racial groups, language groups, and socioeconomic groups) has prompted a resurgence of deficiency talk. The fact that schools do a better job with students who are White, middle class, and native English speaking than with students of color, students from poverty communities, and second-language learners is not new. But the achievement gap has sparked discussion of this problem among many educators and community leaders, who in previous years had taken gaps for granted. Frequently, such discussions take for granted notions of cultural deficiency.

One line of thinking, promoted by Arthur Jensen (1969), then later by Herrnstein and Murray (1994), holds that children in poor families, disproportionately of color, have inherited flaws from an inferior genetic stock, and their failure in school and society simply reflects that flawed inheritance. Most educators, ourselves included, do not accept this line of thought, so we will not review it here.

Another line of thinking explains the failure of students of color (especially African American students) and students from impoverished homes in terms of general environmental conditions. In their description of trends in disadvantaged populations, for example, Pallas, Natriello, and McDill (1989) explained that they "view educational experiences as coming not only from formal schooling, but also from the family and the community. Students who are educationally disadvantaged have been exposed to inappropriate educational experiences in at least one of these three institutional domains" (p. 16). As Noguera and Akom (2000) pointed out, "More often than not, explanations for the achievement gap focus on deficiencies among parents and students. Dysfunctional families, lazy and unmotivated students, and the 'culture of poverty' in inner-city neighborhoods are all frequently cited as causes of the gap."

The "culture of poverty" idea, largely discredited during the 1970s, is increasingly being used once more to explain why some succeed and others do not. For example, Payne (2001) describes the homes of people in poverty as commonly disorganized and loud with the television always on, and the culture of poverty as focusing on survival, living in the moment rather than planning ahead, and placing high priority on entertainment.

The culture of poverty perspective attributes a number of specific psychological deficiencies to those who grow up in "substandard" environments. Many educators believe that poor children lack appropriate role models, which damages their development. For example, Silber (1988) described welfare dependency and sexual hedonism as the moral code now characterizing the "underclass" and perpetuating the cycle of poverty. A description of inner-city families noted that "A mother is sometimes present in these homes, but she is often a drug addict or a teenager who comes and goes. ... Scarred by years of abuse and neglect, many of these children are angry and disruptive" (Gross, 1992, pp. 1, 616). African American males today face enormous barriers, and many people still blame the African American family and community (for example, by attributing problems to female-headed households). African American educators, however, who address the needs of African American males much more assertively than White educators do, frame the issues in terms of access to resources and support systems rather than to moral depravity and psychological instability.

Language is another area popularly attributed to the "culturally deprived." Many educators believe that the language that lower-class children have learned is so concrete and disorganized that it prevents them from learning to think abstractly. For example, Orr (1987) attributed the difficulties of African American students with mathematics to the grammatical structure of Black English: "They come to school without an as … as structure in the language they speak" (p. 195). She argued that in thinking through a mathematical expression such as "twice as large as," Black-English-speaking students merge the structure into their own grammatical frame of reference—ending up with, in this case, "twice as larger than"—and confuse themselves in the process.

Children whose native language is not English are often viewed as "lacking" language. It is not uncommon for language-biased teachers and counselors to place language-minority children in classes for the mentally retarded or learning disabled (Harry, 1992; San Miguel, 1987; Sheets, 1995; Trueba, 1989). Furthermore, many educators believe that Mexican migrant children fail to develop enough competence in either English or Spanish to enable complex learning, which is why their IQ scores are lower than those of Anglo children. Compensatory education for Latino students has focused on, as the primary determinant of underachievement, language rather than other factors (such as the quality of the teaching or the relevance of the concepts being taught). Consequently, Latino students' achievement is rarely discussed without reference to bilingualism, Spanish dominance, or lack of English skills, and other factors related to achievement are often overlooked (Walker, 1987).

Maternal drug use during pregnancy affects the development of children and can have very damaging consequences for later learning. A stereotype we encounter in schools is that drug use is more common among low-income mothers than among middle-income mothers; thus, if a child from a low-income family is performing poorly in school, the child is probably "unteachable" because of brain damage resulting from the mother's drug use. Such a conclusion is a very dangerous leap for a teacher to make. A medical study of the use of illicit drugs during pregnancy found virtually no relationship between drug use and race or socioeconomic status. Yet, poor and African American women were much more likely to be reported to health authorities for suspected abuse than were middle-class and White women (Chasnoff, Marvey, Landress, & Barrett, 1990). Teachers who hold a deficiency orientation toward low-income people, people of color, or both, may be susceptible to making unwarranted assumptions about maternal drug use rather than looking for other reasons that a child is not learning.

Richardson, Casanova, Placier, and Guilfoyle (1989) studied how teachers decide who is at risk and how they attribute causes of risk. They found that

> [t]he teachers were generally unwilling to attribute a student's lack of success to a characteristic inherent in the child or to their own instructional programs. They therefore moved outside the classroom to find the cause of the student's problems. These causes most often rested on their students' home lives and parents. (p. 37)

The teachers viewed students not at risk as coming from strong families and so-called at-risk students as coming from deficient families. Therefore, "teachers appeared to accept any negative statement about families of at-risk students from other teachers or adults in the building" (p. 37).

In schools, we commonly encounter use of the cultural deprivation model to explain lower achievement of students from low-income and minority homes. For example:

> Where are they coming from? … What's going on in their brains, you know? Because sometimes I realize how irrelevant it is to stand up here and talk, and I have a very close family … [my husband and I] have been very strong disciplinarians and we encourage the work ethic.… I realize how foolish and presumptuous [it is] to think all these kids are coming from the same thing.… Just to have a totally helter skelter house where there is nothing regular and the people who are your parent figures come and go and—you don't know, you know what I mean, just what is going on in their brains and where they are coming from. (Sleeter, 1992, p. 172)

As teachers observe changes in the demographics of schools, many interpret these changes as suggesting that more and more students are coming to school incapable of advanced learning. In response to such problems, Hirsch (1996) has even recommended the adoption of an official national curriculum, a measure largely understood as compensatory in nature and essential for the success of culturally deficient students.

The problem with cultural deficiency thinking is that it obscures attention to opportunity gaps (for instance, access to high-quality teachers, a relevant curriculum, good health care, decent school facilities) and to strengths and resources that students from low-income communities have. In addition, assumptions about cultural deficiency link into racist stereotypes, which many youth internalize. As Noguera and Akom (2000) pointed out, "Despite the daunting odds of success in professional sports and entertainment, many young people of color believe they have a greater chance of becoming a highly paid athlete or hip-hop artist than an engineer, doctor or software programmer."

Furthermore, cultural deficiency thinking feeds into low academic expectations. Researchers consistently find expectations of many teachers to vary according to student race and class background. Commonly, teachers justify low expectations on the basis of student family background, particularly teachers' beliefs about the extent to which parents value education (Codjoe, 2001; Contreras & Delgado-Contreras, 1991; Cooper & Moore, 1995; Hauser-Cram, Sirin, & Stipek, 2003; Pang & Sablan, 1998; Tettegah, 1996; Warren, 2002). In practice, the cultural deficiency orientation supports low expectations and precludes many teachers from examining and improving their own teaching. Under pressure to raise test scores, teachers who hold a cultural deficiency perspective about their students are faced with the dilemma of how to help students learn more, while being unsure whether they can. Anagnostopoulous (2003), for example, studied teachers in two urban high schools. The teachers attributed students' low test scores to deprived home environments and problematic peer groups rather than to poor teaching. The teachers dealt with the pressure to raise test scores by drilling students on test material rather than developing more effective teaching strategies. Thus, although we do not deny that children in impoverished communities face many difficulties, we question the usefulness of viewing students in a way that causes us as educators to scale back our expectations for teaching.

Physiological and Mental Deficiency

Historically, much of the work in special education has sought to understand and remediate physiological and mental deficiencies. You can accurately catalog these deficiencies (or supposed deficiencies) simply by listing the special education categories: visual impairment, hearing impairment, physical and health impairments, mental deficiency (in fact, a leading special education journal and professional organization both have the term *mental deficiency* in their titles), emotional or behavioral disorders, learning disabilities, and, more recently, attention disorders. For the most part, the field of special education has assumed these disorders to have primarily an organic or psychological basis, although mental retardation and emotional disturbance have also been thought to be strongly linked to the cultural "deficiencies" described earlier.

Today, most special educators regard disabilities in school as products of the interaction of deficits within the child and characteristics of the learning environment (Artiles, Harry, Reschly, & Chinn, 2002):

> Children who enter school without a diagnostic label ... bring with them as yet unspecified cognitive, behavioral, linguistic, and affective characteristics developed over time, which interact with the academic and social ecology. Out of this interaction comes school success or, in about 10% of children, failure and referral for special education. (p. 124)

In the past 25 years, there has been a shift from cataloging presumed deficiencies of students in special education to designing classrooms that accommodate a range of differences. The field of special education, however, has rested historically on assumptions about what is normal learning, behavior, and development. To the extent that one takes these assumptions for granted, one also takes for granted ideas about the deficiencies of some students.

Many of the same deficits in psychological functioning ascribed to the so-called culturally deprived have been ascribed to students labeled mentally retarded, emotionally disturbed, learning disabled, hard of hearing, and visually impaired. Most of these students are described as deficient in language and reading skills. Children classified as mentally retarded, for example, have been described as having "deficits in memory, ability to pay attention, verbal communication, motivation, ability to generalize, and understanding of similarities and differences" (Mandell & Gold, 1984, p. 12). Children classified as learning disabled have been described as deficient in their ability to handle grammatical inflections, comprehend and create complex sentences, define words, classify objects into categories, produce sentences, and recognize their own language errors (Gersten, Scott, & Pugach, 2001).

Students with language and reading problems are often described as lacking information—as well as some of the underlying concepts—that their "normal" age-mates have; this is particularly an issue as mandatory testing has increased, and schools are sanctioned when they do not meet achievement targets. Hearing-impaired children are often behind academically because of their difficulty succeeding in systems for transmitting knowledge through speaking and writing (Hardman, Drew, & Egan, 2002). When you realize that much of what is taught in school is explained verbally or read, this conclusion makes sense: If you can't read the book, you won't learn the material in it.

Finally, many students in special education are described as being deficient in social skills. For example, Friend and Bursuck (1996) described children classified as emotionally disturbed as having "difficulty with interpersonal relationships and may respond inappropriately in emotional situations" (p. 16).

Educators and researchers have used a variety of theoretical frameworks to understand these "deficiencies." The medical model assumes that the problems are caused by an organic defect, such as brain damage, chemical imbalance, or chromosomal abnormality. It attributes a child's problems to characteristics within the child, and, increasingly, prescription drugs such as Ritalin and Prozac are being used as remedies for diagnosed conditions. (For some disability conditions, such causes are clearly documented; for others they are not.) The behavioral model and the ecological model stress interaction between characteristics of the child and characteristics of the learning environment. Increasingly, these models guide special education research on intervention strategies. The behavioral model assumes that the child's problems are due to reinforcement for the wrong behaviors or a failure to have correct behaviors modeled and reinforced. The ecological model assumes that the child's problems are caused by a failure of multiple factors in the child's environment to support positive characteristics and learning behaviors of the child.

The deficiency orientation suggests that areas in which students are behind must be remediated to enable the students to function more successfully in the classroom and later on in society. For that reason, a substantial portion of the school day is commonly spent on remediation.

Sexual Orientation

Because it is so often a taboo topic for discussion, many people regard homosexuality and bisexuality as deficiencies. For example, Sears (1993) describes a study of over 1,000 teenagers in which "three-fourths of the females and 84 percent of the males think that homosexual behavior is disgusting" (p. 128). With the recent concern about AIDS, the gay rights movement, and religious controversies over ordaining gay church leaders, public attention is repeatedly directed toward homosexuality; some media and religious teachings reinforce the notion that it is a deficiency.

Teachers seldom think about sexual orientation as it relates to their students, and they usually are not encouraged to do so. As we will argue later, the failure to attend to this issue leaves students' needs and rights unaddressed. The general silence that schools maintain about sexual orientation reflects the widespread belief that homosexuality is a disease. Frequently, teachers prefer to think: No one is gay in my classroom or personal space. For students who are struggling with a gay, lesbian, or bisexual identity, the great stigma attached to their sexual orientation along with the general reluctance to discuss it leaves them in a very painful position, which adversely affects the school achievement of many (Kissen, 1993). While teachers today often believe that it is no longer acceptable to hold biased attitudes about culture, gender, or social class, many take bias on the basis of sexual orientation for granted (Miller, Miller, & Gwaltney, 1998).

Sears (1991) found that 40% of the students in his study reported their academic work to be suffering as they struggled with their sexual identities, and he speculated that many of the remaining 60% also suffered academically but in less obvious ways (such as settling for mediocre rather than good academic performance). The deficiency orientation toward homosexuality does not provide a teacher with guidance about how to help. Later in this book, we will provide suggestions in the context of other approaches to multicultural education.

DIFFERENCE ORIENTATION

Advocates of the difference orientation to Teaching the Exceptional and the Culturally Different agree with advocates of the deficiency orientation that there are a standard body of knowledge and a set of values and skills that all American citizens need to acquire. However, these advocates believe that there are different models of healthy psychological development fostered by different cultural contexts or constitutional endowments. Rather than focusing on deficiencies that need to be remediated, advocates of the difference orientation focus on strengths to build on so as to help children assimilate into the American mainstream. As Table 2-1 shows, the school goal of this approach is to teach academic knowledge more effectively by building on the knowledge and skills students bring with them.

The difference orientation prompts higher academic expectations than the deficiency orientation. The reason is as follows: Although the deficiency orientation focuses on what students lack, the difference orientation focuses on what those same students bring to the teaching–learning situation, the knowledge and skills that can be built on to develop achievement. Those who subscribe to the difference orientation often argue that the main limitation to students' learning capacity is inappropriate teaching; if students are not learning well, we are not capitalizing on their strengths and resources. Learning to teach from the difference orientation requires expending time and effort in getting to know more about the background and strengths of students.

Cultural Difference

Many educators, particularly those of color, reacted strongly against the deficiency orientation. Their reaction prompted researchers to establish a research base documenting the notion that cultural differences in language and learning style are not deficiencies and can be built on to facilitate learning. You probably have heard educators debate the pros and cons of using Black English or hip-hop to help teach African American, inner-city students or of providing bilingual education programs. You also may have heard educators refer to the importance of understanding the learning and communication styles of students—for example, recognizing that looking down instead of looking the teacher in the eye may be a sign of respect in the student's home culture.

A central idea behind the cultural difference orientation is cultural continuity. Anthropologists have documented the idea that discontinuities between one set of cultural practices and another can be confusing to the individual who must make a rapid transition between the two different sets. Think of how you feel if you have traveled in a foreign country and have found yourself among people who are culturally different from yourself. You may have felt confused, a bit frightened, unsure of yourself, and perhaps annoyed when you repeatedly did or said the wrong thing. After a period of time, you learned to function in the new culture, but initially the discontinuity jolted you.

The same thing happens with children whose home culture is different from the culture of the school. The discontinuity may be particularly aggravating for the child who is expected to function within the school's culture without being taught the culture and who must make the leap between cultures twice a day—once when arriving at school, then again when going home. Teachers who are not knowledgeable about the child's culture often interpret differences in behavior as deficiencies.

The main idea behind the Teaching the Culturally Different approach is to ensure as much cultural continuity as possible in order to teach mainstream academic content, and to maintain high expectations for all students' learning. There is no one right model of psychological development, and cultural context strongly influences how a child will develop. The psychological development of culturally different children may at times conflict with demands of the regular classroom, especially if the teacher is unaware of how children are interpreting and perceiving its demands. However, all cultural groups foster cognitive strengths that can be built on to facilitate classroom learning. As Trueba (1988) put it:

> At the heart of academic success, and regardless of the child's ethnicity or historical background, an effective learning environment must be constructed in which the child, especially the minority child, is assisted through meaningful and culturally appropriate relationships in the internalization of the mainstream cultural values embedded in our school system. (p. 282)

Considerable research on learning in diverse cultural contexts is based on neo-Vygotskian theory, which postulates that intellectual development takes place in natural interactive activities involving a child and an adult. Within a "zone of proximal development," which is the level of development for which a child is ready, a child can be assisted to learn new things. Effective learning requires that the child and adult share cultural values and patterns and that they communicate effectively (Trueba, 1988). Communication and cognitive style are two major areas of research on cultural difference. We will provide examples of some common differences between the cultural style of many children and that of teachers. The important point is that academic learning can be greatly enhanced when teachers learn the cultural style of the child well enough to connect effectively with the child within the child's zone of proximal development.

Shade (1997) distinguished between two different cognitive styles: analytical and synergetic. Her main contention is that schools and mainstream individuals tend to function with an analytical style; African American students as well as many students from other minority groups tend to function with a synergetic style. Analytical learners are competitive and independent, and they focus well on impersonal tasks. They learn well through print, focus best on one task at a time, and work in a step-by-step sequence. Synergetic learners, on the other hand, prefer to work cooperatively rather than independently; they do not block out their peers, but rather attempt to integrate personal relationships into learning tasks. Synergetic learners are stimulated by multiple activities and become bored when only one thing is happening. They often prefer kinesthetic and tactile involvement as well as discussion. Shade argues that teachers who are analytical learners often misread the behavior of synergetic learners, viewing them, for example, as talking too much, being off task, or cheating rather than as building on their preference for cooperative work. When the teaching style of the classroom matches the learning style of students, students can achieve well; synergetic learners need not be low achievers. Stressing a similar appreciation for multiple cognitive styles, Markova (1992) developed a typology of learners on the basis of thinking patterns along auditory, kinesthetic, and visual channels and also called for greater educational sensitivity to such diversity.

Some educators shy away from discussions of learning and cognitive style, feeling that such discussions only promote stereotypes. It is important to recognize that within any cultural group, individuals vary greatly. However, groups share certain tendencies, which are the result of each group's historic culture as well as its experience with oppression in the United States (Shade, 1997). Sensitivity to group tendencies can enable a teacher to read students' behavior more accurately and to try more alternatives when teaching. It is also important to recognize that minority groups differ. For example, whereas African American students tend to prefer oral communication and kinesthetic activities for taking in new information (Shade, 1997), Native American students tend to have excellent visual skills (Gilliland, 1988).

Cultural groups also differ in communication style, sometimes to the detriment of students' classroom experiences. For example, Pewewardy (2002) pointed out that many indigenous tribal languages are structured quite differently from English. Students who grow up speaking a tribal language that has minimal rules governing word order may find the highly rule-governed order of English words and phrases to be confusing. Rather than viewing students' language as confused, teachers should become familiar with the linguistic structure of students' tribal language.

Students who act out behaviorally or drop out psychologically from the classroom may be bored or may not see the relevance of what they are being asked to learn. Bored students often do not respond enthusiastically to many of the learning tasks they confront. But when the students are African American or Latino, teachers often think the problem stems from lack of motivation or lack of home support rather than boredom with the classroom routine. These misguided assumptions combine with low expectations for academic achievement to form insurmountable obstacles for these groups (Brown, 1986, p. 13).

Acting out or dropping out may also indicate that the student is under stress because of a lack of cultural continuity between the child and the classroom. The degree of cultural continuity between home and school can vary; the larger the gap, the harder schools need to work to construct bridges. For example, Phelan, Davidson, and Cao (1991) distinguished among four patterns: (1) congruent worlds among home, school, and peer group, with smooth transitions from one setting to the next; (2) different worlds with boundary crossings from one to the next that are manageable; (3) different worlds with unbridged boundary crossings that are hazardous for the student; and (4) different worlds with insurmountable barriers. In their research, they found that students did reasonably well academically with teachers who tried to adapt their teaching to the students. When forced to choose between the peer group and the school, or between home and school, many students did not choose school and consequently failed.

Language

Historically, most U.S. schools actively maintained an English-only policy, often prohibiting the use of any language other than English for instruction, although European immigrants in the 1880s and early 1890s used bilingual programs (particularly German-English) quite extensively. However, children of color whose native language was not English tended to be viewed as deficient and their home language and culture as inferior. Early strategies for teaching linguistically and culturally different students included submersion in the English language curriculum or placement in special English as a Second Language (ESL) classes. Neither approach successfully integrated the language-minority student into the mainstream. By the 1960s, spurred on by increased immigration from Cuba and the growing civil rights movement, education policymakers were desperately seeking another more promising approach. At the same time, parents, concerned teachers, and community activists began calling for the use of children's native languages in schools.

From their inception with the passage of the Bilingual Education Act in 1968, bilingual education programs were pushed into a compensatory mold. Although there are bilingual programs that use all the approaches to multicultural education described in this book, the majority continue to use the Teaching the Culturally Different approach. Such programs use the child's native language as a medium of instruction in content areas as a transition, while teaching the child the English language, until the child has learned enough English to be redesignated to an English-only program. In general, most bilingual education programs in the United States follow the transitional approach, in which the child moves from native-language instruction to English-only instruction as soon as possible (three years or less). Regardless of a particular program's structure, all bilingual education models assume that the language and culture a child learns at home can promote normal and healthy language acquisition, psychological development, and communication competence.

As Cummins (2000) explained, the basic challenge for students whose first language is not English is that they "must learn the language of instruction at the same time as they are expected to learn academic content *through* the language of instruction" (p. 57). Evidence indicates that children with well-developed first-language skills acquire their second language with greater ease and success than children who are still learning their first language. This phenomenon is explained by Cummins's "common underlying proficiency" model of language acquisition, which holds that many language skills and attitudes, once learned well, can be translated fairly easily into any language and that they are best learned in one's strongest language (Cummins, 2000). Such language skills include using verbs in different tenses, employing language to describe objects or feelings, and connecting print with meaningful oral language. Once a child has learned to use a particular language skill in one language, it can be transferred into the second language. Cummins points out that there is no single formula for how much instructional time a children should receive in which language, or which language skills should be transferred to the second language in what order. Rather, the most significant factor is how committed a school is to developing students' ability to use both first and second language for academic learning.

Educators tend to worry excessively about whether students whose native language is not English will learn English, and in the process, they attend too little to students' overall academic development. Based on a review of research on bilingual education, Pease-Alvarez and Hakuta (1992) concluded: "Don't worry about English; they are learning it; instead, worry about the instructional content; if you are going to worry about language, worry about the lost potential in the attrition of the native language, for all of the languages of the world are represented in this country" (p. 6).

A problem in today's standards and testing context is that tests that count toward a school's Annual Yearly Progress (AYP) are, for the most part, given in English. While there are limited provisions for first-language testing of recent immigrant students, the fact that most students' learning is being measured in English is pushing many schools away from primary language development. For example, in a study of language programming in California, Wiley and Wright (2004) found that, "In a large urban California school district, ... pressure to raise scores on high-stakes tests was even more influential in ending bilingual programs than Proposition 227 [which limited use of bilingual education]. District leaders rationalized that only by eliminating bilingual education and immersing students in all-English instruction starting in kindergarten would students have a chance of being able to read and answer the test questions in English" (p. 158). This policy is having the effect of reducing bilingual education programs to remedial programs for students who are the farthest behind, and discarding efforts to build students' language skills in their strongest language first.

In addition, ignoring or denigrating a child's native language may not only damage the child's language growth and self-concept but also cut off normal communication development between the child and his or her parents or grandparents. Many immigrant students, when enculturated with the Anglo, middle-class culture of the school, respond with shame and even hostility toward their parents, home language, and culture.

Many of the same considerations apply to dialect as well. Several different dialects are spoken within the United States; in addition to Standard English, dialects in current use include Appalachian, Hawaiian Creole, Tex-Mex, and Black English. Proponents of the cultural deficiency orientation view the speech of lower-class, African American children (and other non-Standard English dialect speakers) as incorrect, poor, and "destitute" (Newton, 1966). Since the mid-1960s, however, considerable research has established dialects as linguistically sound, governed by their own rules of phonemics, syntax, morphology, and word meaning (Labov, 1969). This being the case, educators have wondered whether dialect interferes with teaching conducted in Standard English. Such concerns, for example, have shaped debates over the usage of Black English in school settings (e.g., Oakland, California).

In a review of debates about Black English, Smitherman (1981) argued that the attitudes of educators toward the "Blackness" of Black English is a larger problem than communication mismatch per se. Speakers of Black English come to school having mastered one dialect, and they are cognitively equipped to master a second one—Standard English—as well as the content encoded in it. Unfortunately, they are penalized by being required to take tests that assume competence in Standard English before they have been taught to use it, administered by teachers who assume that Black English is substandard or poorly learned language and that those who speak it are incapable of advanced learning.

African American students who exhibit competence in oral games, such as sounding, understand the use of figurative language better than White students. Teachers who incorporate these students' verbal skills in language arts instruction have a definite strength on which to build their achievement (DeLain, Pearson, & Anderson, 1985). Incorporating students' language into instruction, for example by using quality literature written in the community vernacular, can effectively create a bridge between students' home dialect and standard academic English (Hollie, 2001; Maybin, 1994; Moss, 1994; Siegel, 1999).

Deafness as a Cultural Difference

Hearing people very often regard deafness as a deficiency, and they discuss people with deafness as lacking in normal language development and, as a result, full cognitive development. "The cultural view of the deaf community, on the other hand, views deaf people as a group that shares a common language and a common means of communication" (Stewart & Akamatsu, 1988, p. 238). American Sign Language (ASL) has been in existence since at least the early 1880s, and ASL and the difference orientation to educating deaf children have competed with the deficiency orientation for a long time. Oralism (teaching hearing-impaired children to speech-read and to speak orally) and signed English systems (which put English grammar and morphology into signs) have been used heavily in schools to attempt to approximate the English language as accurately as possible.

Although both oralism and signed English systems provide access to spoken English for children who have some hearing loss, American Sign Language is an alternative language system that is more accessible to children with profound or total hearing loss. As linguists have gained interest in studying ASL, appreciation has developed for this language's sophistication and integrity as a language and for its broad acceptance in a community that uses it as the primary language of communication. As a language-minority community, the deaf community also has other cultural strengths and resources in which deaf children can learn to participate, such as a wide range of organizations, arts produced by the deaf community, and interpersonal. "It is not possible to understand deaf people until the language is acquired but it is not possible to achieve in the language until there is contact with the culture. One does not become deaf to do this anymore than one becomes French in France" (Kyle & Pullen, 1988, p. 57). Increasingly, the deaf community is asking to be regarded and taught as a language-minority group rather than as a disabled group.

Mental Difference

Children whose school performance is far below average are often considered mentally deficient. A teacher who views students such as those in classes for the learning disabled or special needs as different rather than deficient is more likely to use an approach discussed later in this book than the approach discussed in this chapter. For example, imagine a ninth-grade teacher with some special education students who read on a fourth-grade level. The teacher who wishes to assimilate these students may not believe they are permanently deficient but may view the task of assimilating them into the classroom as virtually impossible if their reading deficiency is not corrected first. An alternative is to rethink the idea that there is a standard body of knowledge that all should learn and that this knowledge should be acquired through reading. Once a teacher examines this alternative, he or she is moving away from the Teaching the Exceptional and Culturally Different approach.

On the other hand, children who excel in certain areas and who may be classified as gifted and talented can be considered mentally different. Conceptions of what the word "gifted" means range widely, from narrow definitions that include only the top 1% to 5% in academic achievement (Terman et al., 1976) to broad definitions that view many people as having gifts or talents in a variety of areas. For example, Gardner (1993) described seven intelligences: linguistic, local and mathematical, musical, spatial, bodily and kinesthetic, interpersonal, and intrapersonal. Many people believe that, regardless of how one defines giftedness, gifted children need educational experiences that are different from those of "normal" children and that these experiences should ultimately help them provide the leadership needed in our technological society.

Proponents of the Teaching the Exceptional approach for gifted students believe that failure to offer enriched or accelerated programming often results in the failure to develop abilities, the development of frustration and sometimes psychological problems among the gifted, and the waste of a social resource. Over one-third of students scoring at or above the 95% percentile on achievement tests are not in any kind of program for gifted students (Swiatek & Lupkowski-Shoplik, 2003). Advocates of gifted students condemn the belief that they will make it on their own. On the basis of two research studies, Robinson, Roedell, and Jackson (1981) concluded that "superior abilities that are not nurtured will not develop" (p. 130). Advocates point to underachievers, dropouts, and even suicide victims, who have become frustrated with schooling and sometimes with life in general because their abilities were not being challenged or valued (Robbins, 1984). They also point to medical, scientific, artistic, and social accomplishments that have been achieved for society by gifted people whose abilities were cultivated. For these reasons, these proponents argue, some sort of differential education needs to be provided for this different group of children, whether it be a program within the regular classroom, a pullout program, an accelerated program, a special class, or some type of extra enrichment program (Reis, 1994).

Gender Difference

Gender differences in performance in math and science have decreased markedly over the past few decades. It used to be taken for granted that males naturally outperform females in these fields. During the 1970s and 1980s, concerted efforts were made to raise teachers' expectations for female achievement and to equalize opportunities in classroom practices (for instance, helping teachers make sure both sexes are called on equally) and course selection (making sure both sexes take upper-level math and science courses). In addition, efforts were expended to help girls to see math and science as relevant to their future plans (Leder & Fennema, 1990; Linn & Hyde, 1989). This work resulted in increased success among girls in math and science achievement. Today, although some gender gaps in achievement remain, most have closed significantly (Hanna, 2003).

At the same time, women are still underrepresented in many areas of science and computer science. For example, although women make up about 46% of the workforce in the United States, they occupy only about 10% of the upper-level jobs in technology, and women's participation in computer science majors has dropped recently after having made gains during the 1990s (Gatta & Trigg, 2001).

In K–12 classrooms, girls tend to think about and work with computers differently from boys. Whereas girls are more likely than boys to use computers collaboratively to solve problems, boys are more likely to enjoy the mechanics of the technology itself (Solomon, 2002). Brunner (1997) examined some popular video games and determined to which sex they were made to appeal. Referring to a series of studies conducted by the Center for Children and Technology/Education Development Center on gender-related attitudes toward technology, Brunner explained that, for boys, "technology is seen as a source of power" and as a means to "one-way communication," whereas girls tend to view technology "as a medium" that enables people to "communicate, connect, and share ideas" (p. 55). It is important, therefore, that teachers develop approaches to computer instruction that are sensitive to their students' gendered ideas about technology.

There is some debate about the extent to which gender differences that still exist in science and technology are due to biology. We believe that the success in closing gender differences in achievement in math science reflects the power of intervention, once educators have become aware of an equity issue and what can be done about it, and are convinced that it is worth addressing. As a result of differential socialization, the sexes bring to school different skills, interests, and confidence levels for mathematics, science, and computer science learning which, when taken into account, need not lead to gender differences in learning.

There is debate about the extent to which single-sex schools benefit each gender. Some researchers have found that girls develop more leadership skills and self-confidence in single-sex schools, where they do not have to compete with boys who tend to dominate in leadership roles. In a study of the effects of single-sex schooling on general achievement, Riordan (1990) found that "minority females profit most from single-sex schooling, followed by minority males, and then by white females" (p. 147), largely because single-sex schools reduce the effect of the adolescent subculture that tends to disadvantage females. Research on the benefits of single-sex or mixed-sex education is not yet conclusive, however.

No matter how similarly teachers may try to treat boys and girls in school, some compensation is in order for the differential socialization that the sexes experience outside of school. Interestingly, there is very little discussion about how to assimilate boys into traditional female domains—for example, evaluating techniques that might be successful in preparing boys to become office workers. We think that this example gives some indication as to which sex has controlled the more interesting, prestigious, and well-paying work.

RECOMMENDED PRACTICES

Since no classroom is completely homogeneous, teachers learn to expect differences among their students. The problem the teacher faces is what to make of those differences, and the more students vary from the teacher's standards, the greater the problem. Teachers who see strong reasons for maintaining traditional conceptions of what students need to learn and who want to see all their students achieve these goals as well as possible will search for ways to teach all of their students. Whatever adaptations teachers make for diverse students, they usually expect adaptations to be temporary until the students are able to swim on their own.

Program Structure
Before discussing classroom adaptations for diverse students, we will comment on the range of program structures schools use to accommodate them. These structures range from efforts to make the regular classroom as inclusive as possible for diverse students to design of separate programs for specific populations.

Programs for students with disabilities have shifted markedly over the past several decades. While students used to be removed from the regular classroom and integrated back into it only when they were deemed ready, "the student now starts in the general education classroom [and] goes to the more restrictive environment of the resource room or self-contained classroom only if the specified goals are not attained in the general education classroom" (Haskell, 2000). Inclusive classrooms are specifically designed to accommodate students with a wide range of learning abilities and approaches to learning. Often this is done by teaming a special education and general education teacher in the same classroom. This shift from removing students with disabilities from the regular classroom to keeping them there and transforming the regular classroom is reflected in the Individuals with Disabilities Act, passed in 1990. Philosophically as well as pedagogically, making classrooms inclusive for students with disabilities involves much the same thinking as making classrooms inclusive for a wide range of other students.

At the other end of the continuum are programs designed for specific populations. Students with severe retardation and multiple disabilities are frequently educated most of the day in a separate, self-contained class. Immigrant children are often placed in separate "Newcomer" programs for a period of time to ease transition into U.S. schooling in English. Some large school districts have implemented African American immersion schools to attempt to raise the achievement and promote the overall development of African American students, thereby offering African American students an experience comparable to that of most White students, who attend Euro-American immersion schools staffed mainly or exclusively by White teachers, offering a largely Eurocentric curriculum and Euro-American cultural style of doing things. Although research on the effectiveness of such schools is inconclusive, historically Black colleges, have a much higher success rate in graduating African American students than do White colleges (Farrell, 1992).

Between inclusive classroom structures and separate program structures is a range of possibilities. A dual-language program structure, for example, separates students by language for most of the day during the first years of the program. For example, at the first-grade level students may spend 90% of the school day being educated in their primary language and learning the second language, and only in 10% of the school day are they mixed by language (for instance, for music or physical education). As members of both language groups develop competence in the second language, the groups are gradually mixed for instruction more and more, until they are mixed all day, and instruction alternates for everyone between English and the other language (usually Spanish).

What follows are bridges teachers can build between the child and the curriculum to support achievement and assimilation in inclusive classrooms. We have organized these bridges under the broad areas of curriculum content, instructional process, and parental involvement. Examples of what these concepts look like in practice can be found in Chapter 2 of our companion book, *Turning on Learning* (Grant & Sleeter, 2006).

Curriculum Content

The standards movement directs schools to offer a grade-level curriculum to all students, including those who are academically behind grade level. We support the recommendation that curriculum be as challenging as possible. Unless students are genuinely mentally retarded, we believe it should be oriented toward academic excellence rather than remediation, with college access as the goal. Jaime Escalante, for example, has been a highly visible advocate of a challenging curriculum for inner-city students. When asked whom he recruited for his Advanced Placement math program, he replied that he did not specifically recruit students identified as "gifted." Rather, he says, "I often chose the rascals and kids who were 'discipline problems' as well as those who simply liked math. I found that the 'class cut-ups' were often the most intelligent, yet they were extremely bored by poor teaching and disillusioned by the perceived dead end that school represented for them" (Escalante & Dirmann, 1990, p. 409).

In high-poverty schools or schools with large proportions of students of color, often teacher expectations are low and teachers may be new, underprepared, or inexperienced, so curriculum is often weak. To address this problem, many schools and school districts are adopting "off-the-shelf" curriculum packages such as Success for All, America's Choice, or Open Court as a way of getting all teachers on board with a grade-level curriculum that is coordinated across grade levels. For example, Sherman (2002) described a school on the Flathead Indian Reservation that adopted Success for All, largely because it utilizes a considerable amount of cooperative learning, which the community saw as fitting with indigenous culture. The school used Success for All teaching processes along with books that connected with the Indian community and now reports significantly increased test scores. Such programs report increases in student achievement mainly because they align curriculum very closely to state curriculum standards and provide considerable structure for how to teach standards-based content (e.g., Borman & Hewes, 2002).

The Teaching the Exceptional and the Culturally Different approach does question what students should be learning in school. Rather, its advocates begin with state curriculum standards and seek ways of helping a diverse student population master those standards. As Table 2-1 shows, if students are not learning the standard curriculum satisfactorily, bridges need to be built between them and the curriculum. Lesson plans in *Turning on Learning* (Grant & Sleeter, 2006) illustrate putting these bridges into practice.

The experiences and interests of students serve as one bridge. Students sometimes do not try hard when they fail to see that what they are being taught is useful or personally interesting. In addition, students often need familiar concrete examples to help them acquire new concepts. For example, Moses and Cobb (2001) described a successful program for teaching algebra to inner-city middle school students. Directionality was a concept students had not learned to attach to numbers, and many students were having difficulty with positive and negative numbers. So the teachers sent the students to the local subway and had them diagram the subway system in terms of directionality. The teachers then helped the students represent their experience with the subway numerically, in the process helping them to translate the familiar—subway routes—into the unfamiliar—positive and negative numbers.

TABLE 2-2.
A Sample of Household Funds of Knowledge

Agriculture and Mining	Economics	Household Management	Material and Scientific Knowledge	Medicine	Religion
Ranching and farming	Business	Budgets	Construction	Contemporary Medicine	Catechisms
Horsemanship (cowboys)	Market values	Childcare	Carpentry	Drugs	Baptisms
Animal husbandry	Appraising	Cooking	Roofing	First aid procedures	Bible studies
Soil and Irrigation systems	Renting and selling	Appliance repairs	Masonry	Anatomy	Moral knowledge and ethics
Crop planting	Loans		Painting	Midwifery	
Hunting, tracking, dressing	Labor laws		Design and architecture		
	Building codes			Folk medicine	
Mining	Consumer knowledge		Repair	Herbal knowledge	
Timbering	Accounting		Airplane	Folk cures	
Minerals	Sales		Automobile	Folk veterinary cures	
Blasting			Tractor		
Equipment operation and maintenance			House maintenance		

Source: L. C. Moll (1992), Bilingual classroom studies and community analysis. *Educational Researcher, 21*(2), 20–24.

Moll (1992) helped teachers work with parents to construct a curriculum that built on what were, in his words, the funds of knowledge held by families in the community. Table 2-2 summarizes the funds of knowledge in the local community with which he worked. With practice, teachers became increasingly skilled at developing classroom lessons and homework assignments that tapped into community knowledge, creating more congruence between school knowledge and the students' lives.

To make the curriculum relevant to the lives of students, teachers need to ask two questions: (1) What is the academic concept I am trying to teach? and (2) What examples or experiences do my students have that connect to this concept? A science teacher in a low-income rural area thus seeks out everyday examples, such as plants or animal life familiar to students, to teach science concepts. A social studies teacher on an Indian reservation connects social studies concepts with the history of the tribe(s) of which the students are members. In so doing, the teacher attempts to broaden what students know—keeping mastery of a challenging academic curriculum as the goal but making the concepts taught "user friendly" and familiar to the students.

A second bridge is language. Academic content and skills must be meaningful if students are to learn them; meaning is best conveyed in whatever language a student understands. Schools with curricula structured to promote academic achievement for language-minority students provide the most difficult content in a student's native language, content that uses many context clues (such as hands-on work) in sheltered English, and content in fluent, mainstream English as students become able to handle it. It requires five to seven years to develop competence in learning new academic content in a second language (although it takes a much shorter time to achieve conversational fluency); it is important to recognize that the academic benefits of bilingual instruction may not show up for several years (Cummins, 2000).

Most English language learners are not in bilingual education programs, however. Teachers can learn to make academic content reasonably comprehensible to students whose native language is not English. Part of this involves giving students explicit instruction in English and plenty of opportunity to practice using the language in a nonthreatening context. Teaching subject matter in English is not the same thing as providing English Language Development (ELD), or actually instructing students in English vocabulary, grammar, and syntax. Focusing on meaning that students communicate through language rather than on correcting their errors when teaching content is less threatening to students as they practice using a new language. If a child makes a comment or answers a question using grammar or words incorrectly, the teacher can incorporate into a reply a corrected restatement of the child's utterance. The communication focus is on meaning; sometimes children will repeat the corrected restatement, which helps with the learning process.

When teaching reading and writing to students whose native language or dialect is not Standard English, teachers need to distinguish between mechanics and meaning. For example, Taylor (1989) described a process in which she taught

Black English-speaking students to write in Standard English. Her goal was to help students convey their own ideas and meanings as effectively as possible to particular audiences. She helped students learn to identify specific patterned differences between Black English and Standard English; students also analyzed writings by Black and White authors in order to understand writing style. Most of all, she stressed the importance of what students have to say, helping them gradually learn to control the mechanics. In a study of reading instruction, Moll, Diaz, Estrada, and Lopes (1990) found that teachers were equating Spanish-speaking students' skill in decoding English with their ability to comprehend meaning. As a result, instruction was too simple for the level of content that many students could comprehend and tended to bog down in the mechanics of decoding. The mechanics of language do need to be taught in isolation, but with a meaningful use of language to convey the ideas being presented in the class.

Another bridge involves filling in important academic gaps. For example, for mainstreamed special education students, Reynolds and Birch (1988) recommend that the curriculum be developmentally appropriate (e.g., do not teach long division before students have mastered addition and subtraction) and that teachers make sure students are taught what the authors call cultural imperatives: language skills, mathematics, health and safety, social skills, and career skills. They point out that mainstreamed special education students may not be able to learn everything that is in the standard curriculum; the teacher should decide what to emphasize, using these recommendations as guidelines.

Too often teachers become so overwhelmed with what students have not learned that they become bogged down in remediation. If there are large gaps in the students' knowledge, teachers should be selective about what students need to learn, focusing on the most important content for helping them catch up and start to excel.

Instructional Process

More attention has gone into modifying instruction than curriculum content for the Teaching the Exceptional and the Culturally Different approach. Teachers who take this approach usually feel fairly confident about what students should learn but less confident about how to help them learn it. The approach suggests several ways of modifying instruction to serve diverse learners more effectively. In *Turning on Learning* (Grant & Sleeter, 2006), we illustrate these in the second chapter, which coordinates with this chapter in this book.

Achievement can be enhanced when teachers work with the child within her or his zone of proximal development, which was described earlier. The Center for Research on Education, Diversity and Excellence (CREDE) (Tharp et al., 2000) developed five standards for effective pedagogy using the zone of proximal development, based on their research into academically successful classrooms of culturally and linguistically diverse students. The standards are (1) teachers and students working together in small groups to jointly create an idea or a product; (2) teachers connecting lessons to students' lives, including their experiences at home, in the community, and at school; (3) teachers developing language and literacy across the curriculum; (4) teachers engaging students with challenging lessons that maintain high standards and design activities to advance students' understanding to more complex levels; and (5) teachers emphasizing teacher-student dialogue over lectures, especially academic, goal-directed, small-group conversations.

The standards emphasize finding out what students know and can do, and working interactively with students to build new knowledge and skills on the understandings, language, learning strategies, and interests they bring into the classroom. Tharp and colleagues summarized research results on the connection between these strategies and student academic achievement: "Teachers who were stronger implementers of the Five Standards produced significantly greater gains in reading performance" (p. 228). The most long-term demonstration of the effectiveness of building on students' culture using these five standards was the Kamehameha Elementary Education Program (KEEP) in Hawaii, a primary-grade program for Native Hawaiian children (e.g., Jordan, 1985).

Scaffolding is a useful process that makes use of the CREDE standards. This process refers to temporary support for students as they learn to do something new and complex (like training wheels on a bicycle); scaffolding also helps teachers embed lower-level skills and content in higher-order thinking. It involves starting with, and accessing, what students already know, then guiding students in producing a new academic skill or product from there. For example, Gibbons (2002) described a process of scaffolding complex writing on intellectually challenging topics for English language learners. In Stage 1, students learn various ways of retrieving what they already know (such as using discussion) and linking it with new knowledge. In Stage 2, the teacher talks through the construction of text, modeling writing text similar to what students will write, involving students in writing portions of the text. The new text makes use of the writer's prior knowledge, connecting it with new ideas and new writing skills. In Stage 3, the teacher jointly constructs text with students, starting with the student's verbalization of what is to be written and then helping them construct sentences, choose word working, and so forth as needed. The teacher may also give students an outline of the text they are to produce, with spaces for them to write, to help students visualize the writing assignment. In Stage 4, students write independently.

Adapting instruction to the learning styles of students is another way to engage them in learning. Instruction that uses mainly print, whole-class teaching, and individual work is not engaging for many students. In fact, students who tune out or do not seem to concentrate well may be reacting to instructional strategies that do not work well for them. For example, whole-language, collaborative learning is compatible with the style of many Native American children because it emphasizes meaning and process over product, uses cooperative work, capitalizes on oral language, and integrates subject areas. These features are compatible with the preference of many Native American students for communal learning and personal meaning, use of time, and holistic worldview (Kasten, 1992). Many African American students tune in more in a classroom that encourages interpersonal interaction, multiple activities, and multiple sensory modalities (for example, use of body movement and sound) than in quiet classrooms in which students are supposed to pay attention to tasks more than people, print more than sound, and do only one thing at a time (Shade, 1997).

Many formal and informal methods are available to assess students' learning styles, including both paper-pencil and computerized instruments. The important point is for teachers to find out which strategies hold their own students' attention and engage their minds and then to use those strategies, particularly when teaching material that is new or difficult.

Many of the same teaching strategies that make content accessible to English language learners also help special education students in inclusive classrooms. As Haskell (2000) noted, "dependency on the textbook/ lecture instructional model without accommodations or alternative strategies 'handicaps' the student with learning disabilities." Students are handicapped by instructional processes that do not work for them and are facilitated by processes that do work for them.

For example, teachers can make content accessible to a range of students by using strategies such as pictures, diagrams, and role play to supplement spoken or written language. Structured small-group activities in which children talk through material helps English language learners to use vocabulary they know in order to make sense out of new ideas. Classwide peer tutoring is highly useful in diverse inclusive classrooms. In a longitudinal study of special education students who experienced classwide peer tutoring, Greenwood (1999) found that these students performed better on standardized tests, were less likely to drop out of high school, and after seventh grade less likely to need special education support services than those who were taught in classrooms that did not use this strategy. In classwide peer tutoring, students are taught how to tutor each other, and then everyone has an opportunity to serve as both tutor and tutee.

It is also helpful for teachers of English language learners to identify new or potentially confusing words and phrases ahead of time, and plan how to teach or clarify these during instruction. (For example, the phrase "run with an idea" is not necessarily meaningful to someone learning English.) The language skills of language-minority students tend to improve when they are encouraged to talk with peers in cooperative learning contexts. For example, Garcia (1988) found that language-minority students learn math and literacy skills most effectively when student–student discussions took up at least 50% of the instructional time.

All of the strategies mentioned here start with identification of what students already know and can do, and then go on to adaptation of instructional processes to use and build on what students can do in order to help them learn something new. These are not crutches, but rather serve as ways of helping students learn successfully.

Parental Involvement

Public schools are frequently a source of alienation for low-income and minority parents (Calabrese, 1990). For a wide variety of reasons, such parents often do not participate in schools the way teachers expect. Some parents feel it is the teacher's job to teach and that parents should stay out; some parents who were low achievers themselves in school feel uncomfortable dealing with teachers; and some parents, when they try to participate, are turned off by school personnel (Harry, 1992; Soto, 1997). It is important for teachers not to lower their expectations for children's learning, regardless of whether or not parents participate. However, there are many recommended practices teachers can use in attempting to connect more effectively with parents. For example, teachers can try to meet parents on the parents' turf rather than in the school. Initial meetings with parents should focus on a child's strengths rather than on problems. Problem solving should involve genuine two-way rather than one-way communication. Schools can encourage parents to network. Teachers can also collaborate with institutions and organizations in minority communities, such as the church (Billingsly & Caldwell, 1991; Cummins, 2000; Frase, 1994; Gilliland, 1988; Soto, 1997).

A model of building parent involvement on community strengths was developed by James Comer (Comer et al., 1996), who has helped several schools serving low-income, African American students to raise the achievement levels on standardized achievement tests to well above the district average. The school staffs learn to use child development principles and build support systems for healthy development, rather than blaming children and their parents for problems. Parent teams are formed, and parents begin to work cooperatively with the teachers and administrators. This process of bridge building takes several years, requiring teachers as well as parents to learn to change their behavior with each other; but the process pays off in terms of the children's achievement.

To illustrate the implementation of Teaching the Exceptional and the Culturally Different, we offer two vignettes.

MS. ROSS

Ms. Ross has been teaching fourth grade in Los Angeles for several years. This teaching assignment was her first after acquiring her teaching certificate. Her students this year are typical of those she has taught since she began. They are African American and Latino residents of a poor socioeconomic community. The community members, including the parents of Ms. Ross's students, respect the school and look on it as the main institution that will improve life chances for their children.

Of the 33 students in Ms. Ross's class, 16 are girls—7 African American, 4 Mexican American, 4 Mexican immigrants, and 1 Salvadoran immigrant. Of the 17 boys, 7 are African American, 5 are Mexican immigrants, 3 are Mexican American, 1 is Chilean, and 1 is Guatemalan. Although several students speak Spanish as their first language, Ms. Ross teaches in an English-only program. The immigrant students' familiarity with English varies widely; although all of them can carry on conversations in English, several have difficulty when it comes to reading and writing in English.

On entering Ms. Ross's classroom, you are struck by the richness and warmth of the environment. Colorful bulletin boards, lively posters (mostly of nature), bushy plants in decorative pots, two aquariums, and two hamsters (in cages) capture your attention. Ms. Ross mentions that she needs to find more time to teach science; most of her day is spent with reading, writing, and math. However, students will be tested the following year in science, and she loves science herself, so she works it in as she can.

Ms. Ross follows a highly structured curriculum package for reading and language arts, and another package for math. As you enter the classroom, you notice her working with a small group at the reading table, while the rest of the class is completing workbook pages at their desks. She glances up at you, then goes back to her work with six children. This is ELD time, or English Language Development time, and she is currently working with the children who tested lowest in English. Right now they are reading and discussing a story in their ELD text. Ms. Ross has a very warm and lively way of interacting with the children as she instructs them in vocabulary and sentence structure, using the story as a tool for language teaching.

They finish, and Ms. Ross instructs them to return to their seats. She then tells everyone to open their reading text to the story they are working with this week. It is a fairly long story about a family that makes their living fishing off a boat. Ms. Ross tells the group that she knows they are all familiar with this story since the class has read it and worked on the vocabulary previously. She tells students to sit with their buddy in pairs and to take turns reading the story orally to each other. The buddy is supposed to think of a question to ask the reader at the end of each page. When they finish, they will switch roles. Students begin, and she circulates, helping and checking on progress. Several of the students have difficulty formulating a question to ask their partner, so she helps them with this.

The bell rings, and it is time to line up and go out for recess. Ms. Ross then has a few minutes to talk with you. She tells you that this class is really super, but most of the students are behind grade level. The school did not make its AYP (Annual Yearly Progress target) last year, and teachers are under tremendous pressure to bring up test scores. So, she spends a good deal of time each day drilling students on basic reading and math skills. She comments that she thinks her students will do reasonably well this year but that it is hard because those who are new to English won't be ready to test well in English by the time tests are given in April. There isn't much time for social studies, and even less for art and music, but she mentions that she tries to work these things in here and there, as she finds time. She tries to keep class work interesting, but it's hard because she feels that she needs to stick closely to the text so that students will be prepared for the tests.

She also finds herself becoming frustrated with parents who do not speak English because she is unable to communicate with them and they are unable to help their children with homework that is in English. "It's not their fault, they came here for a better life," she comments. "But I only know a few words of Spanish myself, and a couple of the families speak indigenous languages rather than Spanish anyway. All I can do is try my best." She says that she really likes teaching in this school, but if test scores don't come up and the school eventually is closed, she will probably move to a suburban teaching job because that seems like it would be easier and more stable.

MRS. STEPHENS

Mrs. Stephens is a high school learning disabilities teacher. She has been teaching for five years in a suburban high school. During the course of a day, she sees about 30 students, most of whom are boys. Her classroom is small; it is furnished with two round tables, a number of chairs, several carrels, three well-stocked bookshelves, and a teacher's desk. Student work is displayed prominently around the room.

Mrs. Stephens tells you that her main job is to teach the students whatever she can to help them make it in the regular classroom and survive in the outside world. She has informally divided her students into two categories: those who can probably be remediated well enough to handle regular classes and maybe even college, and those who are too far behind to catch up with regular classwork and who need real-world survival skills, such as vocational training, skill in handling a checkbook, ability to fill out job applications, and so forth. The class about to be described consists of 10 students who are preparing themselves for a more academic course of study.

As the bell rings, the students enter class, laughing and shoving each other on their way to their seats. Mrs. Stephens jokes with them in a friendly manner. The second bell rings and the students quiet down. Mrs. Stephens says, "Today we will continue with grammar. We will learn about the preposition." One boy jokes to a girl, "I'm gonna preposition you!" Mrs. Stephens says, "I'm gonna preposition you, too. Brian, come up here." She gives him a poster with a word written on it. She says, "You are a preposition. Hold this."

Mrs. Stephens calls up other students and gives them posters with other words on them. She has the students arrange themselves in various combinations to form various sentences, having them identify the subject and verb of each sentence. For each sentence, she has students explain what words go with "to" and why. Then she says, "You can all sit down. You are really getting the idea."

Dave raises his hand. "My friend Marc, in the regular English class, said they studied this stuff last month."

Mrs. Stephens nods her head. "Right. So far they have studied a lot more parts of speech than you have, but by the end of the semester you should have pretty well caught up." Joe asks, "Does that mean we won't need to be in here anymore?"

Mrs. Stephens replies, "Not yet. You still don't have the vocabulary and reading skills the English teachers require, although by next year some of you may be ready to handle Mr. Ross's class. Now, let's get back to these prepositions."

Mrs. Stephens gives the students a list of prepositions on a handout. She then writes several sentences on the board and asks the students to identify the parts of speech and explain which word is the preposition. The last 10 minutes are spent playing a game with prepositions.

After class, you ask how many of her students actually learn to make it in school on their own. She replies, "Not that many. A lot of this stuff I teach does stick—for a while at least—but they are so far behind; it's like running after a moving train. Most of them won't completely graduate from LD, but they will become more successful in their other classes, and some will need LD less and less. Reading-oriented work just isn't their thing, so every day it's a struggle."

You ask if the regular teachers assume any responsibility for teaching these students. She replies, "Oh, sure, a number of them do. They give me new vocabulary words to review with the students—study guides to help them with. Some let me give tests orally. Some make allowances on their written work—have them do stuff orally, have them work with a buddy. They don't change their whole approach to teaching, of course. But a lot of them make modifications here and there so my students can at least get something out of the class and experience some success. A lot of high school teaching is heavy reading and lecture. Sometimes I wonder if it has to be that way, but that's the way it is. I've got kids who would drop out before they'd endure another day of heavy reading and lecture in a regular class. I mean, I've got eleventh and twelfth graders who read on a fourth-grade level. Without LD or something like it, they'd be on the streets, and most regular teachers aren't at all equipped to deal with them. But the teachers are very cooperative about trying to modify things for the students who are reading on maybe a junior high level."

CRITIQUE Ms. Ross and Mrs. Stephens are both very concerned and caring teachers, and they give their best effort to implementing the approach described in this chapter. If they care about their students and do their jobs as well as they can, what criticisms can we have of what they, or others adopting this approach, are doing?

Let us first summarize the main criticisms of the cultural deficiency orientation, which were very cogently stated in 1970 by Baratz and Baratz. The notion of cultural deficiency was promoted by educators and social scientists who lacked an anthropological background and who took middle-class Anglo culture as their reference point for judging other cultures. Those people whose behavior, language, and cognition differed from this narrow standard were judged as "sick, pathological, deviant, and underdeveloped," with blame placed on their genes or their environment, or both (Baratz & Baratz, 1970, p. 31). "Instead of explicating the strengths of African American [and other minority] youth, a number of educators, opinion shapers, and policy-makers have persisted over the years in characterizing these young people as culturally deprived, educationally disadvantaged, learning disabled, and (using a term in vogue nowadays) at risk" (Madhere, 1991, p. 59).

Abundant anthropological and linguistic data amply demonstrate that lower-class people and people of color have well-developed cultures that are different in some ways from those of middle-class Whites. Culture can be understood as a way of making sense and coping with the resources and opportunities a community has or of coping with what a community lacks. Low-income people do lack access to economic resources, but lacking that access is not the same thing as lacking knowledge and culture. School failure to support and develop the knowledge, skills, and language abilities that low-income and minority students have is disabling, promoting academic failure rather than growth (Cummins, 1989).

However, the cultural deficiency interpretation continues to experience renewed popularity. In the 1980s, this took the form of describing children as being "at risk." In the 2000s, it is taking the form of attributing low test scores to the culture of poverty. Critics of this interpretation do not deny that families and communities live in severe poverty. Rather, they question the usefulness of dismissing the knowledge people from impoverished or culturally different communities have, rather than seeking ways to build on that knowledge in the classroom. Educators who persist in thinking of their students as "culturally deprived" are choosing not to learn a good deal that could help them teach more effectively.

The notion of mental deficiency is also flawed, especially the categories of educable mental retardation, emotional disturbance, and learning disabilities. It is very likely that you view these categories as real deficiencies that educators have discovered and are learning how to treat. Most nonspecial educators believe that special educators agree, for example, on what mental retardation is, how to identify a retarded child, and what to do about mental retardation. Actually, special educators do not agree on these issues, particularly as they apply to the largest special education category—learning disabilities. Ysseldyke and Algozzine (1982) distinguished between objective categories—blindness and deafness—which have an objective, sensory basis, and subjective categories—learning disabilities, emotional disturbance, and mental retardation—which are "completely subjectively derived" (p. 43). Objective categories are fairly clearly caused by a physiological defect, and it is not necessary to be a professional to recognize members of these categories. For example, blindness is caused by damage to the eye or optic nerve, and usually you do not need to give a series of complicated tests to determine whether someone is blind, although it may be necessary to give such tests to determine the visual limitations of a partially sighted person.

Subjective categories are different. How, for example, do you determine who is learning disabled and what causes learning disabilities? Although learning disabled individuals have been thought historically to be neurologically impaired, there is no evidence of such impairment in most students classified as learning disabled, and in practice, the concept of learning disability is a product of schools that have institutionalized particular conceptions of "normal" learning and what it means to succeed and to fail (Dudley-Marling, 2001; Skrtic, 2003). Students certainly do differ, but the question is what to make of their differences. In addition to the categories themselves being based on subjective criteria, they feed into the cultural deficiency paradigm through which children of color, children from poverty communities, and immigrant children are still too often viewed. For example, despite decades of professionals of color trying to reduce the extent to which African American students are referred for special education, they are still greatly over-referred.

Problems with the deficiency orientation can be illustrated with a story. Imagine that you are forming a neighborhood basketball team and you decide that substantial height is the main characteristic team members should have. You round up your neighbors and discover you have more than enough people for a team. You line them up by height, and because you can afford to, you define the shortest 5% of the neighborhood as deficient. The neighborhood could treat shortness as a serious problem and expend considerable energy looking for a remedy. Perhaps some of the shortest neighbors could even be cured of their defect by eating well. Soon there is a concerted effort among the neighbors to see that their children are fed well enough to grow tall. A year passes and heights sprout up. The next season, you line everybody up again, choose the tallest people for your team and most of the rest for the bench, and again define the shortest 5% as deficient. Crazy? This process is exactly like using norm-referenced tests to determine who is mentally deficient. Norm-referenced tests are specifically constructed to rank-order people—to line them up by height, so to speak, except instead of according to height, we line people up according to reading level, skill in certain thinking processes, or general knowledge. We then decide where to draw the line between "normal" and "deficient." As long as we have enough workers for available jobs, we can afford to classify those on the lower end of our rank order as deficient.

To some extent, Mrs. Stephens in the case study recognizes these problems. She realizes that the content and skills taught in the regular classroom form a yardstick for judging the extent to which her students are normal. Some of what she teaches has functional value outside school, and some has value mainly in helping her students cope with the demands of the regular classroom. Hence, she spends considerable time teaching concepts such as prepositions, although she wonders if such time might be better spent helping her students develop their talents and interests more. She has sufficient sustained contact with her students so that she gets to know most of them as interesting people with a variety of abilities, and she sometimes wonders if it is accurate or fair to call them "handicapped." Nevertheless, she also knows that our society has little tolerance for people who lack functional literacy skills, and so she builds her instruction around attempting to remediate these so-called failings.

Even when someone has an obvious disability, there is still the problem of professionals defining what the other person's needs are, which is a form of oppression. We would be foolish to argue that a blind person is not impaired physiologically or that a severely retarded person has no learning difficulties. But again, the question is what to make of these things, and who decides. McLarty and Gibson (2000), for example, argued that a problem that verbally disabled, multiply impaired young people face is that their attempts to communicate are routinely ignored and go unrecognized. They explained that "[t]his inattention, or lack of awareness on the part of educators or carers, of behaviour which constitutes communication often leads to the labeling of non-verbal communicators as 'non-communicators' and, consequently, even 'non-thinkers'" (p. 140). They used video as a tool to capture children's communication efforts, so that they could learn to understand what so-called nonverbal students were trying to say in order to involve them in helping make decisions about everyday life.

Impairments to one's body do not usually prevent learning, although they may necessitate the development of skills and strategies that most people do not need. For example, manual communication lends itself better to a deaf person than does oral communication, but there is no evidence that deafness itself (or other physiological impairments, except clearly identifiable brain damage), manual communication, or the strategies that deaf people use to compensate for hearing loss retard their learning ability. Thus, although there may be differences in how some physiologically impaired people learn, these differences are not learning deficiencies. Even still, disability-related judgments reflect conceptions of normal, so that disability is seen as "a 'problem' of the body gone wrong" (Titchkosky, 2000, p. 198).

In spite of objections to it, the deficiency orientation maintains considerable popularity, resurfacing periodically with new terminology. In the first edition of this book, we predicted that this orientation was waning, especially the notion of cultural deprivation. However, the concept was then revived in the children at-risk discourse. The notion of children at risk, like that of the culturally deprived or socially maladjusted, may direct our attention toward services that need to be provided. But more often such a term locates the source of a child's problems within the child, as if the problems were personal or biological characteristics, and directs our attention away from larger social problems such as poverty or racism that create barriers and problems for many children (Fine, 1990).

The difference orientation corrects many flaws in the deficiency orientation. It focuses on strengths, recognizes the legitimacy of various cultural experiences and routes to becoming a mature person, and does not advocate that a child be ashamed of or give up anything he or she is. Certainly, the difference orientation also has its critics, although they are fewer in number. Educators who are trying to be positive but know relatively little about a group often stereotype, in order to oversimplify and to take an either-or position where none is needed. Stereotyping, whether it occurs through attempts to be constructive, implies that all members of a given group share the same cultural and behavioral patterns. Witness, for example, the teacher who comments, "Mark is probably doing well in math because Asians are so good in that area; he doesn't seem to talk much or have many friends, but then Asians are quiet." The teacher is turning group tendencies in achievement and style into a stereotype she is using to "explain" Mark, which leads her to refrain from actually looking closely at Mark's math skills, wondering why Mark doesn't have many friends, and what she can do about it. Positive stereotypes, such as those attributed to Asians, are almost as damaging as negative stereotypes because both deflect attention away from individual needs and characteristics (Pang, 1990).

Furthermore, the difference orientation tends to assume that minority-group people lack competence in the dominant culture. Most speakers of Black English, for example, comprehend Standard English very well, and a teacher who assumes they do not is underestimating people's ability to become bicultural. Indeed, such a teacher may be less bicultural than the students! Failing to recognize errors in these assumptions, many educators make needless adaptations—and excuses—for their culturally different students. Based on a review of research on learning styles, Kleinfeld and Nelson (1988) concluded that, although ample evidence documents that learning style preferences do vary cross-culturally, there is no demonstrable impact on achievement when teachers try to match specific teaching strategies to specific aspects of student learning style. Achievement does improve when teachers use variety but not necessarily when specific teaching and learning styles are matched.

The difference orientation to Teaching the Culturally Different as it relates to language-minority students has focused almost exclusively on addressing the "language problem" by transitioning students into English as soon as possible. This has pushed much of bilingual education into a compensatory model. Cummins (1995) argued that bilingual education and compensatory education have been unsuccessful because they have not significantly altered the relationships between educators and minority students and between schools and minority communities. This condition has prompted one researcher on Latino education to state, "Programs that attempt to address the educational outcomes of Hispanic students without a consideration of the school-based variables which give rise to those problems will only scratch at the surface" (Arias, 1986, p. 55).

Now let us look more broadly at the entire approach that has been presented in this chapter. Some of you probably agree with the foregoing criticisms but still see the approach as sound. After all, many of the recommended practices seem to be sensible, effective strategies that good teachers use. Furthermore, both research and experiential evidence confirm the usefulness of these practices. For example, most teachers know that students become more interested in a concept that the teacher has tried to make relevant. Who would argue with the recommendation that the level of instruction be matched to a student's readiness level? What criticisms, then, have been directed toward this approach?

One of the main criticisms is that it is assimilationist, and, as such, it seeks to eliminate minority cultures and make everyone like White, middle-class people. Banks (1994) summarizes several problems that "Third World writers and researchers" have had with this approach (p. 66). One problem is that people of color have viewed assimilation as a "weapon of the oppressor that was designed to destroy the cultures of ethnic groups and to make their members personally ineffective and politically powerless" (p. 66). Another problem is that the melting-pot idea never worked for people of color, even when they wanted to melt. No matter how hard some people have tried to melt, White society is not color-blind and still devalues people of color. Finally, the assimilationist ideology is a "racist ideology that justified damaging school and societal practices that victimized minority group children" (p. 66), for example, using culturally biased tests to classify minority children as mentally retarded. As Banks points out, "The assumption that all children can learn equally well from teaching materials that only reflect the cultural experiences of the majority group is also questionable and possibly detrimental to those minority group children who have strong ethnic identities and attachments" (p. 68).

By seeing the cultures of people of color, women, and lower-class people as problems, the approach deflects attention from the majority group and how it perpetuates discrimination and inequality. As long as majority-group children are not seen as needing to learn another culture, implicitly they are being taught to accept "cultural elitism, meaning that minority groups are treated like second-class citizens, either in terms of a refusal to take their traditions and beliefs seriously or with a patronizing acceptance aimed at seducing or manipulating them" (Pratte, 1983, p. 23). Racism within the White culture, sexism within male institutions, homophobia, and the competitive individualism and Horatio Alger myth that uphold classism all remain unexamined. As Mukherjee (1983) puts it, this approach allows Whites to "externaliz[e] the issue" of race rather than "owning up to that racism" (p. 279).

For example, Ms. Ross sees her main task as teaching a largely White, middle-class English language curriculum to African American and Latino children. She does not ask whether the curriculum itself reflects broad power relations, nor whose knowledge and points of view it includes and excludes. Furthermore, when doing this work becomes difficult over time, she thinks about simply relocating to where teaching might be easier, rather than wondering why schools serve some communities better than others, and what can be done to address that problem.

Teaching the Exceptional and Culturally Difference, as an approach to multicultural education, also allows males to externalize problems related to sexism. As long as sexual equity is seen only as helping women to compete in male-dominated domains, women are the only ones seen as needing to change. This viewpoint deflects attention from the need for men to learn, for example, nurturing skills and attitudes that women normally learn in the process of their socialization. It also takes attention away from examining the competitiveness, impersonality, and violence that often characterize the male-dominated world. Because of these limitations, most female educators and researchers who study sexism do not subscribe wholly to the Teaching the Culturally Different approach for female students.

Finally, the approach completely ignores structural and institutional bases of oppression. It assumes that people do not succeed in life because they have not learned a certain repertoire of skills and knowledge. This assumption implies that success is open to as many people as will expend the time and energy necessary to earn it. The assumption ignores the fact that our economy sustains a certain level of unemployment and a stratum of low-paying jobs, regardless of people's qualifications. (Witness the last recession and ask yourself whether the unemployment and suffering that people faced were caused by a sudden lapse in the cultural competence of the recession's victims.) Also ignored is the fact that people develop culture around their life conditions and that cultural patterns tend not to change until the conditions supporting them change. Almost 40 years ago, Liebow (1967) illustrated the problem with an example that still holds:

Many similarities between the lower-class Negro father and son (or mother and daughter) do not result from "cultural transmission," but from the fact that the son goes out and independently experiences the same failures, in the same areas, and for much the same reasons as his father. What appears as a dynamic, self-sustaining cultural process is, in part at least, a relatively simple piece of social machinery which turns out, in rather mechanical fashion, independently produced look-alikes. The problem is how to change the conditions which, by guaranteeing failure, cause the son to be made in the image of the father. (p. 223)

Most educators who study multicultural education, as well as most members of oppressed groups, do not subscribe exclusively to the Teaching the Exceptional and the Culturally Different approach for their own groups, although they do incorporate the approach's best features into other approaches. During the civil rights era in the United States, the approach gained some popularity and is still used by many. However, most of its acceptance has been by White, middle-class teachers who take their own background and culture for granted and are searching for a way to incorporate or deal with those backgrounds and cultures they view as different. The approach also tends to be accepted by those who see American society as the land of opportunity and as a good, technological society that is constantly improving itself. People who do not share this view of American society tend to subscribe to one of the approaches discussed later in this book.

Let us hasten to add that most of these educators would not wish to throw the baby out with the bath water. The approach does contain elements that are very useful in other approaches. Critics of this approach do not believe, for example, that all children should master one standard body of knowledge—which happens to be based primarily on the experience of White, middle-class males—but many do believe that there are some things, such as reading skills, that all citizens do need. The question is, How much of the existing curriculum should be retained and taught to everyone? Many critics who warm to the idea of making the curriculum relevant take issue with the idea that relevance should be a temporary bridge. This approach offers some useful concepts of instruction, such as building instruction around student learning styles. Nevertheless, critics become concerned when teachers are searching desperately for instructional techniques that will help them fit square pegs into round holes. If a body of information is not being accepted well or is not making sense to a class of Appalachian students, for example, perhaps the solution lies not in hitting on the right teaching strategy but in examining possible biases or lack of relevance in the information itself. Students' problems in schools may reflect problems with schools, rather than merely technical problems revolving around the teacher selecting the best instructional strategy.

REFERENCES

Anagnostopoulous, D. (2003). The new accountability, student failure, and teachers' work in urban high schools. *Educational Policy, 17(3)*, 291–316.

Arias, M. B. (1986). The context of education for Hispanic students: An overview. *American Journal of Education, 95*, 26–57.

Artiles, A. J., Harry, B., Reschly, D. J., & Chinn, P. (2002). Over-identification of students of color in special education: A critical overview. *Multicultural Perspective 4(1)*, 3–10.

Banks, J. A. (1994). *Multiethnic education: Theory and practice.* Boston: Allyn & Bacon.

Baratz, S. S., & Baratz, J. C. (1970). Early childhood intervention: The social science base of institutional racism. *Harvard Educational Review, 40,* 29–50.

Billingsly, A., & Caldwell, C. H. (1991). The church, the family, and the school in the African American community. *Journal of Negro Education, 60(3),* 437–440.

Borman, G. D., & Hewes, G. M. (2002). The long-term effects and cost-effectiveness of Success for All. *Educational Evaluation and Policy Analysis, 24(4),* 243–266.

Brown, T. J. (1986). *Teaching minorities more effectively.* Lanham, MD: University Press of America.

Brunner, C. (1997). Opening technology to girls: The approach computer-using teachers take may make the difference. *Electronic Learning, 16(3),* 55.

Bryan, T. H., & Bryan, J. H. (1978). *Understanding learning disabilities,* 2nd ed. Sherman Oaks, CA: Alfred.

Calabrese, R. L. (1990). The public school: A source of alienation for minority parents. *Journal of Negro Education, 59(2),* 148–154.

California Business for Education Excellence. (2002). *Reaching higher: Restoring excellence to California public education.* Sacramento, CA: Author.

Chasnoff, I. J., Marvey, J., Landress, A. C., & Barrett, M. E. (1990). The prevalence of illicit-drug or alcohol use during pregnancy and discrepancies in mandatory reporting in Pinellas County, Florida. *The New England Journal of Medicine, 322(17),* 1202–1206.

Codjoe, H. M. (2001). Fighting a "public enemy" of Black academic achievement—The persistence of racism and the schooling experiences of Black students in Canada. *Race Ethnicity and Education, 4(4),* 343–375.

Comer, J. P., Haynes, N. M., Joyner, E. T., & Ben-Avie, M. (Eds.). (1996). *Rallying the whole village: The Comer process for reforming education.* New York: Teachers College Press.

Contreras, A. R., & Delgado-Contreras, C. (1991). Teacher expectations in bilingual education classrooms. In J. J. Harris III, C. A. Heid, D. G. Carter, Sr., & F. Brown (Eds.). *Readings on the state of education in urban America* (pp. 75–96). Bloomington: Indiana University Center for Urban and Multicultural Education.

Cooper, H., & Moore, C. J. (1995). Teenage motherhood, mother-only households, and teacher expectations. *Journal of Experimental Education, 63(3),* 231–248.

Cummins, J. (1989). *Empowering minority students.* Sacramento: California Association for Bilingual Education.

Cummins, J. (1995). *Negotiating identities: Education for empowerment in a diverse society.* Ontario, Canada: CABE (California Association for Bilingual Education).

Cummins, J. (2000). *Language, power and pedagogy.* Buffalo, NY: Multilingual Matters.

DeLain, M. T., Pearson, T. D., & Anderson, R. C. (1985). Reading comprehension and creativity in black language use: You stand to gain by playing the sounding game! *American Journal of Educational Research, 22,* 155–174.

Dudley-Marling, C. (2001). Reconceptualizing learning disabilities by reconceptualizing education. In L. Denti & P. Tefft-Cousin (Eds.). *New ways of looking at learning disabilities* (pp. 5–18). Denver: Love Pub. Co.

Escalante, J., & Dirmann, J. (1990). The Jaime Escalante math program. *Journal of Negro Education, 59(3),* 407–423.

Farrell, C. L. (1992). Black colleges still carrying their load—and then some. *Black Issues in Higher Education, 9(5),* 10–13.

Fine, M. (1990). Making controversy: Who is "at risk"? *Journal of Urban and Cultural Studies, 1(1),* 55–68.

Frase, L. (1994). Fostering school, community, and family partnerships. In L. Frase (Ed.). *Multiculturalism and TQE: Addressing cultural diversity in schools* (pp. 67–88). Thousand Oaks, CA: Corwin Press.

Friend, M. P., & Bursuck, W. D. (1996). *Including students with special needs: A practical guide for classroom teachers*. Boston: Allyn & Bacon.

Garcia, E. E. (1988). Attributes of effective schools for language minority students. *Education and Urban Society, 20(4)*, 387–398.

Gardner, H. (1993). *Frames of mind*. New York: Basic Books.

Gatta, M., & Trigg, M. (2001). Bridging the gap: Gender equity in science, engineering, and technology. Center for Women and Work, Rutgers University. New Brunswick, NJ. Retrieved May 27, 2005 from http://www.rci.rutgers.edu/~~cww/dataPages/smet.pdf

Gearheart, B., DeRuiter, J., & Sileo, T. (1986). *Teaching mildly and moderately handicapped students*. Upper Saddle River, NJ: Prentice-Hall.

Gersten, R., Scott, B., & Pugach, J. (2001). Contemporary research on special education teaching. In V. Richardson (Ed.). *Handbook for research on teaching*, 4th ed. (pp. 695–722). Washington, DC: American Educational Research Association.

Gibbons, P. (2002). *Scaffolding language, scaffolding learning*. Portsmouth, NH: Heinemann.

Gilliland, H. (1988). *Educating the Native American*. Dubuque, IA: Kendall-Hunt.

Grant, C. A., & Sleeter, C. E. (2006). *Turning on learning*, 4th ed. New York: Wiley.

Greenwood, C. R. (1999). Reflections on a research career: Perspective on 35 years of research at the Juniper Gardens Children's Project. *Exceptional Children, 66*, 7–21.

Gross, J. (1992, March 29). Collapse of inner-city families creates America's new orphans. *The New York Times National*, pp. 1, 616.

Hanna, G. (2003). Reaching gender equity in mathematics. *Educational Forum, 67(3)*, 204–214.

Hardman, M. L., Drew, C. J., & Egan, M. W. (2002). *Human exceptionality: Society, school, and family*. Boston: Allyn & Bacon.

Harry, B. (1992). *Cultural diversity, families, and the special education system*. New York: Teachers College Press.

Haskell, D. H. (2000). Building bridges between science and special education: Inclusion in the science classroom. *The Electronic Journal of Science Education, 4(3)*.

Hauser-Cram, P., Sirin, S. R., & Stipek, D. (2003). When teachers' and parents' values differ: Teachers' ratings of academic competence in children from low-income families. *Journal of Educational Psychology, 95(4)*, 813–820.

Herrnstein, R., & Murray, C. (1994). *The bell curve*. New York: The Free Press.

Hirsch, E. D. (1996). *The schools we need and why we don't have them*. New York: Doubleday.

Hollie, S. (2001). Acknowledging the language of African American students: Instructional strategies. *English Journal, 90(4)*, 54–59.

Jensen, A. S. (1969). How much can we boost IQ and scholastic achievement? *Harvard Educational Review, 39*, 1–123.

Jordan, C. (1985). Translating culture: From ethnographic information to educational program. *Anthropology & Education Quarterly, 16*, 105–123.

Kasten, W. C. (1992). Bridging the horizon: American Indian beliefs and whole language learning. *Anthropology and Education Quarterly, 23(2)*, 108–119.

Kissen, R. (1993). Listening to gay and lesbian teenagers. *Teaching Education, 5(2)*, 57–68.

Kleinfeld, J., & Nelson, P. (1988). Adapting instruction to Native Americans' learning style: An iconoclastic view. In W. J. Lonner & V. O. Tyler, Jr. (Eds.). *Cultural and ethnic factors in learning and motivation: Implications for education* (pp. 83–110). Bellingham, WA: Western Washington University Press.

Kyle, J. G., & Pullen, G. (1988). Cultures in contact: Deaf and hearing people. *Disability, Handicap & Society, 3(1)*, 49–62.

Labov, W. (1969). *The logic of non-standard English*. Monograph Series on Languages and Linguistics, 22. Washington, DC: Georgetown University School of Languages and Linguistics.

Leder, G. C., & Fennema, E. (1990). Gender differences in mathematics: A synthesis. In E. Fennema & G. C. Leder (Eds.). *Mathematics and gender* (pp. 188–200). New York: Teachers College Press.

Liebow, E. (1967). *Tally's corner: A study of Negro street-corner men.* Boston: Little, Brown.

Linn, M. C., & Hyde, J. S. (1989). Gender, mathematics and science. *Educational Researcher, 18(8),* 17–27.

Madhere, S. (1991). Self-esteem of African American preadolescents: Theoretical and practical considerations. *Journal of Negro Education, 60(1),* 47–61.

Mandell, C. J., & Gold, V. (1984). *Teaching handicapped students.* St. Paul, MN: West.

Markova, D. (1992). *How your child is smart: A life-changing approach to learning.* Berkeley, CA: Conari Press.

Maybin, J. (Ed.). (1994). *Language and literacy in social practice.* Philadelphia: Multilingual Matters.

McLarty, M., & Gibson, J. W. (2000). Using video technology in emancipatory research. *European Journal of Special Needs Education, 15(2),* 138–148.

Miller, S. M., Miller, K. L., & Gwaltney, L. K. (1998). Teacher educators' cultural attitudes and behaviors. *Teacher Education and Practice, 14(1),* 30–42.

Moll, L. C. (1992). Bilingual classroom studies and community analysis. *Educational Researcher, 21(2),* 20–24.

Moll, L., Diaz, S., Estrada, E., & Lopes, L. M. (1990). Making contexts: The social construction of lessons in two languages. In M. Saravia-Shore & S. F. Arvizu (Eds.). *Cross-cultural literacy* (pp. 339–366), New York: Garland.

Moses, R. P., & Cobb, C. E., Jr. (2001). *Radical equations.* Boston: Beacon Press.

Moss, B. J. (Ed.). (1994). *Literacy across communities.* Cresskill, NJ: Hampton Press.

Mukherjee, T. (1983). Multicultural education: A black perspective. *Early Childhood Development and Care, 10,* 275–282.

National Commission on Excellence in Education. (1983). *A nation at risk: The imperative for educational reform.* Washington, DC: U.S. Government Printing Office.

Newton, E. S. (1966). Verbal destitution: The pivotal barrier to learning. In S. W. Webster (Ed.). *The disadvantaged learner: Knowing, understanding, educating* (pp. 333–337). San Francisco: Chandler.

Noguera, P. A., & Akom, A. (2000). Disparities demystified. *Nation, 270(22),* 29–31.

Orr, E. W. (1987). *Twice as less: Black English and the performance of black students in mathematics and science.* New York: W. W. Norton.

Pallas, A., Natriello, G., & McDill, E. L. (1989). The changing nature of the disadvantaged population: Current dimensions and future trends. *Educational Researcher, 18(5),* 16–22.

Pang, V. O. (1990). Asian-American children: A diverse population. *The Educational Forum, 55(1),* 49–65.

Pang, V. O., & Sablan, V. A. (1998). Teacher efficacy. In M. E. Dilworth (Ed.). *Being responsive to cultural differences* (pp. 39–58). Washington, DC: Corwin Press.

Payne, R. (2001). *Framework for understanding poverty.* Highlands, TX: Aha Process.

Pease-Alvarez, L., & Hakuta, K. (1992). Enriching our views of bilingualism and bilingual education. *Educational Researcher, 21(2),* 4–6.

Pewewardy, C. (2002). Culturally responsive teaching for American Indian students. *Journal of American Indian Education, 41(3),* 22–56.

Phelan, P., Davidson, A. L., & Cao, H. T. (1991). Students' multiple worlds: Negotiating the boundaries of family, peer, and school cultures. *Anthropology and Education Quarterly, 22(3),* 224–250.

Pratte, R. (1983). Multicultural education: Four normative arguments. *Educational Theory, 33,* 21–32.

Ralph, J. (1989). Improving education for the disadvantaged: Do we know whom to help? *Phi Delta Kappan, 70(5)*, 396–401.

Reis, S. M. (1994). How schools are shortchanging the gifted. *Technology Review, 97(3)*, 38–45.

Reynolds, M. C., & Birch, J. W. (1988). *Adaptive mainstreaming,* 3rd ed. New York: Longman.

Riccio, C. A., Ochoa, S. H., Garza, S. G., & Nero, C. L. (2003). Referral of African American children for evaluation of emotional or behavioral concerns. *Multiple Voices, 6(1)*, 1–12.

Richardson, V., Casanova, U., Placier, P., & Guilfoyle, K. (1989). *School children at risk.* London: Falmer Press.

Riordan, C. (1990). *Girls and boys in school: Together or separate?* New York: Teachers College Press.

Robbins, W. (1984). Student's suicide stirs new interest in gifted. In C. A. Grant (Ed.). *Preparing for reflective teaching* (pp. 281–283). Boston: Allyn & Bacon.

Robinson, H. B., Roedell, W. C., & Jackson, N. E. (1981). Early identification and intervention. In W. B. Barbe & J. S. Renzulli (Eds.). *Psychology and education of the gifted,* 3rd ed. (pp. 128–141). New York: Irvington.

San Miguel, G., Jr. (1987). "Let all of them take heed": Mexican Americans and the campaign for educational equality in Texas, 1910–1981. Austin: University of Texas Press.

Sears, J. T. (1991). *Growing up gay in the South.* New York: Hayworth Press.

Sears, J. T. (1993). Responding to the sexual diversity of faculty and students: Sexual praxis and the critically reflective administrator. In C. Capper (Ed.). *Educational administration in a pluralistic society.* New York: SUNY Press.

Shade, B. J. R. (1997). Culture, style and the educative process, 2nd ed. Springfield, IL: Charles C. Thomas.

Sheets, R. H. (1995). From remedial to gifted: Effects of culturally centered pedagogy. *Theory into Practice, 34(3)*, 186–193.

Sherman, L. (2002). From division to vision. *Northwest Education, 8(1)*, 22–27.

Siegel, J. (1999). Stigmatized and standardized varieties in the classroom: Interference or separation? *TESOL Quarterly, 33(4)*, 701–728.

Silber, J. (1988). Education and national survival: The cycle of poverty. *Vital Speeches, 54*, 215–219.

Skrtic, T. M. (2003). An organizational analysis of the overrepresentation of poor and minority students in special education. *Multiple Voices, 6(1)*, 41–57.

Sleeter, C. E. (1992). *Keepers of the American dream: A study of staff development and multicultural education.* London: Falmer Press.

Smitherman, G. (1981). What go round come round: King in perspective. *Harvard Educational Review, 51(1)*, 40–56.

Solomon, G. (2002). Digital equity: It's not just about access anymore. *Technology & Learning, 22(9)*, 18–20, 22–24, 26.

Soto, L. D. (1997). *Language, culture, and power.* New York: State University Press.

Stewart, D. A., & Akamatsu, C. T. (1988). The coming of age of American Sign Language. *Anthropology and Education Quarterly, 19(3)*, 235–252.

Swiatek, M. A., & Lupkowski-Shoplik, A. (2003). Elementary and middle school student participation in gifted programs: Are gifted students underserved? *Gifted Child Quarterly, 47(2)*, 118–130.

Taylor, H. U. (1989). *Standard English, Black English, and bidialectalism.* New York: Peter Lang.

Terman, L. M., Baldwin, B. T., Bronson, E., DeVoss, J. C., Fuller, F., Goodenough, F. L., Kelley, T. L., Lima, M., Marshall, H., Moore, A. H., Raubenheimer, A. S., Ruch, G. M., Willoughby, R. L., Wyman, J. B., & Yates, D. H. (1976). *Genetic studies of genius: Mental and physical traits of a thousand gifted children.* Stanford, CA: Stanford University Press.

Tettegah, S. (1996). The racial consciousness attitudes of White prospective teachers and their perceptions of the teachability of students from different racial/ethnic backgrounds: Findings from a California study. *Journal of Negro Education, 65(2)*, 151–163.

Tharp, R. G., Estrada, P., Dalton, S. S., & Yamaguchi, L. A. (2000). *Teaching transformed: Achieving excellence, fairness, inclusion, and harmony.* Boulder, CO: Westview.

Titchkosky, T. (2000). Disability studies: The old and the new. *Canadian Journal of Sociology, 25(2)*, 197–224.

Trueba, H. T. (1988). Culturally based explanations of minority students' academic achievement. *Anthropology and Education Quarterly, 19(3)*, 270–287.

Trueba, H. T. (1989). *Raising silent voices: Educating the linguistic minorities for the 21st century.* New York: Newbury House.

Walker, C. L. (1987). Hispanic achievement: Old views and new perspectives. In H. Trueba (Ed.). *Success or failure? Learning and the language minority student* (pp. 15–32). Cambridge, MA: Newbury House.

Warren, S. R. (2002). Stories from the classroom: How expectations and efficacy of diverse teachers affect the academic performance of children in poor urban schools. *Educational Horizons, 80(3)*, 109–116.

Wiley, T. G., & Wright, W. E. (2004). Against the undertow: Language-minority education policy and politics in the "Age of Accountability." *Educational Policy, 18(1)*, 142–168.

Ysseldyke, J. E., & Algozzine, B. (1982). *Critical issues in special and remedial education.* Boston: Houghton Mifflin.

CHAPTER THREE

Human Relations

What comes to mind when you hear the term *human relations?* "Getting along," "tolerance," "interactions between individuals and groups," and "learning how to resolve differences between individuals and groups" were some of the responses our students gave to this question. Our students also said that human relations means trying to reduce prejudice and stereotypes among the races, helping men and women to eliminate their gender hang-ups, helping people to accept religious diversity, and helping all people to feel positive about themselves. Central to most definitions was the development of positive interactions between individuals or groups.

GOALS

Our students' statements were consistent with the goal statements of educators who advocate a Human Relations approach. As we note in Table 3-1, the goals of this approach are to create positive feelings among students and reduce stereotyping, thus promoting unity and tolerance in a society composed of different people. Johnson and Johnson (2002) explained, "The goals of human relations training are (1) to improve relationships between majority and minority citizens by eliminating prejudice and discrimination, primarily through teaching all subsequent generations to value and respect diversity among individual; and (2) to increase participants' competencies for interacting effectively with diverse individuals by teaching participants procedures and skills" (p. 13). In order to engage successfully with another person, we must develop skills that enable us to recognize our common humanity, as well as acknowledge and respect individual differences. Human relations training helps us learn these skills. In this chapter, we will examine how advocates of the Human Relations approach suggest developing positive relationships among individuals or groups that differ from one another.

Some proponents of the Human Relations approach relate it directly to the study of prejudice and intergroup hostility. This is in part due to its history. According to C. Banks (2005), the intercultural movement began in the early 1930s and continued into the 1950s as intergroup education. Intercultural educators were concerned with the problems and issues that European immigrants, especially those from Southern Europe, were experiencing. Banks states, "A major goal

TABLE 3-1.
Human Relations

Societal goals:	Promote feelings of unity, tolerance, and acceptance within existing social structure
School goals:	Promote positive feelings among students, reduce stereotyping, promote students' self-concepts
Target students:	Everyone
Practices:	
Curriculum	Teach lessons about stereotyping, name-calling; teach lessons about individual differences and similarities; include in lessons contributions of groups of which students are members
Instruction	Use cooperative learning; use real or vicarious experiences with others
Other aspects of classroom	Decorate classroom to reflect uniqueness and accomplishments of students; decorate with "I'm OK, You're OK" themes
Other schoolwide concerns	Make sure activities and school policies and practices do not put down or leave out some groups of students; promote schoolwide activities, such as donating food to the poor, aimed at peace and unity

of the intercultural education movement was to reduce the fears and misconceptions of mainstream Americans about the immigrants and improve intergroup relations" (p. xv). She tells us that a related and "important goal was to increase the social status of immigrant children" (p. xv).

Intergroup education advocates claim that because so many complex factors, such as home background, social situations, health, income, intelligence, and aspirations affect human interaction and human relationships, intergroup education must take into account one's total personality. They support Grambs's (1960) observation "that intergroup relations cannot properly be understood in a narrow sense at all but must be considered in terms of the total personality, the interaction of persons in groups, the sources of group tension and conflict, and the cultural context within which people grow and learn" (p. 5).

The Human Relations approach is directed toward helping students communicate with, accept, and get along with people who are different from themselves; reducing or eliminating stereotypes that students have about people; and helping students feel good about themselves and about groups of which they are members, without putting others down in the process. This approach is aimed mainly at the affective level—at attitudes and feelings people have about themselves and others. It attempts to replace tension and hostility with acceptance and care. Advocates of human relations, or intergroup education, believe the approach needs to be fostered in everyone, and in all schools, to make our democracy work and bring about world peace.

Systematic attention to intergroup, intercultural-human relations education began during World War II and grew rapidly right after the war ended (Banks

2005; Johnson & Johnson, 2002; Taba, Brady, & Robinson, 1952). Prior to the war, organizations such as the Anti-Defamation League of B'nai B'rith, the Urban League, the National Association for the Advancement of Colored People, and the National Conference of Christians and Jews had fought to eliminate discrimination and prejudice and were encouraging legislation that would help to accomplish their aims. World War II brought about some specific changes that fueled these organizations' efforts to draw serious attention to their concerns. World War II created jobs, and people often had to move to other regions to take advantage of these opportunities. These relocations brought together people who were not used to being together, which sometimes resulted in intergroup conflicts—for example, when African Americans and Whites from the South moved to the North and West and interacted under different rules (e.g., no legal segregation). As poor people and people of color took advantage of the increased economic opportunities and began to experience a more fulfilling and enriched life, they started to demand social justice. War veterans, especially those of color, believed that they and their people deserved fair treatment because they had fought and died for democracy—democracy not just for some citizens but for all citizens. Intergroup, intercultural, and human relations education was seen as a way to bring about harmony among these different groups.

During the war, the United States was especially concerned about maintaining and improving its relations with its neighboring countries, Canada and Mexico. Roosevelt's Good Neighbor policy had implications for educators in Texas. Pressure from the Mexican government was exerted to expose the poor treatment of Mexican American students in schools. In response, the Inter-American Education movement developed, holding conferences, developing curricula, and conducting studies aimed at improving relations between Anglos and Mexicans in the schools.

Another factor supporting intergroup education was the belief that America's concern about human interactions was being ignored while we invested the country's financial and human resources in the technological race. There was more interest in the atom than in relationships among people. Many believed that our role as free-world leader and as champion of the democratic way of life throughout the world was inconsistent with the way of life experienced by many U.S. citizens.

It was not enough to advocate justice and fair play abroad; we had to put these ideals into practice at home. Minority and majority group relations had to be improved. Finally, the war itself had produced some devastating consequences that pointed strongly to a need to promote better intergroup relations. The Holocaust demonstrated how inhumanely one group can treat another group, and the bombing of Hiroshima and Nagasaki revealed to the world a more terrible and destructive kind of weapon than had ever been used in human history.

These events and circumstances gave human relations and intergroup education a big push, and interest in this concept grew rapidly. Many books, pamphlets, articles, lectures, and discussions at professional association meetings concentrated on this concept during a short period of time and thus provided the momentum for its growing acceptance. Another big push for human relations came a decade later with the school desegregation and civil rights movements. School desegregation meant that, in many cases, people of color and White people would have to share the same facility (school). Human relations and intergroup education programs were often put into place (and some still exist) to help promote harmony among racial groups.

During the late 1970s and 1980s, following the passage of PL 94-142 (the Education for All Handicapped Children Act), the Human Relations approach was viewed as useful in mainstreaming special education students. As students who previously had been kept segregated were increasingly placed in the regular classroom and school, educators became concerned about negative attitudes among both regular students and teachers, particularly because one reason for the mainstreaming movement was to encourage the acceptance of students with disabilities. By the early 1980s, books and articles began to appear with some frequency that discussed how to modify attitudes toward people with disabilities and increase their social integration.

The late 1980s and early 1990s witnessed a resurgence of name calling and racial hostility in schools, on college campuses, and in cities and suburbs, and the Ku Klux Klan engaged in cross burnings, an expression of hate that many Americans had believed to be extinct. This period also saw a rise in attention to sexual harassment, particularly following television coverage of Anita Hill's testimony in Congress against Supreme Court nominee Clarence Thomas. As a result, educators and the general public became increasingly concerned about what is proper for members of different groups to say to each other, resulting in debates about what constitutes legitimate free speech. In addition, teachers who previously had not been concerned with Human Relations or any other approach to multicultural education began to ask themselves—especially if their own students were becoming more diverse—What can I do?

September 11, 2001, brought a new concern to teachers who advocate the Human Relations approach. Whereas they saw an increase in patriotism among Americans, they also observed that many Arab and Muslim Americans, and even those who just looked Middle Eastern, encountered hostility and were fearful of their children attending school. Again these teachers asked what can I do and what should I do?

This same question was responsible, in fact, for the emergence of the first conflict resolution programs in the early 1970s, programs that were "sparked by the increasing concern of educators and parents about violence in the schools" (Girard & Koch, 1996, p. 111). Growing out of these earlier efforts, the National Association for Mediation in Education was established in 1984, further contributing to this growing movement. Now known as the National Institute for Dispute Resolution (NIDR), the organization works toward the development and implementation of conflict resolution and peer mediation programs in the schools.

Thus, the 1990s and the beginning of the twenty-first century have seen schools dedicate more time and attention to conflict resolution, peer mediation, and the elimination of violence. Some school districts advocate beginning training as early as kindergarten and the primary grades where children learn about resolving conflicts such as playground disputes over balls, use of swings, and so forth. Children are taught skills related to speaking, using "I messages" to identify feelings, needs, and desires. They are taught to listen, negotiate, mediate, apologize, postpone gratification, and compromise. In the middle grades and in secondary school, conflict resolution skills are also taught to help students get along better with one another and to deal with different people and perspectives they encounter throughout society. A variety of materials that deal with such issues as peer mediation, anger management, and violence prevention have been and continue to be published. (See, for example, publications from Conflict Resolution Media, Ellicott City, Maryland.) Programs and materials have especially begun to proliferate in the area of violence prevention. Creighton and Kivel (1992), for example, have developed a step-by-step program aimed at preventing violence in teen relationships, and Gazda et al. (2006) are in their seventh edition of a human relations development manual for educators.

Peer mediation and conflict resolution also became a very important curriculum topic starting in the 1990s for fostering better student-teacher interaction. In order to teach tolerance, Valentine (1997) suggests that educators begin by examining their own cultural perspectives. This means that teachers need to examine who their friends are, who comes to their homes, and who attends their houses of worship. In schools, suggestions for teaching tolerance include examining instructional material for biases, modeling empathy and respect for others, addressing intolerance as it arises, and creating opportunities for people from different cultures to work with one another (see Calabrese, 2002; Johnson & Johnson, 2002; Watson, 2002). Some states, such as Wisconsin, require that prospective teachers receive training in conflict resolution; other states offer programs through which students can obtain advanced degrees in conflict resolution itself.

What is the relationship between diversity, which is increasing in its many and varied forms, and human relations? There is a strong relationship. The next time you go to a shopping mall, notice the ethnic diversity, including the diversity that is the result of interracial marriage, and listen for language diversity. If you observe closely, you may see religious and other forms of diversity. Johnson and Johnson (2002) connect diversity to human relations when they state: "In facing the promise and problems of diversity, there should be no doubt that avoidance of diversity is not an option. Diversity exists and it is increasing. Diversity is pervasive and inevitable. Acquiring the skills to interact with diverse individual effectively is not a luxury; it is a necessity" (p. 4).

THEORIES BEHIND HUMAN RELATIONS

The theoretical underpinnings of the Human Relations approach have come mainly from general psychology and social psychology. Human relations is a field that examines relationships among people, regardless of whether race, social class, gender, disability, or sexual orientation is involved. For example, there is a body of literature on human relations in formal organizations and a cadre of people who conduct human relations workshops for businesses. For this chapter, we will draw only on the research that develops human relations as an approach to multicultural education. Nevertheless, it is important to remember that this approach is a subset of a larger body of thought and rests on many of the same theoretical foundations.

Some theorists have emphasized the development of prejudice and stereotyping within individuals. Others have emphasized the development of prejudice and hostility between groups. Still others pay more attention to individual self-concept. These ideas are not mutually exclusive. In fact, as Allport (1979) noted, no one theoretical formulation by itself can account for prejudice, although different people see different theories as being the most persuasive, and much of the current social science research in the area supports this observation.

Development of Prejudice within Individuals

Gordon Allport (1979) was probably the main theorist to write about the development of prejudice in individuals, and his work still forms the basis for much of the Human Relations approach. He focused on individuals for two reasons: Not everybody in any given society is prejudiced, which raises the question of why some people are much more prejudiced than others and why prejudice and discrimination are acted out by certain individuals. Allport drew mainly on cognitive development theory and psychoanalytic theory. We will explain these theories, incorporating examples (some used by Allport, some not) to show how they apply to race, gender, social class, disability, and sexual orientation. We will also provide elaborations of these ideas that have been offered by other theorists.

According to cognitive development theory, the mind has a need to relate, organize, and simplify phenomena in order for experiences to make sense. Thus, on the basis of concrete experience, people create categories to organize similar phenomena. As people mature and acquire an increasingly broad range of experience, they attempt to assimilate as many of their new experiences as possible into existing categories. Occasionally, people have to restructure (accommodate) categories to fit experience. How does this apply to prejudice?

By age 2 or 3, children are aware of visible differences among people, including skin color (Katz, 1982; Van Ausdale & Feagin, 2001), physical impairment (Diamond, 1996), and gender (Kohlberg, 1966). Initially, these differences do not suggest stereotypes or evaluations, although Allport suggested that children often associate dark skin with dirt. At the same time, children are also learning language, and with it, labels for categories and the emotional overtones of those labels. In fact, children sometimes learn a label and its emotional overtone (e.g., homosexuals) before they have constructed a category to which the label applies or before they have connected the label with a category.

A research study on young children by Van Ausdale and Feagin (2001) supports the early awareness of differences in 3-year-old children and reports why this is so. Ausdale and Feagin state:

> As we have demonstrated in the survey in Chapter 1 and in our data, racist thought and practice remain strong in the United States, and young children cannot avoid participating in and perpetuating them. Racism surrounds us, permeates our ideas

and conversations, focuses our relationship with one another, shapes our practices, and drives much in our personal, social and political lives. There are few social forces so strong. Children are neither immune to it nor unaware of its power. A social reality this mighty is bound to become an integral part of their lives, and thus it endures from generation to generation, perhaps changing somewhat in form, but still strong in its impact. (pp. 197–198)

Student teachers in preschool or kindergarten classes are sometimes struck by the degree to which children play together without seeming to notice or to care about differences among themselves. Student teachers sometimes comment that maybe the younger generation is growing up without prejudice, or that because children don't "see race" the teacher should not bring up the subject of differences. A more accurate interpretation is that the children have not yet learned the meanings society attaches to the differences they do see. As they mature, they will be bombarded with interpretations of human characteristics: in the media, at school, at home, in jokes and stories, and from friends.

By late childhood, children tend to overcategorize and stereotype many things. Their categories will have acquired many descriptive attributes that they apply to whoever or whatever seems to fit the category. Thus, all dogs are large and brown, or all people in wheelchairs are friendly (or quiet, or stupid, or whatever the child has experienced with one or two members of that category). Finding their system of organizing experience useful, children overuse it, often without recognizing its limitations.

As children mature, their categories modify by varying degrees to fit reality better. As one encounters people who do not fit a designated category, one tends to view them as exceptions to the rule. For example, upon meeting a man who is a homemaker, a person who sees homemakers as women will consider the man an exception rather than restructure the category to make it genderless. Most people learn to allow for numerous exceptions and qualifications and do not see the boundaries of their categories as fixed and rigid. Thus, a person can say, "Some of my best friends are Jews," allowing the retention of a stereotypical image of "Jew" although admitting to many exceptions to the stereotype (Allport, 1979, p. 309). However, the more diverse examples of a category to which a person has been exposed, and the more that person examines the category itself, the less rigid and stereotypical the person's system of mental categories becomes. For example, a child who has been exposed to a wide range of Asian Americans has a good experiential basis to question stereotypes, such as "Asians are good at math."

Allport noted the important role of perception in this process. When the mind perceives, "it selects, accentuates, and interprets sensory data" (p. 166). To view a diverse group of people (such as the poor) as a category, we find it necessary to pay special attention to the attributes that members of the category are believed to have in common. In attending to these attributes, we tend to accentuate them unconsciously. For example, we look for skin color so that we can identify a person's race; in the process, we exaggerate the importance of skin color and minimize the significance of attributes people have in common. As another example, when teachers hear they are receiving a new student who is "at risk," certain images and personal characteristics assumed of such students often rush forward. Research on stereotyping also finds people to be more accepting of individuals who fit a stereotype than individuals who do not. Stereotypes seem to give us a map of reality that suggests how to interpret and act toward people, and individuals who do not fit that map make us uncomfortable. Rather than questioning the stereotypes, however, we often avoid or put down the persons who do not fit.

You may be wondering whether, if the development of prejudice is so natural, prejudiced beliefs can be changed. Yes, they can. Earlier we noted that answering children's questions accurately and providing them with multiple different examples of members of a category helps them to develop more accurate, complex interpretations of people. Beliefs can be changed or broadened by making use of dissonance theory. According to Watts (1984),

> Dissonance occurs whenever an individual simultaneously holds two cognitions (ideas, beliefs, opinions) which are psychologically inconsistent. Because dissonance is an unpleasant motivational state, people strive to reduce it through a cognitive reorganization that may involve adding consonant cognition or changing one set of opinions. (p. 44)

An example Watts provided is that of a person who believes that cigarette smoking is dangerous to one's health but who smokes nonetheless. All of us live with some degree of dissonance, especially if we are not forced to confront opposing beliefs. To reduce dissonance, if it were to become uncomfortable, the person could belittle the research on lung cancer or decide to quit smoking.

Consider the child who thinks retarded people are unpleasant but then begins to play with a neighbor with mental retardation. The child could reduce the dissonance between attitude and behavior either by clinging to the attitude and ceasing to play with the retarded child or by adopting a more positive attitude that would support their play relationship. Teachers can create planned dissonance. For example, a teacher with a class that regards Arabs as terrorists can present the students with multiple examples of American Arabs who are outstanding patriotic American citizens. Students can resolve their dissonance by treating such Arab Americans as exceptions, but eventually the number and power of the exceptions will make the stereotype increasingly difficult to maintain.

Thinking in terms of categories and stereotypes is natural and does not necessarily, by itself, lead to prejudice and hostility. Why do some people hate groups unlike themselves, whereas other people are simply curious and accepting of others? For an answer to that question, Allport (1979)—and others—turned to psychodynamic theory. Essentially, psychodynamic theory holds that the mind has built-in urges and capacities that manifest themselves in feelings and needs. Only a portion of these urges and capacities reach the conscious level in any individual. A larger portion remain at the unconscious level, where they nevertheless direct our thoughts and behaviors, but in ways of which we are unaware. Allport described several needs or capacities that are built into the human mind: aggression, affiliation with others, fear of strangers, need for status, and need for a positive self-image. Early in life, children attempt to form relationships with others, build positive self-images, and acquire status, with some children experiencing more success than others. Lack of success leads to frustration. Many people learn to channel frustration productively (e.g., it becomes a motivation to try harder until success is achieved), whereas others allow the frustration to smolder inside. People who do not learn to handle frustration develop a free-floating hatred that can be directed against any convenient group or individual, and the hatred can turn into active aggression against that target.

Projection is the main process by which frustration becomes directed against a group. Allport defined projection as "the tendency to attribute falsely to other people motives or traits that are our own, or that in some way explain or justify our own" (p. 382). Projection is based on feelings of guilt, fear, or anxiety about traits or urges within ourselves or factors in our own lives. For example, many people develop feelings of guilt about their own homosexual thoughts, and because they are unable to deal with these feelings at a conscious level, they project fear of their own urges onto others who are openly homosexual. These others become a target for hate. People who fear losing their jobs, either because of their own inadequacies or because of economic conditions, may project this fear onto a group, often a minority group, that they can blame for stealing jobs from people who deserve them. Such a group becomes a scapegoat.

You may be thinking that although this makes some sense, many people do not externalize their problems and blame others. Why are some people prone to hate much more than others? Earlier psychodynamically oriented research suggested that certain child-rearing styles develop personality types that are prone to be either prejudiced or open (Adorno et al., 1950; Harris, Gough, & Martin, 1950). Recent research still contends that parental influence on children's personalities is significant, but offers a more cautionary perspective. O'Bryan, Fishbein, and Ritchey (2004) argue that some studies (Aboud, 1988; Fishbein, 2002; Ritchey & Fishbein, 2001) do not agree that parents are the major contributors to a child's personality type. Ritchey and Fishbein (2001) ask, "[w]here do individual differences in prejudice and stereotyping come from?" They answer as follows: "Parents have a weak influence, and friends, apparently none. The research on authoritarianism, our findings about authoritative parenting and consistent sex differences suggest that the place to look for influences is within the adolescent and not in significant reference groups. It is possible that differences in personality and values among adolescents may differentially lead them to adopt the various prejudices and stereotypes that are well known in a culture" (p. 206). Given the ambiguity in the literature, teachers should be cautioned in concluding that a student's act of prejudice is based on one's parents. Instead, teachers may wish to "look within the student."

Development of Prejudice and Hostility between Groups
Many social psychologists see the preceding theories as inadequate for understanding prejudice and discrimination. For example, can we say that the Germans constructed death camps for the Jews in the 1930s because, for some reason, most Germans experienced levels of frustration they could not handle and so projected

their individual guilt and failings on the same target group? Although to some extent this theory may have some validity, it does not account very well for groups mobilizing against groups. To understand intergroup relations, we turn to reference group theory, developed by Sherif and Sherif (1966). The Sherifs conducted numerous observations and some experiments with small groups to understand how groups form interactions with other groups, One notable set of experiments, which is very much cited in the literature today, took place in a number of boys' summer camps at which situations were constructed in order to encourage groups to form. These groups were then studied in isolation from one another as well as in contact with one another. Those of you who have attended camp yourself may well remember the sense of "we-ness" that can develop among tent-mates or cabin-mates and the friendly rivalry that often develops between cabins.

According to reference group theory, people derive much of their identity from association with others. All people belong to a set of in-groups, beginning with one's family during early childhood. As one matures, the number of groups to which one belongs expands. People identify with some groups more than others; one can even identify with a group to which one does not even belong. Recently, researchers confirmed reference group theory from their study of group life and its importance on people's self-concept and their behavior. Goethals (1999) argues that interpersonal relations within groups have a significant impact on a person's self-concept, and this can lead to an acceptance of the group. This takes places, Goethals contends, because (a) people evaluate important personal qualities—opinion and abilities, and so on, through social comparison; (b) through interpersonal interaction and communication people learn what others think of them; and (c) people identify with others, mainly members of their own group, and strive to be like them in significant ways. As Goethals explains, all three of these processes—social comparison, reflected appraisal, and identification—affect people's sense of their identity and their value (p. 19).

We all willingly conform to groups with which we identify, and we may deliberately behave in ways that distinguish us from other groups. For example, the Sherifs found that each group of boys in camp adopted a color as its own; having chosen a color, each group then avoided wearing the colors of other groups. During the late 1970s, many girls adopted the "preppie" look, which identified them with conservative, upper-class or upper-middle-class White girls. One visible badge of group membership was a string of real pearls; particularly if the rest of one's garb on a given day was ordinary, the pearls would indicate that one had the money to sport expensive jewelry, even with jeans.

During the 1980s, many African American young people wore Malcolm X caps and T-shirts to signify that the wearer regarded race as a significant social division and identified with Black power strategies to strengthen the African American community rather than with White-controlled strategies. Presently, gang members can be identified by the colors they wear. The wearing of these colors symbolizes a form of status and belonging. However, the wearing of colors in school has led to so much tension and violence related to "group belonging" that school policy now often outlaws the wearing of colors.

In and of itself, group formation does not necessarily cause prejudice and discrimination. However, the Sherifs noted that when groups come in contact with each other they begin to make a concerted effort to define and maintain group boundaries. To encourage all group members to stay within the group and to remain loyal to the group, individual group members begin to depict the group as superior to out-groups and try to convince one another in the group of this superiority. Hostility develops as soon as groups perceive themselves to be in competition with one another. Sherif and Sherif noted that groups need not even really be competing; as long as group members believe another group is competing for something they want, hostility and rejection of the out-group can result.

Reference group theory can easily be applied to ethnic, gender, social class, gay and lesbian, and disability group relationships, as well as to relationships among other kinds of groups. In applying the theory, one can combine it with psychological theories described earlier. For example, take gender. According to cognitive development theory, children learn early that sex is an important way to categorize people. Children also learn early to which category they belong. Once they know, most children actively strive to conform to that category as part of constructing a self-identity. If a little girl believes that girls wear only dresses, she will not wear anything but dresses. In early childhood, there is some sex segregation and rejection between the sexes as each group seeks to maintain its boundaries and to conform to its image of its own sex. "Fags" and "tomboys," as they are disdainfully called, threaten the integrity of group boundaries, group norms, and personal understanding of what the terms *male* and *female* mean. As children grow up, the opposite sex becomes a target group for individuals with the psychological problems described in psychoanalytic theory; hence, rape and wife beating take place. When people perceive the sexes to be competing over such matters as jobs, stereotyping and hostility develop: Males are seen as "chauvinist or sexist" and females as "aggressive" people who are failing to provide a secure home for their children.

When victimized, according to Allport (1979), most individuals and groups react, and some reactions further intensify the problem. Reactions that intensify the problem include becoming obsessively concerned with prejudice (e.g., reading anti-Semitism into remarks that are not intended as discriminatory); withdrawing or becoming passive (thus, for example, reinforcing stereotypes that characterize people with disabilities or Asian Americans as unassertive); covering up hurt by clowning; strengthening in-group ties (which can make outsiders see the group as too clannish or too different); rejecting one's own group; striving extra hard to succeed in spite of discrimination (which reaffirms stereotypes that the group is cunning or works too hard); acting militant (which reaffirms the idea that the group is hostile); and allowing the prophecy to be self-fulfilling. Such reactions can unwittingly intensify prejudice and stereotyping, but they are normal reactions to victimization.

Think, for example, about a time you were treated unfairly, picked on, or put down. How did you react? The reactions of a group should direct our attention to the unfair treatment that prompted the reactions. However, when we expect to see stereotyped behavior (such as passivity, violence, or lack of effort), the appearance of such behavior may cause us to conclude, "That's just how they are," rather than forcing us to pay attention to how the group was mistreated in the first place.

Self-Concept Theory

The Human Relations approach deals with self-concept as well as intergroup relationships. Purkey and Novak (1984) defined self-concept as "our view of who we are and how we fit into the world" (p. 25). By far the most influential and eloquent voice in self-concept theory was that of Carl Rogers. Purkey and Schmidt (1987) tell us that Rogers, a psychologist who developed client-centered therapy, introducing an entire system of helping built around the importance of the self. Purkey and Schmidt state:

> In Rogers' view, the self is the central ingredient in human personality and personal adjustment. Rogers described the self as a social product, developing out of interpersonal relationships and striving for consistency. He maintained that there is a basic human need for positive regard both from others and from oneself. He also believed that in every person there is a tendency towards self-actualization and development so long as this is permitted and encouraged by an inviting environment. (p. 22)

Advocates of the Human Relations approach are particularly concerned about how members of different sociocultural groups view themselves and their place in the world. Intergroup and interpersonal relationships can be thought of as attitudes toward other people, and self-concept and self-esteem as attitudes toward oneself and toward groups of which one is a member.

Self-concept and self-esteem are very complex phenomena that educators frequently oversimplify, especially when considering children who are members of other sociocultural groups. In *Why Are All the Black Kids Sitting Together in the Cafeteria?*, Tatum (1997) offers a complex portrait of the formation of self-concept. She emphasizes the importance of understanding why students, as members of cultural groups, cohere in school settings. Forming social groups with peers "like oneself" facilitates the formation of a positive identity as well as a sense of belonging. At times, too, group formation serves to protect students whose identities are devalued by the school setting and curriculum. Discussing the formation of racial identity, Tatum stresses the need to appreciate the development of self-concept and to engage in conversations across currently existing racial and ethnic divides.

The narrow manner in which teachers frequently address issues of self-concept is illustrated by the following observations. We heard a teacher remark that a particular Mexican American child who frequently comes to the teacher for a hug must have a poor self-concept because he is not getting much love at home and comes to school hungry for attention. Similarly, we have heard teachers describe African American children from low-income families as not trying very hard on assignments because they bring low self-esteem from home. To attempt to build up their students' self-esteem, some teachers insert lessons into the curriculum about heroes or heroines of the children's cultural group, often without considering the genuine complexities involved in the development of self.

We must caution educators against assuming that children from low-status groups develop poor self-concepts at home, especially if they are not behaving as the teacher expects. Often the assumptions of these educators are not true. For example, considerable research has been done on various dimensions of the self-concepts and self-esteem of African American and White children. As a review of this research concludes, "it is repeatedly found that young African Americans express above-average levels of self-esteem often higher than those of White youngsters of the same age" (Madhere, 1991, p. 47). Knowing the social hostility their children will have to face, many African American parents and other parents of color deliberately build up their children's sense of self and sense of belonging to a strong group, so that they enter school feeling good about themselves, their personal abilities, and their racial or ethnic group. Furthermore, children who seek hugs from teachers often are used to being hugged by adults—at home as well as in school.

Beane and Lipka (1986) listed four common dimensions of a young person's self-concept: self as a member of a family, self as a peer, self as a student, and self as a person with attributes. Each dimension can be further broken out; for example, "self as a student" can refer to self as a learner, a participant in school activities, or an academic achiever. One may further differentiate, say, between self as a math achiever versus self as a music achiever. Beane and Lipka also distinguish between self-concept and self-esteem. Self-concept, they state, is "the description an individual attaches to himself or herself," and self-esteem "refers to the evaluation one makes of the self-concept description" (pp. 5–6). Self-concept and self-esteem are complex; one cannot make sweeping statements about a child's self-concept based on how the child behaves in one setting. Moreover, although the child's behavior in a particular setting, such as a classroom, may reflect the child's self-esteem developed in other contexts, it may also reflect a direct response to that setting itself.

Children develop their self-concepts through interactions with other people in various contexts. The home and neighborhood provide contexts, as does the school. Schools, however, to the degree that they reflect institutionalized inequalities, support the self-concepts of students differentially. Beginning with kindergarten, children gain feedback regarding their ability to perform school tasks, in the form of verbal praise or criticism, grades, test scores, and assignment to an ability group. Some children learn to view themselves as capable in school, and some learn very early to view themselves as incapable. Children also gain feedback from teachers and peers regarding their likeability. In addition, schools transmit images of various sociocultural groups—images that can act like mirrors in which children view people like themselves. For example, if the accomplishments of males are celebrated repeatedly in the curriculum, children learn which sex is capable of doing interesting things, and children often do notice. A teacher we know remarked that one of her fifth-grade girls commented one day about their reading text, "Oh, good, this story is about fish! The girls in this book never do anything interesting." Upon reviewing the text, the teacher agreed; the student had noticed a pattern the teacher had not.

By late elementary school and middle school, the self-esteem of some categories of students begins to drop. Madhere (1991), for example, found the self-esteem of African Americans, and particularly boys, to drop in seventh grade. A study by the American Association of University Women (1992) found that the self-esteem of girls dropped more than that of boys in secondary school. Gay and lesbian students first experience homoerotic feelings around the age of 9, on the average, and by adolescence are struggling with feelings they have learned are socially unacceptable, which takes a toll on their self-esteem (Sears, 1993). As children gain exposure to the wider society and its evaluation of themselves and people like themselves, their self-esteem and esteem for their reference group are affected.

The school is a part of that wider society and may be transmitting damaging messages to which children then react. Many children of color react negatively to the celebration of White people that most curricula embody. Low-income people are generally looked down upon by the broader society, including most schools; many students from low-income families learn to regard the school as an alien institution. Many Spanish-speaking students learn in school that speaking Spanish is regarded as a problem rather than as an asset, and so these students eventually refuse to speak Spanish.

Some homes do not support the development of healthy self-esteem, but teachers often misread the home. Rather than blaming the home for a child's behavior, it is more fruitful to examine the kind of context one's own classroom may be providing for children's self-concepts. Are some categories of children reprimanded, ignored, or praised disproportionately? Does the curriculum celebrate the importance of some sociocultural groups more than others? Does every child have a regular opportunity to succeed and appear talented and capable at something? What kind of interpersonal relationship do you have with each child? These kinds of questions direct teachers toward factors they can control. The classroom is only one context of several within which self-concept and self-esteem develop, but it is an important context.

Many teachers react to these kinds of questions by saying, "I don't see color; I just see children." We must point out that nobody does not literally "see" color or other differences. If we only associate negative images with color or other human characteristics, we may try not to see those characteristics so that our negative associations do not come into play. However, as we noted earlier, children do see visible differences, and they are curious about what those differences mean. Teachers using the Human Relations approach try to construct classrooms that celebrate individual differences. Race, language, personal talents, body size, hair color, physical abilities, interests, and so forth, are presented to children as characteristics that we all have but that differ among us; the differences are not only normal, but they are interesting and worthwhile. Furthermore, such teachers try to provide a range of experiences in which different children are successful and to develop the self-esteem of diverse children. Theirs is an approach based on the philosophy that everyone has something to offer and that no one is perfect.

Some Thoughts on Theory

We believe that reference group theory and cognitive development theory provide the strongest explanations for the development of prejudice and discrimination, primarily because both theories deal with groups of people. Cognitive development theory helps us understand how individuals learn to categorize people into groups and apply stereotypical descriptions to those groups. In a society that is already somewhat segregated and stratified on the basis of race, sex, family background, and disability, cognitive development theory explains how individuals construct sense out of the social world they encounter. Reference group theory helps explain why racial, gender, social class, and disability prejudice are group phenomena rather than isolated individual problems. This theory helps us understand why people tend to hold tenaciously to certain values and perceptions and to reject people they see as nonmembers of their group and why tension can exist between groups even when individuals have no personal reason to dislike those who belong to the out-group.

Psychodynamic theory and social learning theory help explain why some people are more prone than others to reject out-group members, but their focus on the individual does not help explain intergroup relations on a large scale. Viewing prejudice and discrimination as emotional disturbances overlooks the advantages that social stratification confers on the dominant group. By acting in ways that help maintain racism, Whites preserve certain economic and political benefits for themselves. By maintaining sexism, males preserve benefits for themselves. Acting on the basis of self-interest may at times be morally questionable, but it is not necessarily the product of emotional instability.

For example, take the wealthy White neighborhood in which families hire women of color as "cleaning ladies." The White employers may harbor positive attitudes toward their employees, may have learned positive behaviors for interacting with them, and may manifest great emotional stability in their own lives and in their acceptance of people. Yet, at the same time, they may accept as natural that only women do housework and that women of color do other people's housework for minimum wages. They may accept stereotypes about this category of person and see the category as an out-group, albeit a group having a useful function. It is possible that individual members of the neighborhood may harbor negative feelings about women of color; some in the neighborhood may dislike these women intensely. On the other hand, others may feel they treat their cleaning ladies well and like them personally. At the same time, they still see them as different, perceive them in terms of stereotypes about women of color, and accord them a lower status.

The strategies that follow are based mainly on reference group, cognitive development, social learning, dissonance, and self-concept theories.

STRATEGIES

Human relations strategies for classrooms are based on the theories we have just discussed, with the major exception being psychoanalytic theory. Allport (1979), Carter (1995), Dana (1997), and Helms and Cook (1999) recommended individual counseling and therapy to help people who have unusually hostile attitudes toward others. Counselors and therapists have at their disposal psychotherapeutic techniques for helping people resolve their inner frustrations and conflicts and develop more positive attitudes toward others. This therapy is not normally done in classrooms, nor is it recommended for classrooms.

Advocates of the Human Relations approach have developed several strategies for classroom use, summarized in Table 3-1. These advocates have also developed four underlying principles that teachers should consider before selecting specific strategies. We will present these principles first.

General Principles

First, the human relations program should be comprehensive. This means that it should be infused into several subject areas, and it should be schoolwide to avoid giving children mixed messages. For example, a school attempting to promote social acceptance of students with mental retardation is working at cross-purposes if lessons in social studies are aimed at reducing prejudice, but language arts and mathematics classes are ability grouped, with retarded students composing the lowest group, and school clubs are dominated by the most academically successful students.

Second, diverse strategies should be used. We will present a variety of strategies that can be considered for implementation. Different strategies accomplish different things, and no single strategy has been found to be the one best strategy for promoting positive human relations. However, strategies actively involving children tend to be most effective. Although there is value in presenting information or in demonstrating an action, those strategies that place children in a passive role have less impact than those that place them in an active role.

Third, the program should start with the children's real-life experiences. Educators recommend, for example, starting with interpersonal relationships in the classroom or intergroup hostilities in the school. These familiar experiences enable the children to more easily grasp the point of developing human relations involving more distant and abstract groups.

Finally, each child should be able to experience academic and social success in the classroom, and the success of some students should not be contingent on the failure of others. Often in classrooms children compete for grades or rewards. This competition teaches a child to devalue the feelings and accomplishments of others because others must do poorly in order for the child to look good. Those students who consistently come out at or near the bottom tend to suffer some rejection by others and may develop feelings of personal inadequacy. These feelings run counter to the goals of the Human Relations approach.

These principles govern the use of a number of strategies: providing accurate information, using group process, using vicarious experience and role playing, involving students in service learning projects, and teaching social skills.

Providing Accurate Cognitive Information

Ignorance supports prejudice; accurate information can help to reduce prejudice. Young children are naturally curious about what they see, and they want information. Derman-Sparks (1989) provided an example of a young child's question and an appropriate response:

> "How do people get their color?" asks 3-year-old Heather. "What are your ideas?" her teacher responds. "Well, I was wondering about pens. You know, the pens you can put red or blue or brown on your skin if you want to." Teacher: "I'm glad you are trying to figure things out, but that's not how people get their skin color. We get our skin color from our mommies and daddies. Your skin is the same color as mine. Marizza's skin color is like her mommy and daddy's. Denise's skin is lighter brown because she is a mixture of her mommy's white skin and her Daddy's black skin." (p.33)

The information the teacher provided is accurate and about as conceptually sophisticated as a 3-year-old can grasp. Older children could learn about melanin, how melanin protects the skin, and why people who developed in geographical areas near the equator developed more melanin than those nearer the North Pole. Providing such information is much more constructive than ignoring the issue or telling students not to ask about such matters.

In multicultural education programs, providing accurate cognitive information means providing accurate information about various racial, ethnic, disability, gender, social class groups, and people who are gay or lesbian. At the very least, it means making sure that classroom materials do not contain overt stereotypes and biases. Most educators advocate going beyond the removal of stereotypical materials by presenting accurate and comprehensive information. This strategy is important because, as noted earlier, people learn stereotypes, and they focus attention on attributes of categories of people (such as skin color) that exaggerate traits, oversimplify, and in many cases misrepresent people. Accurate cognitive information seeks to replace stereotypes and misconceptions that children may already have.

Human relations educators agree that this information should stress "the commonality of people as well as their individuality" (Colangelo et al., 1985, p. 1). Following World War II, Taba et al. (1952) recommended that teachers teach children about cultural differences by stressing ways in which culture is a reasonable response people make to their particular life conditions in an effort to resolve common human problems. These educators gave an example regarding teaching about the Chinese diet. Anglo children may view the preponderance of rice in the Chinese diet as peculiar until they are made aware of the preponderance of wheat in the Anglo diet and until they learn why all people need a grain product in their diet. Educators today such as Johnson and Johnson (2002) and Gazda et al. (2006) support Taba's ideas, but more explicitly work at teaching students to understand culture by participating in a range of human relations activities that teach about valuing diversity, starting with analyzing one's own culture, and from such an analysis exploring the similarities and differences across cultures.

Calloway (1999) applied these ideas to disability. She recommended that teachers in inclusive classrooms answer children's questions about disability accurately and honestly; provide pictures, books, and dolls so that children can learn about disability in a comfortable way; and create plenty of opportunities for nondisabled and disabled children to interact with each other. Examples of how to transform one's existing curriculum and teaching processes to do this can be found in the Human Relations chapter of *Turning on Learning* (Grant & Sleeter, 2006), such as how one might integrate information about disability into a health lesson.

As noted earlier, young children ask questions freely before they learn that some kinds of questions are impolite. Adults often treat questions about human differences as rude, so children stop asking them. Instead, they learn to verbalize differences in the form of jokes, snide remarks, and name calling. Sears (1992), for example, notes, "Too many school children remain ignorant of the diversity of human sexuality, and too many teachers and students fear discussing sexuality beyond whispered conversations, cruel jokes, or sexual innuendo" (p. 147). By late elementary or junior high age, students may be very uncomfortable engaging in initial lessons about differences they have learned not to discuss openly.

One of us witnessed a junior high teacher trying to discuss ethnic background with a group of students who apparently had never talked openly about this issue; her invitation for students to share their ethnic background was met with silence, then embarrassed giggles, and finally joking behavior (such as African American students saying that they were Chinese). Unprepared for the students' reaction, the teacher stopped the lesson and moved on to something else. With older students, teachers may wish to begin instruction by acknowledging that this subject may be one students have never openly discussed, reflecting on the teacher's earlier discomfort in discussing the subject (such as racial differences). Then the discussion proceeds to the highly interesting information the teacher learned and wishes to teach (giving an example). As the teacher provides correct terminology and accurate information, modeling comfort while discussing a human difference or characteristic, students soon open up and begin asking questions that have been suppressed, often since early childhood.

In order to teach students about "the other," teachers often invite a live representation into the classroom for the students to meet. They believe, for example, that a student in a wheelchair speaks far louder about disability than any words they could say. We wish to issue a caution here and state that much of the research in this area argues that "contact" in and of itself is not enough. For one thing, such learning can be at the expense of the guest to the classroom, who may be asked to highlight her or his "differentness" and painful responses to discrimination. Furthermore, increasingly over the past several decades, researchers have contended that teachers must create conditions and opportunities for personal interactions between the students, who are, for example, in a wheelchair and students not in wheelchairs in order for positive relationships to develop and stereotyping and prejudice to decrease. Also, these researchers argue that both groups of students need to be of equal status (Marcus-Newhall et al., 1993; Urban & Miller, 1998; Wright et al., 1997). The key points here are "personal interactions" and "equal status."

Yet the teacher should not rely exclusively on members of other groups to teach about themselves; if the teacher does not have enough information to get started, there are excellent teaching resources to use. For example, numerous books provide insightful vignettes and focus activities that may help teachers to construct meaningful lessons (e.g., Grant, 1995; Gazda et al., 2006; Johnson & Johnson, 2002; Tiedt & Tiedt, 1995). In addition, children's literature books can be an excellent source of information about diverse groups.

Teachers also need to educate themselves about what is worth teaching. When teachers first begin to teach about differences, they often construct what Derman-Sparks (1989) refers to as a "tourist curriculum," which focuses on artifacts of other countries, such as food, traditional clothing, folk tales, and household items (p. 7). For example, on Cinco de Mayo (a Mexican American holiday in May), children eat tacos and learn to count to 10 in Spanish; or to study Native Americans, children make headdresses or totem poles, eat fry bread, and listen to a folk tale. Derman-Sparks criticizes the "tourist curriculum":

> Tourist curriculum is both patronizing, emphasizing the "exotic" differences between cultures, and trivializing, dealing not with the real-life daily problems and experiences of different peoples, but with surface aspects of their celebrations and modes of entertainment. Children "visit" non-White cultures and then "go home" to the daily classroom, which reflects only the dominant culture. The focus on holidays, although it provides drama and delight for both children and adults, gives the impression that that is all "other" people—usually people of color—do. What it fails to communicate is real understanding. (p. 7)

Instead, she recommends starting with a variety of differences—cultural, physical, and gender—that students actually see and experience, here and now. Rather than treating differences as exotic, teachers should treat differences in the community as normal. Teachers should also discuss stereotyping and prejudice, so that students comprehend how people react to differences they do not understand.

How much impact can the teaching of cognitive information have? Banks (1991) reviewed numerous research studies on the impact of content about race and gender on students. He found that, although results of the studies are inconsistent, curriculum interventions can have a positive impact on students' racial and gender attitudes. The studies he reviewed were conducted in a variety of ways, using a variety of measures of impact. However, many of them reported a positive change in students' attitudes; none reported a negative impact. Most of the interventions were short term; the impact of a long-term course of study has not been investigated to any appreciable extent.

Educators see limitations to presenting information as a primary teaching strategy; by itself, presenting information does not necessarily change behavior or attitudes. For example, based on a review of research studies on the impact of persuasive information on attitudes, Watts (1984) found that information is most likely to change attitudes when a person is not already committed to the target attitudes or when the attitudes are not directly connected to core beliefs. Attitudes that help anchor a person's core beliefs are resistant to change, and the information presented may simply be ignored. Sniderman and Piazza (1993) argue that a person's education level is the strongest predictor of prejudice. In other words, education reduces prejudice. Teachers who couple the presentation of information with additional strategies are likely to create a stronger impact on students. In discussing teacher education, for instance, King (1991) discourages the isolated presentation of factual information about social inequality. Rather, she stresses the need students have for "an alternative context in which to think critically about and reconstruct their social knowledge and self-identities" (p.143). Similarly, Berlak (1996) emphasizes the possibilities of narrative in challenging student perspectives and raising awareness.

Presenting children with positive information about their own group can be very helpful, however, especially if it counters negative perceptions. People want to feel good about themselves and look for information that will validate their self-worth. School curricula do not tend to include much substantive information about many groups, such as women of color, contemporary American Indians, or people with disabilities. This lack of information sends the message to members of these groups that they are relatively unimportant, which can be detrimental to their self-concepts. For example, when an Indian child is taught about his or her tribe's accomplishments, this information is embraced with more enthusiasm than information that suggests that Indians in the twenty-first century are an artifact of U.S. history. The strategies that follow involve students actively; they are very useful when coupled with information presentation.

Using Group Process

In 1954, Cook and Cook defined group process as the "use of the group to educate its members" (p. 243). Over the years this definition has remained consistent. Kahn (1999) describes group process as two or more people coming together to discuss an issue of collective concern. Human Relations educators usually advocate the use of heterogeneous groups (i.e., race mixed, sex mixed, or groups containing both special education and regular students); cooperative learning in particular has become very popular. Group process strategies make use of two of the theories discussed earlier. One is *cognitive development theory*. As a result of direct contact with members of another group during carefully structured situations, students should be able to gain accurate information that will probably challenge stereotypes about members of that group. For example, if a student believes that hearing-impaired people are unsociable but then works on a class project with one who is gregarious, that stereotype might be weakened or eliminated. The other theory that group process builds on is *reference group theory*. By building groups of heterogeneous students, teachers attempt to construct in-groups with students who had previously regarded each other as out-group members. For example, in a sex-segregated classroom, cross-sex team members begin to identify with teammates of both sexes, as well as with members of the same sex who are on other teams. Also, the peer group within the entire class develops a norm against sex discrimination (or race or disability discrimination) as students on each team see the value of interacting with teammates of the opposite sex.

Depending on how a teacher structures group work, it can be either very successful or disastrous. Some teachers mistakenly believe that contact by itself among members of different groups is beneficial. Actually, as we noted above, contact in and of itself is not sufficient and in some cases can encourage stereotyping, prejudice, and social rejection. For example, imagine a teacher in a desegregated school who has White, middle-class students, who have attended suburban schools with good teaching, and African American, low-income students, who have previously attended schools with inferior teaching. Suppose that this teacher establishes racially mixed groups that are assigned to complete a library research project on the Industrial Revolution. It is quite possible that the African American students would not be as well prepared for this task as the White students. Consequently, if the White students believe that African Americans are inferior, the contact experience might reaffirm that belief. Conversely, if the African American students believe that Whites are arrogant, this belief, too, might be reaffirmed.

Allport (1979) specified conditions under which cross-group contact can be beneficial:

> Prejudice (unless deeply rooted in the character structure of the individual) may be reduced by equal status contact between majority and minority groups in the pursuit of common goals. The effect is greatly enhanced if this contact is sanctioned by institutional supports ... and provided it is of the sort that leads to the perception of common interests, and common humanity between members of the two groups. (p. 281)

Cooperative learning is a form of group work that is receiving considerable attention. Johnson, Johnson, and Holubec (1998) differentiate cooperative learning from traditional grouping on the basis of several factors. In cooperative learning groups, students must work together to complete the task successfully; the work is structured to promote their interdependence. Cooperative learning should involve individual as well as group accountability; the teacher should give both individual and group feedback. In cooperative learning groups, students share responsibility for leadership functions; they also share responsibility for each other's achievement. The teacher makes sure students are rewarded for sharing these tasks. Teachers of cooperative learning groups help students develop group process skills, such as conflict management and listening. Considerable evidence points to the use of cooperative learning in classrooms as a successful strategy for reducing stereotyping and social rejection across disability, race, and gender lines (e.g., Cohen & Lotan, 1997; Johnson & Johnson, 2002; Slavin, 1990, 1991). Examples of how to integrate cooperative learning into teaching in various disciplines can be found in *Turning on Learning* (Grant & Sleeter, 2006).

Various models of cooperative learning exist. The *group investigation model* involves students working in small heterogeneous groups to create a product that requires diverse talents, skills, or viewpoints (see Johnson, Johnson, & Holubec, 1998). The product may be as elaborate as a multimedia production in which students synthesize information they have gathered about a topic; or it can be as small as a list of ideas generated during a short discussion. Group investigation assignments require considerable advance planning by the teacher because the tasks must draw on the strengths or abilities of each student in the group; no group should be assigned a task that sets up some of its members to fail. For example, creating a newspaper as a way of investigating a topic requires different skills, such as preparing articles that have diverse writing styles, creating drawings, doing interviews, and designing layouts. By contrast, sending groups of students to the library to do a research paper usually sets up some students for failure, unless all of them are skilled in doing library research or unless the teacher has identified in advance those materials that are of interest to and within the skill levels of all the students.

The *jigsaw model* uses two groupings to complete an assignment. In the first grouping, each group studies a different but related piece of a topic, and group members work together to make sure they all understand the material and become "experts" on it. The students are then regrouped so that each new group has one or two "experts" on each piece. A task is then given, requiring students to pool their expertise. For example, suppose students in an English class are studying sonnets. The teacher divides the class into groups and gives each group a different sonnet to study; each group member is given a copy of the sonnet and questions to use as a guide in discussion. Students are then regrouped with others who have read different sonnets, so that each new group is composed of "experts" on one sonnet. Their task could be to determine the essential characteristics of a sonnet by comparing the different sonnets studied. Many teachers like this particular model of cooperative learning because when students get to their second group, everyone has an important piece to contribute that the rest of the group members need. Even the lowest academic achievers have some expertise to share.

In the *team games model,* students are divided into heterogeneous groups. All the students are expected to master a body of skills or knowledge, but they compete as a team against other teams in some form of tournament. The main way for teams to succeed is for group members to tutor each other before the competition. Teachers can use team games in a wide variety of ways, ranging from giving fairly short and simple quizzes on the material (in which, say, the group with the best average score wins) to conducting very elaborate tournaments (Slavin, 1986).

Some teachers occasionally use cooperative learning activities as a break from traditional teaching methods; others structure much of their teaching program around cooperative learning. For example, the Tribes Program involves groups of "five or six children who work together throughout each day throughout the school year" (Gibbs, 1987). The teacher plans group process activities to help the students learn to work together and uses the models of cooperative learning described above; students are also encouraged to help each other, even when they are not required to provide such help.

An important part of group process strategies is teaching students the skills and attitudes needed for working together; the benefits of cooperative learning come from students actually learning to work together well. Several curriculum guides are full of activities that are specifically designed to teach students how to cooperate, such as how to listen to each other, how to resolve differences, or how to encourage each other to participate (e.g., Johnson & Johnson, 2002; Johnson, Johnson, & Holubec, 1998; Kahn, 1999; Prutzman et al., 1988; Tinto, 1997).

Teachers who are interested in group process strategies will find many useful books and workshops available to help them. It does take practice to learn to use cooperative learning well. Sometimes teachers try it out and then give up because what they intended did not work automatically. Failures with cooperative learning are usually due not to the concept but to one's skill in using the concept.

Using Vicarious Experience and Role Playing

Umphrey (1999) states that "'First-hand' experiences are those that we have gone through ourselves"; and "'vicarious' experiences are those we get by contemplating what has happened to other people. although we might never have traveled in the arctic on dog sleds, if we watch a movie or read a book about arctic explorers, we can learn much about what that experience is like. This is vicarious experience" (p. 1).

Group dynamics, described earlier, foster direct, face-to-face contact; vicarious experiences promote contact through the use of symbols of reality. Vicarious experiences include contact through role playing, sociodrama, literature, and film, in which the student takes the perspective of a member of another group.

Vicarious experiences are rooted in different theories, depending on how the experiences are structured. These experiences may be structured primarily to reduce stereotyping. For example, if some students who believe that all Japanese Americans are quiet view a film depicting a realistic story involving Japanese Americans who do not conform to that stereotype, the stereotype may be weakened (depending on the believability of the film).

Vicarious experiences can also reduce social distance and develop feelings of empathy. For example, a boy who plays the role of a woman trying to raise a family single-handedly on a secretary's salary may reevaluate his stereotypes about working women as well as discover the problems such women face and may therefore feel more concern for their situation. According to dissonance theory, the boy would experience a discrepancy between his previous negative attitude and his feelings while playing the role. The experience could lead to a change in attitude, provided the role playing was realistic. Simulations of disabilities are currently popular for preparing regular education students for the inclusion of special education students in inclusive classrooms.

Bandura (1997) argues that the social modeling used when carrying out vicarious experiences can affect students' self-efficacy, and that when students see a successful model their self-efficacy can be raised. To the degree that the students feel that the model is similar to them, modeling affects their self-efficacy. However, Bandura observes, vicarious experiences may have more effect when failure is modeled than when success is modeled.

Role playing and simulation have been found to help improve attitudes toward people with disabilities (Johnson & Johnson, 2002; Kitano, Stiehl, & Cole, 1978). Simulations may, of course, facilitate sensitization across a variety of domains. For example, Sylvester (1994) transformed his elementary classroom in a way that reflected economic problems in the surrounding community and society; by having to confront issues such as unemployment, wage structures, and taxation, students gained a deeper understanding of the struggles encountered by social groups. However, simulations can also greatly oversimplify a situation, leading students to view another group's problems as easily resolvable; teachers who use simulations need to be aware of this possible outcome.

Skits are useful for helping students examine group behavior. For example, Prutzman and colleagues (1988) suggest that a teacher can have students stage a skit involving interpersonal conflict. As students act out what they would do or what they have seen others do, the skit can be interrupted periodically for discussion of alternative courses of action. Skits are useful in teaching conflict resolution: "When children encounter a problem similar to one they have already resolved, they are better prepared to meet it with a creative solution" (Prutzman et al., 1988, p. 60).

Involving Students in Service Learning Projects

Service learning is another form of direct contact experience, moving the students out of the classroom and placing them in contact with members of a target group in the community to do some sort of service project. According to Schine (1997): "In the current wave of school reform, service learning is frequently cited as a strategy for engaging disaffected students and for developing the habits and attitudes of constructive citizenship" (p. 2).

Like group dynamics, service learning provides contact in an effort to reduce stereotyping and other personal biases by engaging in real-life experiences. Like role playing, this strategy can create dissonance between behavior and prejudiced attitudes by engaging students in real-life experiences outside of the boundary of the school. Schine (1997) argues that while service learning is not a new concept, it is increasingly regarded as a promising component of schooling.

Teaching Social Skills

Teaching social skills to someone who does not interact positively with members of another group can facilitate cross-group relationships and positive attitudes. This strategy has two rather different kinds of applications. One application is primarily for members of dominant groups who behave toward others in a manner that breeds hostility or simply indifference. LaGreca (1993) and Johnson (1993) illustrate skills one could teach: encouraging self-disclosure, developing and maintaining trust, listening, responding, sending clear messages, expressing feelings both verbally and nonverbally, and confronting others constructively. Some educators have trained teachers and students to use these skills in interracial situations in order to facilitate positive and constructive communication (Banks & Benavidez, 1981).

A particular problem teachers often must deal with involves harassment, name calling, and bullying. Harassment and bullying probably occur to a greater degree than most adults are aware of or will admit. For example, in a review of literature on sexual harassment in schools, Linn, Stein, Young, and Davis (1992) note that there is a high occurrence of sexual harassment among students, with young women being victims much more often than young men, and "more often than not, nothing is done with this information [about allegations of sexual harassment], and the problem and conditions fester" (p. 115). Isernhagen and Harris

(2003) compared bullying behaviors of high school students in two states and found that almost one-third of the girls and one-fifth of the boys often observed bullying, most commonly hurtful teasing and name calling. Boys used more physical violence than girls, but both genders reported being threatened with harm about one-fourth of the time when they were being bullied. Adults may be unaware of bullying harassment among students for a variety of reasons: it often occurs when adults are not around, students are often embarrassed to report it, and adults often trivialize it when it is reported (for example, replying that "boys will be boys" or tacitly agreeing that a particular student is a "fag").

How do human relations advocates recommend handling harassment, bullying, and name calling? Teachers must establish rules and explain to students the reasons for the rules. Young children are often unaware of the hurtfulness of name calling or other exclusionary behaviors; older children may well be aware that such behavior hurts others but may try to get away with it. Teachers should intervene immediately, comfort or support the target, and enforce the rule prohibiting the behavior. Teachers should then consider the underlying reason for the behavior. Sometimes harassment or name calling results from peer pressure or prejudice. Harassment is also often a power play, in which dominate group members try to keep subordinate group members "in their place." For example, sexual harassment is frequently a way of reminding females of their vulnerability, especially if they try to succeed in "male" areas such as sports.

Reactive solutions (i.e., stopping the behavior) have limited long-term effects; teachers who approach harassment proactively assume that the potential for harassment exists and continuously use the strategies described in this chapter and in subsequent chapters to build more positive relationships among students before problems occur (Derman-Sparks, 1989). An application of social skills teaching is aimed at preventing violence among elementary and middle school children. "Second Step" is a project designed for students, which teaches empathy training, impulse control, and anger management (Grossman et al., 1997).

Various programs have been developed to teach skills to special education students, socially unpopular students, and victims of bullying, to facilitate their social relationships with other students and to help them stand up for themselves. The findings of such studies are mixed; they may or may not reduce bullying, but they do seem to help victims of bullying feel better about themselves and their ability to handle situations (Fox & Boulton, 2003; Oden & Asher, 1977).

Social skills are usually taught using a variety of techniques, including modeling, coaching, and role playing. Positive reinforcement is given consistently, immediately following a child's use of a desired positive social behavior. Students need to be helped with skills development until they are able to use the skills appropriately in real-life situations. Many guides, in fact, have been published which provide exercises for fostering students' abilities to respect differences, communicate, and resolve conflict (Drew, 1987; Duvall, 1994; Henkin, 2005; Johnson & Johnson, 2002).

How does a Human Relations approach get into a school? What kinds of considerations and problems make such an approach seem useful? The following vignette describes one morning in a typical middle school, where problems with human relationships suddenly assumed great importance.

A BLUE MONDAY MORNING

Mr. Mack, a middle school social studies teacher, was not feeling his best this morning as he sped along the expressway to Hemingway School, located in the suburbs. He was annoyed with himself for arguing with his wife about where to spend spring vacation. She wanted to go to San Francisco to see their just-born niece and then rent a car and drive along the California coast for a second honeymoon. He wanted to go to Boston to see a few Celtics games and spend some time in the Harvard library doing research on his thesis. Not only was he annoyed for having lost the argument that had occupied most of their attention over the weekend, but he had spent too much time this morning making a final plea for his position (it being the last day for reduced fares) and was now in danger of being late for school. He was well aware that the nonverbal communication conveyed by his principal, Mrs. Wilson, hung staff members by their thumbs, so to speak, when they arrived late; and his anxiety was compounded by having been late Thursday of last week.

When he pulled his car into the first open space in the school parking lot, a glance at his Swatch informed him that he had one and a half minutes before being late. He figured that if he walked fast across the playground, he could make it and not have to endure Mrs. Wilson's scowls. He was halfway across the playground and beginning to feel like he just might get in under the wire when he suddenly saw three boys from his class—Ernest, Ken, and Harold—yelling and chasing Victor Cheng, the new boy in school. He wondered if he had correctly heard what they were shouting. He called the boys over to him. As they arrived—28 seconds left before the scowl—he told Ernest, Ken, and Harold to meet him in his classroom. He then took Victor Cheng gently by the arm and continued his trek to the office. On the way, he asked Victor why the boys were chasing him and what they were calling him.

He scribbled his name and time of arrival on the time sheet just as the bell sounded, alerting all faculty that the workday had officially begun (and telling any teacher who hadn't yet signed in that he or she was late). Victor told him then what the boys had said—that they didn't like wormy Chinese food or people who try to act smart in class. He said that they had told him that if he didn't bring some fortune cookies to school, they would do him in; he hadn't brought the cookies to school.

Mrs. Wilson overheard this conversation from her vantage point near the sign-in sheets, and she moved closer to listen until Victor finished his story. Then she asked Mr. Mack to have Victor wait in the library. She wanted to talk privately with Mr. Mack.

Mrs. Wilson told Mr. Mack that this was the ninth name calling and fighting incident that had come to her attention in the last few days. She said, "We have had basically a peaceful integration of students of color into the school, but the name calling, fighting, and writing of graffiti—words like Nigger and Chink—on the boys' bathroom wall suggest that the students need to have some human relations orientation. They also need to learn what sexual harassment is and that it is illegal. Just yesterday a father came in very angry because his daughter said some boys had been trying to touch her where they shouldn't." She suggested that Mr. Mack organize a committee of three other teachers to recommend some schoolwide and classroom human relations activities that would help reduce the prejudice, eliminate the stereotyping and name calling, and put a stop to any sexual harassment. She suggested that they consider bulletin boards that would point out the similarity of people, the importance of brotherhood and sisterhood, the obligation to respect others, and the need for appropriate behavior between members of the opposite sex. She also suggested that they establish policies for reporting and dealing with name calling and sexual harassment when these practices occur.

Mr. Mack said, "Okay, I'll get back to you this afternoon with the names of the other committee members. I've become increasingly interested in learning more about these matters anyway. Besides, I've heard that getting students to work on these issues in cooperative groups can help."

Mrs. Wilson remarked that she had heard the same thing, although she cautioned that the faculty should not just leap onto one possible solution before investigating an array of strategies.

As he left Mrs. Wilson and headed to pick up Victor Cheng, Mr. Mack thought, "Human relations are important on the job and off!"

CRITIQUE The Human Relations approach seems to be the most popular approach with teachers, particularly White elementary teachers. For example, in a study of 30 teachers participating in a long-term, staff development program in multicultural education, one of us found that teachers define multicultural education as the Human Relations approach more frequently than any other approach (Haberman & Post, 1990; Sleeter, 1992). However, this is not the approach preferred by most people who have studied discrimination or multicultural education in depth. Why is there this discrepancy?

One can criticize the Human Relations approach, not for what it aims to do but for what it does not aim to do. Few can quarrel with the desirability of reducing prejudice, stereotyping, tension, and hostility among groups. The approach itself, however, is limited in its analysis of why discrimination and inequality exist and in its simplistic conception of culture and identity.

Advocates of the Teaching the Exceptional and Culturally Different approach see the Human Relations approach as too soft and ineffective in addressing academic achievement. The approach they advocate directly addresses how to teach the curriculum better, which the Human Relations approach does not. For example, in the vignette the teachers were probably ignoring Victor Cheng's ethnic background, as well as that of other students, until a social problem erupted. They were probably teaching students as if they were all alike, as if the school were predominantly White, and as if all the students were White. Student diversity became an object of concern only when it threatened harmony within the school. However, as we have noted earlier, in most schools the chances are great that, on the average, students of color, students from low-income homes, students struggling with their sexual identity, and students with disabilities are not achieving on a par with the White, suburban students with whom they will be competing to get into college. Advocates of Teaching the Exceptional and Culturally Different (as well as advocates of other approaches we will discuss later) view student achievement as one of the most fundamentally important issues to address. If we simply accept low achievement levels as natural and focus only on how students are getting along, we are not doing our job as teachers.

Actually, the two approaches we have examined thus far—Teaching the Exceptional and Culturally Different, and Human Relations—can be used simultaneously. Nevertheless, teachers who try to do so usually emphasize one or the other—teaching the existing curriculum well or improving feelings in the classroom—simply because there is not time to do everything exceptionally well.

The three approaches to multicultural education that we will discuss next view discrimination, inequality, culture, and cultural identity as much more complex than does the Human Relations approach. Ask yourself, for example, why substantially larger proportions of children of color live in poverty than White children. When asked this question, most White people at first draw a blank, then name things that families of color must lack (such as ambition or education), and sometimes make vague references to discrimination, such as mentioning a relative who will not hire employees of color. Or ask yourself why the poverty rate among women is growing despite the fact that some career opportunities have opened to them. Does stereotyping and sexual harassment fully explain the impoverization of women? Without having investigated these kinds of questions, most people simply don't know the answers. Therefore, in the classroom when symptoms of inequalities are acted out, teachers treat the symptoms only—the name calling, stereotyping, and prejudice.

For example, imagine two children, a lower-income Puerto Rican and a middle-class Anglo, fighting at school. One can teach them to play together rather than to fight, and one can teach that Puerto Ricans are not violent (contrary to the Anglo child's stereotype) or that Anglos are not arrogant (contrary to the Puerto Rican child's stereotype). Unfortunately, these teachings do almost nothing to change the fact that this Puerto Rican child, like many Latino children, is living in poverty; that middle-class Anglos tend to accept another's poverty and see it as the other person's fault; and that the Anglo child will have doors of opportunity open to him or her that will be closed to the lower-income Puerto Rican child and, in many cases, even the middle-class Puerto Rican child, especially if her or his skin is dark. Perhaps this particular Anglo child will deal more humanely with people of color as a result of human relations teaching, but kind treatment by individuals does not of itself eliminate poverty, powerlessness, social stratification, or institutional discrimination.

As in the vignette, the other students may learn to interact pleasantly with Victor and to enjoy Chinese food, but this accommodation is no guarantee that they will learn about issues such as the poverty in Chinatown or the psychological devastation many Asian immigrants face when they realize they must surrender much of their identity to assimilate into American society. McCarthy (1993) has been quite critical of approaches to multicultural education that emphasize the changing of individual attitudes and the need for more positive relationships while failing to address the structural nature of inequality.

McCarthy's critique is both significant and valid, for human relations curricula do not address these issues in much depth, if at all. For example, we reviewed *Multicultural Teaching: A Handbook of Activities, Information, and Resources* (Tiedt & Tiedt, 1995), which contains a variety of human relations lessons for grades K–8. The lessons are in categories that include supporting individual self-esteem, achieving empathy for others, and recognizing and providing equity for all people living in the United States. Written objectives inform the user that the lessons aim to teach children that diversity is something to be valued, that people of different colors have contributed to America, and that the "range of diversity to be represented in a multicultural curriculum includes young and old, male and female, the physically able and disabled, as well as those who can be grouped by language, national origin, race, or religious belief" (pp. xiii–xiv). Included in the goals for the lessons are the ideas that there is diversity within ethnic groups, that individual uniqueness should be cherished, that no cultural group is better or worse than any other, and that everyone has feelings. These are worthwhile purposes, and the lessons are creatively and skillfully written to accomplish them. However, although the authors state that multicultural education should include conversations about "controversial issues," the lessons and the goals for the lessons do not teach about injustices that have happened in the past or are now occurring. They do not examine how groups in real life compete for wealth and power, how power positions in the United States are dominated by White males of wealth, how unemployment is high in central cities partly because businesses do not find it profitable to locate there, and how many businesses are set up to value personal profit more than sharing with others. Such lessons fail to examine why many women who head households and need jobs often lack child care facilities for their children, and are forced to choose between holding a job but having to leave their children unsupervised or staying home with their children but having to live on welfare.

These problems are not resolved by teaching individuals only to get along better and value diversity. In fact, valuing diversity can be interpreted to mean believing, for example, that Mexican Americans should eat beans rather than steak because beans are "more Mexican." Such thinking ignores the fact that beans are also cheaper, and it can glorify the way people have adapted to poverty and powerlessness without acknowledging that many people who eat beans do so because they cannot afford steak.

In a very real sense, the Human Relations approach can be assimilationist. Some educators who adopt a Human Relations approach often do not address issues of assimilation versus pluralism; cultural differences are addressed only as much as necessary to improve feelings toward self and others. Other Human Relations educators do address cultural diversity, stressing mainly the acceptance of differences without necessarily examining critically which differences are of most value and which are artifacts of historic or present injustices. In addition, by failing to focus adequately on social problems and structural inequalities, the approach implicitly accepts the status quo. It asks people to get along within the status quo rather than educating them to change the status quo.

Cooperative learning, as we have mentioned earlier, is currently very popular. Often teachers use it to improve relationships among students in the classroom, but otherwise the teachers maintain business as usual. For example, it is quite possible to use cooperative learning to process textbook assignments that teach about the conquest of Native American nations without ever critiquing the relations between Native Americans and Whites today—relations that for many tribes are not cooperative. As Sapon-Shevin and Schniedewind (1989/1990) point out:

> Learning about and implementing cooperative learning can provide schools an opportunity to examine all aspects of school policy, philosophy, and practice, making these consistent with a belief in the value and educability of all students and a sense of the mutual responsibility that creates communities. (p. 65)

Strategies such as cooperative learning open up larger questions about how groups relate to each other. Advocates of the three approaches to multicultural education that will be discussed next hope that educators will pursue these larger questions.

Because of what the Human Relations approach does not address, it has not been adopted by most educators interested in fighting sexism, heterosexism, or classism, and many people of color who adopted the approach at one time have since shifted to one of the approaches examined later in this book. The Human Relations approach can be incorporated into other approaches, so one need not give up a fight against prejudice and stereotyping to adopt another approach.

The Human Relations approach currently is popular with those who work with special education students, probably because most people who write about and teach students with disabilities do not themselves have disabilities. Educators see human relations problems in schools, but they tend to view people with disabilities from a deficiency or difference rather than an oppressed minority perspective. Therefore, many teachers believe that it is sufficient if children learn to get along and accept other physical or mental characteristics. An oppressed minority perspective, adopted by advocates of the three approaches this book will treat next, as well as by disability rights advocates and Disability Studies scholars, focuses on issues such as access to a wide range of institutions, the cultures of disability communities, and "ablism" within the dominant society.

Early childhood and primary grade teachers feel that we are terribly off base if this critique implies that teachers should teach young children about issues such as job discrimination. Actually, at the early childhood level, good Human Relations teaching can provide a basis for more sophisticated approaches to multicultural education later. The key word here is *good* Human Relations rather than "tourist curricula." For example, in this chapter we have made reference to the *Anti-Bias Curriculum* (Derman-Sparks, 1989) and to *Multicultural Teaching: A Handbook of Activities, Information, and Resources* (Tiedt & Tiedt, 1995). The Anti-Bias Curriculum is explicitly designed to provide children with a basis for learning that is consistent with the three approaches to multicultural education that we will explore next. Multicultural Teaching, though not explicitly so designed, also lays a very good foundation for young children on which it is possible to build the same three approaches. Similarly, King (1990) suggests many activities to help young children explore ethnic and gender differences in their immediate environment. Tourist curricula, teaching about the food and folk customs of other countries, do not lay such a foundation. Early childhood and primary-grade teachers should become familiar with all five approaches to multicultural education, but they may find that much of their work is most consistent with the Human Relations approach.

REFERENCES

Aboud, F. (1988). *Children and prejudice.* Oxford: Basil Blackwell.

Adorno, T. W., Frenkel-Brunswik, E., Levinson, D. J., & Sanford, R. N. (1950). *The authoritarian personality.* New York: Harper & Row.

Allport, G. W. (1979). *The nature of prejudice* (25th anniversary ed.). Reading, MA: Addison-Wesley.

American Association of University Women. (1992). *The AAUW report: How schools shortchange girls.* Washington, DC: AAUW and the National Education Association.

Bandura, A. (1997). *Self-efficacy in changing societies.* New York: Cambridge University Press.

Banks, C. (2005). *Improving multicultural education. Lessons from the intergroup education movement.* New York: Teachers College Press.

Banks, G. P., & Benavidez, P. L. (1981). Interpersonal skills training in multicultural education. In H. P. Baptiste, Jr., M. L. Baptiste, & D. M. Gollnick (Eds.). *Multicultural teacher education: Preparing educators to provide educational equity* (pp. 177–201). Washington, DC: Association of Colleges & Teacher Education.

Banks, J. A. (1991). Multicultural education: Its effects on students' racial and gender role attitudes. In J. P. Shaver (Ed.). *Handbook of research on social studies teaching and learning* (pp. 459–469). New York: Macmillan.

Beane, J. A., & Lipka, R. P. (1986). *Self-concept, self-esteem, and the curriculum.* New York: Teachers College Press.

Berlak, A. C. (1996). Teaching stories: Viewing a cultural diversity course through the lens of narrative. *Theory into Practice, 35(2),* 93–101.

Calabrese, R. (2002). *A companion guide to leadership for safe schools.* Lanham, MD: Scarecrow Press.

Calloway, C. (1999). 20 ways to promote friendship in the inclusive classroom. *Intervention in School and Clinic, 34(3),* 176–177.

Carter, R. (1995). *The influence of race and racial identity in psychotherapy.* New York: Wiley.

Cohen, E. G., & Lotan, R. A. (Eds.). (1997). *Working for equity in heterogeneous classrooms.* New York: Teachers College Press.

Colangelo, N., Dustin, D., & Foxley, C. H. (1985). *Multicultural nonsexist education: A human relations approach,* 2nd ed. Dubuque, IA: Kendall/Hunt.

Cook, L. A., & Cook, E. (1954). *Intergroup education.* New York: McGraw-Hill.

Creighton, A., & Kivel, P. (1992). *Helping teens stop violence: A practical guide for counselors, educators, and parents.* Alameda, CA: Hunter House.

Dana, R. H. (1997). *Understanding cultural identity in intervention and assessment.* Thousand Oaks, CA: Sage.

Derman-Sparks, L. (1989). *Anti-bias curriculum: Tools for empowering young children.* Washington, DC: National Association for the Education of Young Children.

Diamond, K. E. (1996). Preschool children's conceptions of disabilities: The salience of disability in children's ideas about others. Topics in Early *Childhood Special Education, 16(4),* 458–475.

Drew, N. (1987). *Learning the skills of peacemaking: An activity guide for elementary-age children on communicating, cooperating, and resolving conflict.* Carson, CA: Jalmar Press.

Duvall, L. (1994). *Respecting our differences: A guide to getting along in a changing world.* Minneapolis, MN: Free Spirit.

Fishbein, H. D. (2002). *Peer prejudice and discrimination: Origins of prejudice,* 2nd ed. Mahwah, NJ: Erlbaum.

Fox, C. L., & Boulton, M. J. (2003). Evaluating the success of a social skills training (SST) programme for victims of bullying. *Educational Research 45(3),* 231–247.

Gazda, G. M., Asbury, F. R., Balzer, F. J., Childers, W. C., & Phelps, R. E. (2006). *Human relations development: A manual for educators,* 7th ed. Boston: Allyn & Bacon.

Gibbs, J. (1987). *Tribes: A process for social development and cooperative learning.* Santa Rosa, CA: Center Source.

Girard, K., & Koch, S. (1996). *Conflict resolution in the schools: A manual for educators.* San Francisco: Jossey-Bass.

Goethals, G. (1999). Peer influences among college students: The perils and potentials. Williams Project on the Economics of Higher Education. Retrieved May 20, 2005 from www.williams.edu/wpehe/DPs/DP-51.pdf

Grambs, J. D. (1960). *Understanding intergroup relations.* Washington, DC: National Education Association.

Grant, C. A. (Ed.). (1995). *Educating for diversity: An anthology of multicultural voices.* Boston: Allyn & Bacon.

Grant, C. A., & Sleeter, C. E. (2006). *Turning on learning,* 4th ed. New York: Wiley.

Grossman, D. C., Neckerman, N. J., Koepell, T. D., Liu, P.-Y., Asher, K. N., Belan, J. K., Frey, K., & Rivara, F. P. (1997). Effectiveness of violence prevention curriculum among children in elementary school: A randomized, controlled trial. *Journal of the American Medical Association, 277(20),* 1605–1611.

Haberman, M., & Post, L. (1990). Cooperating teachers' perceptions of the goals of multicultural education. *Action in Teacher Education, 12(3),* 31–35.

Harris, D. B., Gough, H. B., & Martin, W. E. (1950). Children's ethnic attitudes: II, Relationship to parental beliefs concerning child training. *Child Development, 21,* 169–181.

Helms, J. E., & Cook, D. A. (1999). *Using race and culture in counseling and psychotherapy: Theory and process.* Boston: Allyn & Bacon.

Henkin, R. (2005). *Confronting bullying: Literacy as a tool for character education.* Portsmouth, N.H.: Heinemann.

Isernhagen, J., & Harris, S. (2003). A comparison of 9th and 10th grade boys' and girls' bullying behaviors in two states. *Journal of School Violence, 2(2),* 67–80.

Johnson, D. W. (1993). *Reaching out: Interpersonal effectiveness and self-actualization,* 5th ed. Englewood Cliff, NJ: Prentice-Hall.

Johnson D., & Johnson R. (2002). *Multicultural education and human relations: Valuing diversity.* Boston: Allyn & Bacon.

Johnson, D., Johnson, R., & Holubec, E. (1998). *Cooperation in the classroom.* Boston: Allyn & Bacon.

Kahn, P. (1999). *The human relationship with nature: Development and culture.* Cambridge, MA: MIT Press.

Katz, P. (1982). Development of children's racial awareness and intergroup attitudes. In L. G. Katz (Ed.). *Current topics in early childhood education* (Vol. 4, pp. 17–54). Norwood, NJ: Ablex.

King, E. W. (1990). *Teaching ethnic and gender awareness.* Dubuque, IA: Kendall/Hunt.

King, J. E. (1991). Dysconscious racism: Ideology, identity, and the miseducation of teachers. *Journal of Negro Education, 60(2),* 133–146.

Kitano, M., Stiehl, J., & Cole, J. (1978). Role-taking: Implications for special education. *Journal of Special Education, 12,* 59–74.

Kohlberg, L. (1966). A cognitive-developmental analysis of children's sex-role concepts and attitudes. In E. E. Maccoby (Ed.). *The development of sex differences* (pp. 82–173). Stanford, CA: Stanford University Press.

LaGreca, A. M. (1993). Social skills training with children—Where do we go from here? *Journal of Clinical Child Psychology, 22(2),* 288–298.

Linn, E., Stein, N. D., Young, J., & Davis, S. (1992). Bitter lessons for all: Sexual harassment in schools. In J. T. Sears (Ed.). *Sexuality and the curriculum* (pp. 106–123). New York: Teachers College Press.

Madhere, S. (1991). Self-esteem of African American adolescents: Theoretical and practical considerations. *Journal of Negro Education, 60(1),* 47–61.

Marcus-Newhall, A., Miller, N., Holtz, R., & Brewer, M. (1993). Cross-cutting category membership with role assignment: A means of reducing intergroup bias. *British Journal of Social Psychology, 32,* 224–253.

McCarthy, C. (1993). After the canon: Knowledge and ideological representation in the multicultural discourse on curriculum reform. In C. McCarthy & W. Crichlow (Eds.). *Race, identity, and representation in education* (pp. 289–305). New York: Routledge.

O'Bryan, M., Fishbein, H., & Ritchey, P. (2004). Intergenerational transmission of prejudice, sex role stereotyping, and intolerance. *Adolescence, 29.* 407, 20 pp.

Oden, S., & Asher, S. R. (1977). Coaching children in social skills for friendship making. *Child Development, 48,* 495–506.

Prutzman, P., Stern, L., Burger, M. L., & Bodenhamer, G. (1988). *The friendly classroom for a small planet.* Santa Cruz, CA: New Society.

Purkey, W. W., & Novak, J. M. (1984). Inviting school success, 2nd ed. Belmont, CA: Wadsworth.

Purkey, W. W., & Schmidt, J. J. (1987). *The inviting relationship: An expanded perspective for professional counselors.* Englewood Cliffs, NJ: Prentice-Hall, Inc.

Ritchey P., & Fishbein H. (2001). The lack of an association between adolescent friends' prejudice and stereotypes. *Merrill-Palmer Quarterly, 47,* 2, 188–206.

Sapon-Shevin, M., & Schniedewind, N. (1989/1990). Selling cooperative learning without selling it short. *Educational Leadership, 47,* 63–65.

Schine, J. (Ed.) (1997). *Service learning.* Chicago: University of Chicago Press.

Sears, J. T. (1992). The impact of culture and ideology on the construction of gender and sexual identities: Developing a critically based sexuality curriculum. In J. T. Sears (Ed.). *Sexuality and the curriculum* (pp. 139–156). New York: Teachers College Press.

Sears, J. T. (1993). Responding to the sexual diversity of faculty and students: Sexual praxis and the critically reflective administrator. In C. Capper (Ed.). *Administration in a pluralistic society.* Albany, NY: SUNY Press.

Sherif, M., & Sherif, C. W. (1966). *Groups in harmony and tension.* New York: Octagon.

Slavin, R. E. (1986). *Using student team learning.* Baltimore, MD: Johns Hopkins Team Learning Project.

Slavin, R. E. (1990). *Cooperative learning: Theory, research, and practice.* Englewood Cliffs, NJ: Prentice Hall.

Slavin, R. E. (1991). Are cooperative learning and untracking harmful to the gifted? *Educational Leadership, 48(6),* 68–71.

Sleeter, C. E. (1992). *Keepers of the American dream.* London: Falmer Press.

Sniderman, P., & Piazza, T. (1993). *The scar of race.* Cambridge, MA: Harvard University Press.

Sylvester, P. S. (1994). Elementary school curricula and urban transformation. *Harvard Educational Review, 64(3),* 309–331.

Taba, H., Brady, E. H., & Robinson, J. T. (1952). *Intergroup education in public schools.* Washington, DC: American Council on Education.

Tatum, B. D. (1997). *Why are all the black kids sitting together in the cafeteria?* New York: HarperCollins.

Tiedt, P. L., & Tiedt, I. M. (1995). *Multicultural teaching: A handbook of activities, information, and resources,* 4th ed. Boston: Allyn & Bacon.

Tinto, V. (1997). Classrooms as communities: Exploring the educational character of student persistence. *Journal of Higher Education, 68,* 599–623.

Umphrey, M. (1999). First hand experiences & Vicarious experience. Writing an essay of place. Retrieved May 22, 2005 from http://www.edheritage.org/tools/eop.

Urban, L., & Miller, N. (1998). A theoretical analysis of crossed categorization effects: A meta-analysis. *Journal of Personality and Social Psychology, 74,* 894–908.

Van Ausdale, D., & Feagin, J. R. (2001). *The first r: How children learn racism.* Boulder, CO: Rowman & Littlefield.

Valentine, G. (1997). Get real! Teaching tolerance strategies that work. *NEA Today, 15(5), 4–6.* Washington, DC: National Education Association.

Watson, R. (2002). *The school as a safe haven.* Westport, CT: Greenwood Press.

Watts, W. A. (1984). Attitude change: Theories and methods. In R. L. Jones (Ed.). *Attitudes and attitude change in special education: Theory and practice* (pp. 41–69). Reston, VA: Council for Exceptional Children.

Wright, S. C., Aron, A., McLaughlin-Volpe, T., & Ropp, S. A. (1997). The extended contact effect: Knowledge of cross-group friendships and prejudice. *Journal of Personality and Social Psychology, 73,* 73–90.

CHAPTER FOUR

Single-Group Studies

Y ou probably have not heard the term *Single-Group Studies* before. If you assumed that we made it up, you are correct. It refers to an approach to multicultural education that is characterized by attention to a single group—for example, women, Asian Americans, African Americans, Latinos, Native Americans, Appalachians, Jewish communities, people with disabilities, gay people, or people of the working class. To refer to this approach as ethnic studies, women's studies, or African American studies would not identify the various populations that can be addressed.

GOALS

Most advocates of the Single-Group Studies approach to multicultural education hope to reduce social stratification and raise the status and power of the group with which they are concerned. In Chapter 1, we described current differences among groups in the United States in terms of their power and access to various resources. The two previously discussed approaches to multicultural education—Teaching the Exceptional and Culturally Different and Human Relations—do not directly confront the persistent inequalities that exist among groups. All advocates of Single-Group Studies want their group to have greater power and control over economic and cultural resources. Table 4-1 shows that their main goal is to promote social equality for and to recognize the group being studied. They hope to broaden what is included in American culture so that the group in which they are interested is an important part, no longer invisible or marginal. Essentially, the Single-Group Studies approach attempts to provide a basis for social action by providing information (in this case through schooling) about the group and the effects of past and present discrimination on the group. In the school, this approach is often implemented through a unit or a course of study, although it can constitute an entire educational program.

Goal statements vary, but the main idea of the Single-Group Studies approach is to empower oppressed groups and develop allies. For example, Mihesuah (2003) explains that the main responsibility of Indian Studies is to tribal communities, using intellectual tools to support "finding decolonization, empowerment, and nation-building strategies" (p. 6). He points out that, in contrast,

TABLE 4-1.
Single-Group Studies

Societal goals:	Promote structural equality and recognition of the identified group.
School goals:	Promote willingness and knowledge among students to work toward social change that would benefit the identified group.
Target students:	Either targeted group or everyone; who students are has implications for curriculum and instruction
Practices:	
Curriculum	Teach units or courses about the culture of a group, how the group has been victimized, current social issues facing the group— from the group's perspective
Instruction	Build on students' learning style, especially style of that group
Other aspects of classroom	Make classroom reflect and welcome members of the group (e.g., through decor, guest speakers, ambience)
Other schoolwide concerns	Employ faculty who are members of the targeted group

many Indian Studies programs have been designed to teach non-Indians about Indians in ways that keep non-Indians relatively comfortable and do nothing at all to improve the lives of Indian people. He argues that Indian Studies needs to be linked directly with Tribes and the issues they are working on, with decolonization as the main goal. Women's studies was created with a "vision of a world in which all persons can develop to their fullest potential and be free from all the ideologies and structures that consciously and unconsciously oppress and exploit some for the advantage of others" (National Women's Studies Association, 2005). Gay and lesbian studies work to "form an intellectual community for students and faculty that is ethnically diverse and committed to gender parity" (A National Survey, 1990–1991, p. 53). Ethnic studies attempts to "help students develop the ability to make reflective decisions on issues related to ethnicity and to take personal, social, and civic actions to help solve the racial and ethnic problems in our national and world societies" (Banks, 2002, pp. 25–26). It may be said, then, that the central mission of Single-Group Studies is to develop in students the ability to think through issues from a critical perspective and to act in an effort to transform unjust social conditions related to a group's oppression.

Single-Group Studies became popular, particularly on college campuses, during the civil rights struggle of the late 1960s as intellectual approaches that are directly connected with political struggle. Some areas of scholarship have roots that extend much farther back; for example, Banks (1997) traces African American studies to the late 1880s and early 1990s. Rothschild (2002) explains that women's studies grew from the women's movement of the 1960s. The first women's studies course in the United States was taught at San Diego State University in 1970, and the National Women's Studies Association was founded in 1977. Initially a movement of White women, women's studies has had to grapple with racial exclusion. A 1981 conference on Women and Racism drew a crowd of over 1,000, which included a large number of women of color who wanted women's studies to link its efforts with those of communities of color working against racism. Forging agreement as to the primary bases of women's oppression has been very difficult and often painful, particularly given the wide diversity of women and the unequal power relations among them. Rothschild explains that the emphasis of women's studies continuously has gone "beyond creating courses that examine the bases of women's oppression to research and methodologies that challenge the intellectual foundations of knowledge as it exists today. Their focus was on feminist education for change" (p. 26). As Lauter (1991) put it,

> The movements for change after the postwar political and intellectual ice age reconstituted a vision of possibility and developed concrete efforts to achieve justice and peace. The meaning of these efforts has more to do with Montgomery and the bus boycott than with the demand a decade later for black studies programs. (p. 19)

Advocates of Single-Group Studies have usually instituted the approach to counterbalance the study of White, middle-class males, which the traditional curriculum emphasizes. A common argument for the study of diverse groups is that the United States is a pluralistic country—racially, ethnically, and culturally. The portrayal of a dominant national, cultural group that controls daily institutional and cultural processes is inconsistent with reality.

You may wonder at whom the Single-Group Studies programs should be aimed. For example, are African American studies for African Americans or for everyone? Are women's studies for women or for both sexes? Our answer is, It depends. Sometimes goals are directed mainly toward empowering students who are members of the target group. This is particularly important when such students have experienced years of schooling that have colonized their minds to view themselves through the dominant society's deficit perspective. Sometimes goals are directed toward students who are not necessarily members of that group, with the aim of educating them. Both kinds of goals usually go into the establishment of Single-Group Studies programs and courses, which, as we will see later, can create something of a problem. Elementary, secondary, and university administrators (who are not necessarily true advocates of Single-Group Studies) often institute these programs to keep peace, in response to student or community demands, rather than on the basis of having thought through their value.

Since the late 1960s and early 1970s, scholars in Single-Group Studies programs at the university level have generated an enormous amount of research and theorizing. Not only has much information about diverse groups been compiled, but scholars have been mapping out new conceptual frameworks within various disciplines and challenging established ideas. Reflecting on the way the work of feminist and ethnic studies scholars has challenged the canon, Maher and Tetreault (1994) explain, "They have created new accounts, new theoretical frameworks, and new bodies of knowledge in every discipline, based on the lives of the marginalized" (p. 4).

Single-Group Studies has had less impact at the K–12 level than at the university level. At the K–12 level, one finds schools such as African American schools with an African-centered curriculum, for example, in Milwaukee and Harlem (Byndloss, 2001), and indigenous schools with a tribal-centered curriculum (McCarty, 2002). Some high schools have ethnic studies or women's studies courses, and in K–12 one can find units of study that focus on specific groups. With the standards movement increasingly defining what is taught in schools at the state level, however, many of these efforts have been dismantled in order to align curricula with state standards. We anticipate the trend away from Single-Group Studies to be temporary, however, because this work is such a strong corrective to schooling organized around the perspective of the dominant society.

Educators who are new to multicultural education usually greatly underestimate the complexity and sophistication of this knowledge. To an important extent, the two approaches to multicultural education presented in Chapters 5 and 6—in addition to the approach discussed in this chapter—depend on this scholarship.

PHILOSOPHICAL FRAMEWORK

The Single-Group Studies approach has its roots in educational, philosophical orientations that argue that education is not a neutral process but is used by government and significant others (e.g., labor and business) for social and political purposes. Whether one examines writings about African American studies, women's studies, or Asian American studies, for example, one will find similar philosophical tenets considering issues such as the nature of knowledge and of society and the purposes of schooling.

Myth of the Neutrality of Education

Many people see education as essentially a neutral process or as not promoting a particular ideology or point of view. For example, we asked an undergraduate class of 36 beginning education students if education (schooling) was neutral, or if their schooling—kindergarten through high school—had a particular message. About half of these college juniors said that education was neutral and that their schooling did not argue a particular point of view or present one group's point of view over another. Several students who took this position pointed out that they could remember their teachers making a point of being neutral, but many others were quick to argue that their peers were naive. These students offered examples of how education serves as a socialization process to help the young buy into and fit into a particular conception of the American way of life. For example, some pointed out that until very recently women were for the most part omitted from textbooks, causing the young to accept male domination of society.

By the time the two-hour discussion was over, the majority of the class had concluded that schooling was not neutral. Schooling, they argued, must be regarded as a social process: It is related to the country's political structure (often its present political scene), to its political and social history, and to its beliefs and ideals. Indeed, what counts as knowledge in schools is the result of complex struggles and cultural politics between identifiable groups and is shaped by the distribution of power within society (Apple, 1993, 1996).

	Dominant groups	Oppressed groups
Nature of society	Fair, open	Unfair, rigged
Nature of "have-not" groups	Lack ambition, effort, culture, language, skills education	Strong, resourceful, work to advance

FIGURE 4-1.
Perspectives about Inequality

However, the two approaches to multicultural education previously discussed—the Human Relations approach and the Teaching the Exceptional and the Culturally Different approach—view schooling as politically neutral. The Human Relations approach concerns itself with what schools teach only insofar they help alleviate stereotyping by providing more information about groups that people frequently stereotype and more positive portrayals of groups to which all students belong. The Teaching the Culturally Different approach modifies what schools teach only as needed in order to make the curriculum more relevant to students who might have trouble catching on. Both approaches see most of the content and processes of schools as essentially fair and desirable and as politically neutral—not biased in favor of any particular group.

Single-Group Studies offers an alternative explanation for why a particular group has disproportionately less than its share of resources. For example, why do full-time working women earn about 78 cents for every dollar men earn? Why are most people with disabilities either unemployed or employed only part time? Why does the poverty level of African Americans and Latinos remain far higher than it is for Whites, in spite of the narrowing education gap between groups? Single-Group Studies offer a different way to approach this issue than the dominant school curriculum or the dominant perspective.

A framework for thinking that is depicted in Figure 4-1 shows two quite different understandings for why inequality exists. The figure focuses on two elements: the nature of society and the nature of nondominant groups. The figure lists those perspectives that the dominant groups in society usually accept. With respect to the nature of society, most of us have been taught repeatedly that the United States offers a fair and open system to all and that everyone can achieve "the American dream" if one works hard enough. Furthermore, those of us who are White, male, heterosexual, and economically secure generally experience a direct relationship between our efforts and our success. The system must be open for everyone because not only is that what we have learned, but we see that the system has also worked fairly for us. Then why have some groups disproportionately not succeeded? Most of us explain this result in terms of the characteristics of such groups, focusing mainly on what they lack: education, culture, ambition, language, modern values, and so forth.

The perspectives of oppressed groups are listed in the right-hand column of Figure 4-1. Society, as it currently and historically has existed, is not open and fair to all groups, in spite of what the dominant rhetoric says. Rather, dominant groups erect barriers to the advancement of people who are identifiably unlike themselves. Oppressed groups do not lack culture or capability; rather, they have rich legacies of intellectual and artistic creativity that attest to their potential to achieve success, if society were open. This perspective is one that schools generally do not teach.

For example, take the question raised earlier regarding a gender gap in earnings of full-time workers. Generally, this discrepancy is not acknowledged or studied in the K–12 curriculum, suggesting that it is not a significant social issue. People who have not systematically looked into this issue often assume that sex discrimination is a thing of the past or is gradually going away, or that women get paid less because women choose lower-paying jobs. Such explanations minimize institutional sexism as a problem and lay the burden for a gender gap on the individual choices of women. Women's studies probe below the surface of these assumptions. Women's studies, for example, question why women have the majority of responsibility for home care and child care, particularly if that responsibility restricts women's ability to take on other roles. Women's studies also examine how sexism operates in the labor market. Tomaskovic-Devey and Skaggs (2002), on the basis of a data-driven analysis of the labor market, found that

> Women are sorted into female jobs and do not gain access to firm-specific training because of that sex segregation. This restricted access to training in turn leads to less complex jobs and lower supervisory authority. When women do not get access to men's jobs, they are also not gaining access to the training opportunities those jobs afford. (p. 120)

One can then ask how it happens that men and women get sorted into different jobs, which then lead to different and unequal opportunities and pay. Asking these questions has shifted much analysis from the left-hand column of Figure 4-1 to the right-hand column and has led to women organizing to eliminate or reduce sex segregation in the labor market, as well as sex-role socialization of children and youth.

Sanchez (1999) argued that immigration studies have too often not focused on concerns represented in the right-hand column. He wrote:

> It is this crossroads of historical interpretation—one in which Latinos and Asians are viewed only as the latest of American immigrant groups, albeit colored differently, versus oppressed racial minorities with longstanding histories in this country, something similar but not equal to African Americans—which continues to frame the ambivalent position of scholars of these groups in relation to the field of immigration history.

As people move globally, he argued that concepts related to race, culture, and power need to inform such studies; otherwise dynamics that are significant to the experiences of people (such as sweatshop labor) are minimized. For example, the health care needs of immigrant communities are shaped not only by immigrant culture, but at least as strongly by racism of the dominant society. Furthermore, he argued, immigration itself is largely a result, of U.S. actions and interventions around the globe.

Thus, Single-Group Studies view education as not neutral in that schools select what to teach and what not to teach and what viewpoint one uses when teaching. Zinn (1994) maintained, "You can't be neutral on a moving train." By that, he meant, "students had had a long period of political indoctrination before they arrived in my class—in the family, in high school, in the mass media" (p. 8). He argued that schools should present multiple points of view and that teachers should make explicit their own point of view. But to pretend that schools teach all points of view equally, or no point of view, is ignorant; this view makes sense only to people who take for granted the dominant belief system as true.

For many groups in society, democracy has been more an ideal to strive toward than a reality. The teaching of a particular point of view in our schools can be traced back through U.S. history. For example, Ellwood Patterson Cubberley (1909), a recognized educational leader in the early 1900s, stated:

> Everywhere these people [immigrants] tend to settle in groups or settlements, and to set up here their national manners, customs, and observances. Our task is to break up these groups or settlements, to assimilate and amalgamate these people as part of our American race, and to implant in their children, as far as can be done, the Anglo Saxon conception of righteousness, law and order, and popular government, and to awaken in them a reverence for our democratic institutions and for those things in our national life which we as a people hold to be of abiding worth. (pp. 15–16)

Tyack (1966) pointed out that to some degree Thomas Jefferson, Noah Webster, and Benjamin Rush all believed that the function of the public school was to teach a balance between order and liberty. Tyack wrote,

> Not content with unconscious and haphazard socialization provided by family, political meeting, press, and informal associations, not trusting in the "given-ness" of political beliefs and institutions, these men sought to instruct Americans deliberately in schools. Having fought a war to free the United States from one centralized authority, they attempted to create a new unity, a common citizenship and culture, and an appeal to a common future. In this quest for a balance between order and liberty, for the proper transaction between the individual and society, Jefferson, Rush, and Webster encountered a conflict still inherent in the education of the citizen and expressed still in the injunction to teachers to train students to think critically but to be patriotic above all. (p. 31)

In other words, schools paradoxically teach Americans to believe not only in democratic participation, but also in allegiance to a culture and social structure defined primarily by Anglo-Saxon men of at least moderate wealth. Spring (1997) discussed in great detail the manner in which schools have historically functioned to suppress cultural diversity, often marginalizing, disrespecting, rendering invisible, or aiming to "civilize" particular groups of students (e.g., Irish, Native Americans, Puerto Ricans)—frequently through assimilationist practices. This teaching is the concern of advocates of Single-Group Studies: Whereas democracy should be fostered in schools, democracy is a sham if it incorporates only the concerns and perspectives of those who already dominate politically and economically. For true democracy, the points of view of oppressed people must also be given full expression, and their concerns and experience must be addressed.

- The United States is the land of wealth and opportunity; it is open to all who try; anyone can get what he works for.

- U.S. history flowed from Europe to the East Coast of North America; from there it flowed westward.

- U.S. culture is of European origin; Europe is the main source of worthwhile cultural achievements.

- National ideals are (and should be) individual advancement, private accumulation, rule by the majority as well as by market demand, loyalty to the U.S. government, and freedom of speech.

- Some social problems existed in the past, but they have been solved.

- Most problems society faces have technical solutions, for which science and math offer the best keys.

- U.S. citizens share consensus about most things; differences are individual and can be talked out (usually in one story).

- Other places in the world may have poverty and problems, but the United States does not; it is our responsibility to solve other nations' problems.

- The United States is basically White, middle-class, Christian, and heterosexual; White Christian men are the world's best thinkers and problem solvers, and they usually act in the best interests of everyone.

FIGURE 4-2.
Themes in a Eurocentric, Patriarchal Curriculum

The curriculum is a central concern of Single-Group Studies advocates because "knowledge is power. Those who have it are more powerful than those who do not. Those who define what counts as knowledge are the most powerful" (Pagano, 1990, p. xvi). Furthermore, "reading is a vital way to gain power in a literate society. That is why marginalized groups have always had to struggle … to obtain access to the power of literacy—or, having obtained it, to get a hearing for their literary productions" (Lauter, 1991, p. 161).

In the 1960s, textbooks presented the experiences and viewpoints of White, middle-class people only—and mainly men. As noted in Chapter 1, textbooks today appear to be more pluralistic; if you thumb through almost any textbook published over the past 20 years, it may appear to be better integrated than it is. You can analyze a textbook using a textbook analysis instrument in Chapter 4 of *Turning on Learning* (Grant & Sleeter, 2006).

Curricula are not merely a collection of facts; they tell a story and present a picture. Some taken-for-granted themes undergird the content of most curricula. We have summarized these themes in Figure 4-2. They are rarely stated directly; rather, they emerge from what is and what is not in textbooks and are reaffirmed in the life experience of students (and teachers) who are White, middle or upper class, and male. For example, few textbooks state that most of society's problems have been solved, but few examine current social problems, even though they may allude to problems such as slavery or the Great Depression that existed in the past. Textbooks never directly state that wealthy White men are the world's greatest problem solvers; the books simply present more members of this group than any other.

Garcia (1982) pointed out that every ethnic group has a unique history set within a definable geographic region and should therefore be studied in an ongoing, in-depth fashion rather than piecemeal, with bits and pieces of its history tacked onto Anglo studies. Note the following statement about the treatment of African Americans, given to undergraduates at the University of Wisconsin–Madison in the Afro-American Studies Department (2000):

> Although the Afro-American community has had a unique historical experience, has evolved a distinct culture, and faces a special set of problems in American society, scholars have tended either to greatly distort or to completely dismiss the African American experience as an unpleasant footnote to the larger American experience. (p. 31)

As another example, consider Linton's (1998) description of how people with disabilities appear in the curriculum. She explains that depictions generally are based in "narrow, pathologized conceptions of disability" that exclude "the voice of the disabled subject and the study of disability as idea, as abstract concept" (p. 87). People with disabilities appear in the curriculum, particularly in the social sciences and humanities, but the idea of disability is rarely "unpacked," analyzed, examined, or historicized outside Disability Studies (p. 88).

Even the teacher who refuses to take a position when presenting an issue makes numerous decisions throughout the school day about what and how to teach—decisions that could suggest a particular point of view. For example, a teacher who decides to teach the American novel could be teaching points of view that have race, gender, sexuality, and class implications. If the teacher decides to use *The Adventures of Huckleberry Finn* (Mark Twain), *The Catcher in the Rye* (J. D. Salinger), *Deliverance* (James Dickey), and *The Grapes of Wrath* (John Steinbeck), then this teacher is also deciding to omit (at least so far) *Manchild in the Promised Land* (Claude Brown), *Woman Warrior* (Maxine Hong Kingston), *Forever* (Judy Blume), and *The Color Purple* (Alice Walker). The points of view given to the students in the two sets of novels are very different because the second set includes novels by three women and three persons of color. If used over an extended period of time, neither set of materials is politically neutral. The question is, what political implications are there in any given set of decisions that teachers make about what to teach, whether those decisions are conscious or unconscious?

In addition to what one teaches, how one teaches is also important and could suggest or influence a point of view. For example, if a teacher of an American authors class, in which only one or two African American students are enrolled, chooses to begin the semester with *Native Son* (Richard Wright) instead of *The Autobiography of Malcolm X* (Malcolm X, with Alex Haley), the African American students may be caused to feel powerless and vulnerable because the major character is powerless—a murderer and a servant. On the other hand, *The Autobiography of Malcolm X* usually inspires African American students, promoting a sense of pride and respect. How the curriculum is presented—particularly the order, timing, and presentation of examples—can have political implications and imply a position the teacher has taken, although it may be taken unconsciously.

Identity and the Social Purpose of Schooling

Schools are society's agencies (or institutions) of socialization. Schools prepare young people for the roles they will have as adults. In that capacity, one can conceive of schooling as an engine of social change in that today's students are tomorrow's citizens. One can also identify myriad ways that schooling serves a form of social control and maintenance of the status quo.

Schools carry out control through the socialization process. Socialization is a lifelong process, basic to human activity and occurring in the classroom as well as in the family and religious institutions. Schools contribute to the process of socialization by helping the student to fit into an established cultural or social tradition and by aiding in the student's development of personality or individual identity. Through participation in various social experiences in the school, the student becomes familiar with or learns knowledge, attitudes, behavior, and values. Schools are considered by many as society's instrument for inculcating the "right" values and social attitudes into the young. For example, some educators claim that in school, habits of obedience, industriousness, neatness, and punctuality are taught as important social values that will help students grow to adulthood and become useful and productive members of society.

Years ago, Bowles and Gintis (1976) showed how schools, by sorting students based on projections of their futures and then socializing them accordingly, reproduce a stratified society:

> Schools foster legitimate inequality through the ostensibly meritocratic manner by which they reward and promote students, and allocate them to distinct positions in the occupational hierarchy. They create and reinforce patterns of social class, racial and sexual identification among students which allow them to relate "properly" to their eventual standing in the hierarchy of authority and status in the production process. Schools foster types of personal development compatible with the relationships of dominance and subordinance in the economic sphere. (p. 11)

For example, lower-class students tend to be sorted into lower-ability and remedial classes, whereas upper-class students tend to be sorted into college-bound classes. On the surface, this process appears fair because it uses objective testing and professional guidance. Once sorted, students learn to view their own status as acceptable and to relate to each other in a leader–follower fashion. The status quo is reproduced but in a manner that appears natural. Furthermore, once sorted, students are taught differently: students designated as college-bound are taught a much richer and more intellectually challenging curriculum than students designated as "general" or remedial. As students proceed through school, they become more and more different, prepared for different futures.

But education can also be immensely liberating and can prompt significant social changes. People have fought for access to reading and writing, understanding these as tools of freedom, even if they are too often not used in that way. As Tyack and Cuban (1995) pointed out, schooling can be understood in terms of both retrogression and progress simultaneously. It is the capacity of education to liberate people both individually and collectively that lies at the heart of Single-Group Studies. But liberation requires learning to grapple with the realities of oppression, as it affects oneself both internally and externally.

Research on development of racial identity helps us understand how schools shape student self-concept and maintain social control, and, at the same time, how education can become liberating (Cross, 1991; Helms, 1990; Tatum, 1992; Thompson & Carter, 1997). This research describes stages of identity development that differ between Whites and groups of color. We will apply these stages to other forms of diversity as well, distinguishing between how dominant group members (i.e., Whites, males, middle- and upper-income people, heterosexual people, people without disabilities) view their identity with a collective and how oppressed group members view their identity. Figure 4-3 summarizes these stages.

Students (and teachers) who are members of dominant groups are usually in the stage of Encapsulation. They have been taught that people like themselves have run this country since its earliest history and have contributed its greatest achievements. This message teaches young people from sociocultural groups that are in control that they have rightfully earned that control and have little need to understand oppression or the experiences of the oppressed. In fact, the idea of "oppression" is foreign to them; they regard the United States as free and open to all. This stage is reinforced by "business-as-usual" schooling.

Advocates of Single-Group Studies seek to help students move to a higher stage. The next stage, Disintegration, occurs when students encounter evidence of discrimination, which Single-Group Studies attempt to provide. Typically, students who are members of dominant groups find such evidence very uncomfortable and often try to escape having to deal with it. Our students have commented, for example, that class sessions revealing powerful information about discrimination "turned their world upside-down." The easiest way for students to deal with their discomfort is described as Reintegration, or a return to the first stage when the course or unit is over (which one can do fairly easily if the course or unit is short). Another way to help students in the disintegration stage is to provide information about the other group and to place students in contact with the members. This is called the Pseudo-independence stage. If the student sticks with the study of another group, eventually he or she may achieve the stage of Autonomy. At this stage, students work to end discrimination against oppressed groups while showing a positive identity with their own group.

For an oppressed group member, the lowest stage is Conformity, in which the individual accepts the status quo and negative images of her or his own group. Members of minority groups, females, the poor, gays, and people with disabilities are often socialized, both in schools and in other social institutions, to occupy this stage. Taught that members of their group rarely make notable achievements,

Dominant Group Members

A. *Encapsulation:* Comfortable with status quo; have never really thought about other groups' experiences or perspectives; accept society's stereotypes of groups

B. *Disintegration:* Faced with evidence of discrimination that clashes with previous perspective—feel guilt, anger

C *Reintegration:* One way of resolving discomfort of Disintegration stage; return as nearly as possible to first stage (Encapsulation)

D. *Pseudo-independence:* Other way of resolving discomfort of Disintegration stage; actively seek information about other group by contacting or hanging around its members; identify more with other group than with one's own.

E. *Autonomy:* Work actively to end discrimination against oppressed group; have positive identity with own group but are not accepting of group's superior status

Oppressed Group Members

A. *Conformity:* Identify with dominant group and its version of society; accept negative images of won group

B. *Dissonance:* Faced with evidence of discrimination that clashes with previous perspective—feel confusion, want to know more

C. *Resistance and immersion:* Actively reject dominant society and its beliefs; thirst for knowledge about own group

D. *Internalization:* Have strong sense of positive identity with own group; willing to reconnect with dominant group but not with subordinated status

E. *Commitment:* Committed to long-term work on antidiscrimination strategies; have positive identity with own group and with members of dominant group who are in states of autonomy.

FIGURE 4-3.
Stages of Identity Development

contributions, or political decisions, children of oppressed groups often see themselves and their group as powerless and worthless. This feeling may be aggravated when they are simultaneously taught that we live in a free democracy in which everyone can do as he or she chooses and people get what they work for. For example, in a discussion of the creation of a Mohawk-centered curriculum, Agbo (2001) explained that "the psychological wounds of assimilation of American Indians into the dominant culture have combined with the Western model of education to the disintegration of traditional beliefs and the lack of identity and self esteem in young people" (p. 44). The message Anglo schooling gives to Mohawk students is one of powerlessness. However, members of the dominant group are often most comfortable with oppressed-group members who are at the stage of Conformity because they tend to be accepting. For example, White teachers tend to be most comfortable with minority group students who accept the teachers' authority and a White-dominant curriculum; the teachers often become uncomfortable with students who assert their racial identity.

The stage of Dissonance is usually triggered by something, such as a personal experience (such as being obviously discriminated against on the basis of sex) or new information that contradicts what one has learned (such as new information about the accomplishments of people with physical impairments). This experience or information often leads the person to want to know more, a need that Single-Group Studies fill. At the stage of Resistance and Immersion, an individual tries to learn as much as possible about his or her group. At this stage, anger emanating from years of experiencing oppression is often expressed. Members of the dominant group, especially those who are themselves at the stage of Encapsulation, are often threatened by a person at the Resistance and Immersion stage.

For example, a young woman experiencing Resistance and Immersion becomes angry about sexism and angry with the behavior of men around her whom she now views as sexist. Her male friends (as well as female friends at the Conformity stage) may respond that she is "too much into that women's lib garbage" and shun her or make fun of her. If both she and her friends are experiencing women's studies together, they are at least being exposed to the same information and can battle out their differences together, helping each other to grow. Eventually, the anger of Resistance and Immersion can give way to Internalization, then long-term Commitment to work for change and an ability to recognize and trust members of the dominant group who themselves have achieved Pseudo-independence or Autonomy. In working for change, the young woman may meet others like herself and achieve Internalization—that is, a positive identity with her own group and a willingness to work with members of the dominant group as an equal member, which may develop into Commitment.

Advocates of Single-Group Studies take a critical view of the nature of society but an optimistic view of human nature and the potential of education. Is human nature essentially active or passive? Do children by nature want to learn, or do they need to be coaxed? Is learning essentially a process of meaning-making or a process of imprinting a body of information on blank minds? The Single-Group Studies approach sees the student as willing and eager to learn, capable of making decisions, and committed to reflection about his or her learning.

Therefore, from the perspective of Single-Group Studies, schools should develop in students what Freire (1970) calls a "critical consciousness." When students learn about their heritage and contributions to society, they participate in a process of self-discovery and growth in social consciousness. This development results in the realization that, contrary to the myth of their inferiority, their actions can be a transforming process in the United States and in the world. In other words, as the students learn about their group, they grow in pride and knowledge about themselves, and as others learn about their group, they, too, will change in relationship to their new knowledge. Dominant groups will learn that their dominance has usually been seized rather than earned and that their use of power more often than not has been biased and unfair. The preamble of the Constitution of the National Women's Studies Association (Graber, 1997) directly addresses the point of consciousness raising when it states: "Women's studies is the educational strategy of a breakthrough in consciousness and knowledge" (p. 6).

Examples of students who have had to be coaxed into learning probably spring readily to your mind. Yet students need to be coaxed only to learn material that has no personal meaning. Schooling for many young people is alienating when it is not about themselves; it is highly motivating when it is.

In summary, the Single-Group Studies approach is aimed toward social change. It questions the knowledge normally taught in schools, arguing that that knowledge reinforces control by wealthy White men over everyone else. "Business as usual" attempts to socialize the young into accepting the status quo as "right," at the same time alienating from social institutions children of color, children of the poor, and female children. Schooling needs to offer an in-depth study of all major social groups for the purpose of empowering group members, developing in them a sense of pride and group consciousness, and helping members of dominant groups appreciate the experiences of others and recognize how their own groups have oppressed others.

RESTRUCTURING KNOWLEDGE AND "THE CANON"

Since the late 1980s, we have witnessed a heated debate in higher education over "the canon." Lauter (1991) provides a definition:

> By "canon" I mean the set of literary works, the grouping of significant philosophical, political, and religious texts, the particular accounts of history generally accorded cultural weight within a society. How one defines a cultural canon obviously shapes collegiate curricula and research priorities, but it also helps to determine precisely whose experiences and ideas become central to academic study. (p. ix)

Earlier we noted that Single-Group Studies had begun to be instituted in higher education during the 1960s. Black studies programs were quickly followed by women's studies, Chicano studies, and Asian studies; then disability studies and gay and lesbian studies programs were created, and a Center of Appalachian Studies was established at Appalachian State University in North Carolina. At first, such programs had a wide array of focuses, allowing faculty and students mainly to examine the history and literature of a particular group. Speaking of early Chicano studies programs, for example, Muñoz (1984) explained, "Ideologically, the spectrum ran from those who defined Chicano Studies as curricula that would emphasize the contributions of Americans of Mexican descent to American culture and society to those who defined it as curricula that would focus attention on racism and the structure of class oppression" (p. 9).

Over time, scholars focused increasingly on questions regarding the persistent oppression of the group and why the mainstream curriculum (and society) so staunchly resists full incorporation of the group. For example, African American women have a long and rich literary tradition, from Frances E. W. Harper through

Toni Morrison. Yet, mainstream literature courses usually add only selective pieces (if any), treated not as examples of great literature but as examples of an add-on category of "minority literature," to be studied only after the "important" literature. Such biased and peripheral treatment sheds light on why, for example, the recent publication of *The Norton Anthologys of African American Literature* (Gates & McKay, 1997) represents such an important and powerful challenge to the status of traditional bodies of knowledge.

As scholars synthesized the main ideas emerging in the study of their group and battled the wider education system's growing resistance to incorporate their work, the debates came to be known as the "battle over the canon": What and whose criteria define what knowledge is worth teaching? The most heated debates took place around Afrocentrism, which many African American scholars juxtaposed to the Eurocentric curriculum.

It is important for teachers to have a sense of the main themes that undergird Single-Group Studies today because these themes should guide the creation of a curriculum about a group. We will briefly outline major common themes, although one must recognize that they play out differently for different groups. It is important to remember that these are intellectual themes about how knowledge is constructed. Earlier, in Figure 4-2, we outlined themes that permeate traditional, White, male-dominant curricula. Single-Group Studies attempt to redefine the canon and disciplinary scholarship by organizing knowledge around different themes that emerge when a group other than White men is the center of attention. Figure 4-4 illustrates themes in a community-created Mohawk curriculum, and Figure 4-5 lists themes that are common to a women's studies curriculum.

The clan system	Food
Ceremonies of the year	Clothing
Thanksgiving	Traditional homes
The Iroquois Confederacy	Survival skills
Cycle of life and the traditional circle	Storytelling and drama
Roles of the family	Native games and sports
Spiritual cleansing and healing	Communication and transportation
Medicines	Art forms and media
The study of Akwesasne	Environmental awareness
Songs and dances	Systems of government

FIGURE 4-4.
Themes in a Mohawk Curriculum
Source: From Agbo (2001).

Gender differences and gender inequality: What is actually fair and what isn't? How biology is used as a control mechanism; to what extent are the sexes innately different, and to what extent does biology determine destiny? Physically, what are women capable of?

The private sphere (the home—dominated by women) versus the public sphere (dominated by men): How does the private sphere limit women's access to the public sphere, and why is the private sphere regarded as "out of bounds" for critique?

Impoverization of women; physical and psychological violence against women; processes used to exclude and devalue women from economic and political activity in the public sphere.

Gender as a cultural construct; how each sex, and how sex itself, is represented in the media, arts, etc.

Creative capacities of women and expressions of women's voices in the arts and domestic arts.

Work women do in producing and educating the next generation.

Women as racially, ethnically, and culturally diverse.

Women as social activists.

FIGURE 4–5.
Themes Central to Women's Studies

Centering: Significance of the Starting Place

In one of our classes, a discussion with a history student illustrated the importance of the starting point in shaping an entire story. This student was attempting to explain why Mexican Americans are not in the curriculum prior to the Mexican War; one might study what happened in Mexico before the United States colonized half of it, but what one learns is not U.S. history. He went on to explain that U.S. history concerns what happened within the political borders of the United States and, prior to its founding, the European events that shaped it. The professor tried to explain that from a Mexican American (and Indian) perspective, the history worth studying goes back to the ancient Mayas and Aztecs, and the U.S. colonization is a relatively recent event in a long history. In this case, the student's starting point was the founding of the political system of the United States; the professor's starting point was the establishment of civilization in a land now known as Mexico, dating back to ancient times. According to the professor's view, just as U.S. history tells us about the life in England that led to the Pilgrims setting sail, and the potato famine and political unrest that led to massive Irish immigration, U.S. history should also tell about Mexican American historical events.

Afrocentrism redefined the starting point of African American history from the time of slavery in the United States to the time when early civilizations lived in

---

People of African Descent: Creators, Thinkers, and Builders

Ancient Egypt, the cradle of civilization

Other precolonial African kingdoms

Colonization and enslavement

Building the church: the emergence of African American institutions

Resisting the yoke of slavery

Reconstruction

The Harlem Renaissance

The Civil rights movement

Black nationalism in Africa, the Caribbean, and South America

Creators, thinkers, and builders today.

FIGURE 4-6.
History Topics from an Afrocentric Perspective

ancient Africa, consciously articulating the importance of the starting place. Asante (1990), one of the founders of Afrocentrism, explains: "All knowledge results from an occasion of encounter in place. But the place remains a rightly shaped perspective that allows the Afrocentrist to put African ideals and values at the center of inquiry" (p. 5). Or, as Murrell (2002) put it, "African Americans have a collective history and a collective memory that circumscribe a significant and tangible cultural heritage" (p. 19). Figure 4-6 outlines topics one could study in an African-centered history course, beginning with Africa in ancient times.

For racial and ethnic groups that have roots in a particular place in the world, defining the starting place shapes the rest of the story. Indigenous people, for example, generally begin with the land and humans' relationship with the land. A group's story may begin in Asia and move east, or South or Central America and move north, or Europe and move west, or right here on the North American continent thousands of years ago. Furthermore, the story is different if one views the group as having started from a position of strength (for example, African civilizations), rather than having been subjugated, and now attempting to rebuild its original strength, rather than starting in a position of weakness (such as slavery) and now attempting to rise. Sample lesson plans in *Turning on Learning* (Grant & Sleeter, 2006), such as "Mexican Americans," illustrate what difference it makes whose experience curriculum starts with.

Social Creation of "Natural" Categories

Most of us take for granted distinctions among categories of people that we have learned to view as natural. For example, there are two mutually exclusive, biologically defined sexes. Racial groups are biologically defined and fixed; everyone knows, for example, how to distinguish White from Black people. People with disabilities are also biologically defined, having a deficiency of some sort. One is either a citizen of the United States or not a citizen.

The "obvious" and assumed fixed nature of such categories has tended to work against oppressed groups, who are now examining how such categories are socially created and reinforced. For example, European and Euro-American people created the Negro, enslaving people of varying physical characteristics and from a variety of tribes in Africa, specifically because their dark skin color would brand them to anyone as slaves. Before slavery, tribal Africans did not think of themselves as African or Negro; the concept of race evolved later, in interaction with Caucasians. Despite what people today often say, no one is colorblind; we still pay attention to color. How, then, do people use color to construct different categories of people?

Moreover, do people of African descent around the world have something in common that transcends their current country of citizenship? Pan-African studies answers in the affirmative. Latino studies does also; many Latinos regard U.S. boundaries as somewhat arbitrary. The term *la raza de Aztlan,* for example, describes the "race" of Mexican people. The U.S. border cuts Aztlan in half; the border was imposed on people indigenous to Mexico. More and more, the "diaspora" of people who have cultural and ethnic ties but have been scattered across modern countries (such as Jewish people, people of African descent, or people of Middle Eastern descent) are being studied based on the importance of their "peoplehood" that transcends their current nation of citizenship (Heller, 1992).

Gender is a concern of women's studies as well as gay and lesbian studies. To what degree does biology determine sex roles? To examine this question, women's studies focus on the biology and psychology of gender, the discrimination of some groups of women by other groups of women, and the movement to have the oppression of woman analyzed from multiple perspectives such as race, gender, and class. The lesson plan "Science and Animal Instincts" in *Turning on Learning* (Grant & Sleeter, 2006) illustrates how to open up a discussion of biology and gender in the classroom. Gay and lesbian scholars argue that male control of society is supported by the reinforcement of a clear distinction between the sexes. People who do not conform to traditional gender identities threaten "ideological beliefs and cultural values [that] prop up existing relations of power and control within society" (Sears, 1992, p. 145).

Social Construct of All Social Theories

A social theory is derived from the theorist's starting place. Even something as "factual" and neutral as a documentary reflects the values and perspectives of the creator: the filmmaker chooses what to film, at what angle and depth, for what audience (Trinh, 1991). The idea of theories as socially constructed is important because it provides a way of questioning what is current practice and of rethinking practice around a different set of ideas.

For example, in his analysis of the Afro-Asiatic roots of Greek culture, Bernal (1981) contrasts two theories: the Ancient theory (commonly believed until the eighteenth century), which traces Greek cultural roots to Egypt, and the Aryan theory (constructed in Europe in the eighteenth century), which holds that Greece emerged from no significant roots. Bernal argues that the Aryan theory was advanced when Europeans were colonizing people of color around the world; it would not do to colonize and enslave people who had contributed significantly to Western culture, so non-Western cultural roots were "disproved" by limiting evidence to that which was archaeologically verifiable and by excluding evidence from linguistic analysis, mythology and legend, and analysis of literary texts.

Special education and the helping professions base their theories about people with disabilities on a medical framework. Questioning the medical model, Woodward and Elliott (1992) argue that the mainstreaming movement set people with disabilities back because it was predicated on the notion that "people with disabilities need Experts to tell them how to live" (p. 15): to define who can or cannot be mainstreamed and to define the "needs" of children with disabilities.

Grumet and Stone (2000) point out that feminist theory has the potential to "make education a process that offers us and our children some new possibilities instead of just the same old couple, dressed up in new clothes" (p. 195). They argue that liberal feminist theory reconceptualizes education for women, but not necessarily for men as well, leaving feminists cast as a special interest group. However, one can use feminist theory to understand how mothers and fathers relate to the project of child rearing differently, and in the process, deal with loss. They explain that "the father's project is to claim the child against an epistemological supposition that asserts separation," meaning that the dominant society proclaims individualism and personal autonomy as the goal of human development, and fatherhood as offering financial but not necessarily nurturing support. For men in this context, fathering means loss. In contrast, "the mother's project is to claim differentiation against an epistemological supposition that asserts connection" (p. 195). Women find themselves seeking space and autonomy in a context that defines these as contrary to nature. Grumet and Stone argue that neither traditional understandings of the family nor liberal feminist understandings envision relations of both connection and individual autonomy for everyone, but that feminist theory has the potential to do so.

Strengths of Oppressed Groups

Mainstream curricula portray oppressed groups as passive and usually as victims: slaves, Indians who were killed off, people with disabilities who need help, Asians who were discriminated against, women who stayed at home. Contrast, for example, the way African Americans are portrayed in most history texts with the portrayal in Figure 4-6, where they are described as creators, thinkers, and builders.

Most traditional textbooks place Native Americans in history and in museums. However, Allen (1986) points out that one of the strongest themes that emerges in American Indian studies is that the American Indian people endure. After 500 years of systematic policies of genocide (by disease, murder, forced sterilization, severe poverty), the American Indian people are still here and still creating. Women, when they are given athletic opportunities, are now breaking

Olympic records that men set years ago (Linn & Hyde, 1989) and have not only caught up with males in other domains to which women now have access, but also surpassed them (Bae et al., 2000). If one can convince an oppressed group that its members are weak and passive, they are more likely to accept their fate. The theme of activity and endurance is important for mobilizing group members to act against their oppression.

Group Identity in Literature and the Arts

The dominant society creates images of oppressed groups through various media: movies, television, scholarly articles, stories and proverbs, literature, and art. These identities usually rationalize the group's position in society. For example, Mazumdar (1989) lists identities that the dominant society has constructed of Asian American women: "the depraved prostitute in nineteenth-century San Francisco; the quiet, courteous and efficient Asian female office worker today. Asian women in America have emerged not as individuals but as nameless and faceless members of an alien community" (p. 1). Churchill (1992) describes the dominant society's construction of Native American identities as *Fantasies of the Master Race*. The dominant society has defined the working class as "middle class," with interests aligned to capital and private gain. The poor have been given negative identities—criminals, welfare queens, the homeless—that validate the status quo and blame the lower class for their condition (Aronowitz, 1992).

Authentic identities of groups—how group members actually see and define themselves—are a major theme of the literature and artistic products created by group members. For example, people without disabilities tend to regard people with disabilities in one of two ways: as deficient people who need help or, as euphemisms such as "differently abled" suggest, as people who are just like nondisabled people with the exception of doing some things differently. In contrast, articles in *The Ragged Edge*, a publication created by people with disabilities, regularly discuss identity in ways that both acknowledge and deal with the limitations associated with disabilities as well as project an image of people with disabilities as complex human beings. When one reads or views literary and artistic creations by a group, one encounters a rich array of diverse identities that are usually quite different from those the dominant society projects.

The video productions of Sadie Benning, a young woman struggling with her lesbian identity in a homophobic culture, and the photographs taken by homeless children participating in Shooting Back, an expanding artistic and social project that began in 1990, are just two more examples of the potential of the arts to bring to the foreground knowledge and experience generally excluded as legitimate (for more detail, see Paley, 1995). Again, such examples call into question the canon's designation of some artistic creations as "universal" and others as group specific.

A Collective Sense

Social changes to improve the conditions of life for an oppressed group usually come about because the group has collectively pressed for change. The civil rights movement, for example, resulted in legal changes and came about primarily because of the work of people of color, particularly African Americans. A sense of the collective is also psychologically strengthening for people who are battling discrimination and alienation every day. However, creating and maintaining this sense of the collective is problematic for groups, although the difficulties differ across them.

For example, women, though identifiable by sight, usually live in family relationships with men. It is often difficult to get women to see gender issues they have in common and to develop a sense of sisterhood. This change in allegiance can conflict with family loyalties; many women resist viewing their husbands, fathers, and sons as part of a controlling group. People with disabilities experience a similar kind of isolation, only to a much more pronounced degree, because a disabled individual may not even have contact with other similarly disabled people. Gay people are not visibly identifiable unless they choose to project symbols of their sexual orientation, and coming "out of the closet" carries great risks because the heterosexual world still strongly rejects homosexuality.

Labor studies attempt to develop a sense of class consciousness in a society that persistently denies that social class has much to do with life chances. For example, Zweig (2000) tries to help students see that, although we are all individuals, our everyday life choices are shaped by social class. In that sense, working-class people are a powerful collective with common concerns. Labor studies, according to Youngstown State University (YSU), which offers an Associate in Labor Studies degree, is to "provide trade unionists, labor relations and personnel specialists, and traditional students with a better understanding of the principles of American trade unionism, while at the same time preparing them for active participation in trade unions and/or employment in the fields of labor relations or personnel." Also, YSU states that "Labor studies involve the examination of the social, economic and political purposes and activities of trade unions in modern society. This includes the study of collective bargaining, labor law, labor history, trade union administration and philosophy, and emerging forms of labor/management relations." However the issue of collectivity plays out for a given group, this theme is one that is regularly encountered in Single-Group Studies and runs counter to the dominant society's stress on individuality.

Labor issues and working-class culture, however, have received attention predominantly at the university level. In elementary and secondary schools, they have frequently received less attention. The authors (Sleeter & Grant, 1991), reviewing elementary school textbooks, found that discussions of class were largely absent. It appears, then, that knowledge produced by labor studies scholars does not constitute a major part of the curriculum. Teachers who wish to include a focus on labor as a group that has profoundly shaped American history and culture may, despite the paucity of information found in the present school curriculum, refer to other texts that specifically emphasize working-class experience. For example, *Labor's Heritage,* a publication of the George Meany Center for Labor Studies, includes a whole range of relevant materials. Stuart Kaufman, founder of this labor publication, described its contributions as follows: "Historians share their latest research; archivists write about the insights and angles to be found in their labor collections; museum curators conduct written and photographic tours through labor exhibits that many would never have the chance to see in person; musicians, artists, and folklorists share their insights into the world of work" (Palladino, 1997, p. 12).

Group Liberation

Oppressed groups that view themselves as having been subjugated want to regain control over the telling of their own stories in order to create the basis for group liberation. For example, Adrienne Rich states,

> It is nothing new to say that history is the version of events told by the conqueror, the dominator. Even the dominators acknowledge this. What has more feelingly and pragmatically been said by people of color, by white women, by lesbians and gay men, by people with roots in the industrial or rural working class is that without our own history we are unable to imagine a future because we are deprived of the precious resource of knowing where we came from: the valor and the waverings, the visions and defeats of those who went before us. (cited by Gaard, 1992, p. 31)

Native American studies, for example, attempts to build the future by reclaiming the past. As Dupris (1981) explained, the U.S. government declared Indians its "wards"; having done so, "the value of the American Indians' culture was designated as 'dysfunctional' and was, therefore, to be eliminated" (p. 70). The elimination of Indian culture began when the task of education was turned over to the White-controlled Bureau of Indian Affairs, in which policies were overtly assimilationist. The results were disastrous. According to Dupris, Cherokees had 90% literacy rates 100 years ago; 70 years of White-controlled schooling have resulted in a Cherokee dropout rate of 75% and a literacy rate of only 60%. Similarly, Deyhle (1995) discusses the cultural conflicts experienced by young Navajo students in the midst of Anglo dominance. The rationale for American Indian education controlled by American Indians is to restore a language and culture that have been partially lost as well as to strengthen the identity and improve the achievement of Indian children.

Group liberation is both political and educational; Single-Group Studies advocates view education as a tool of collective emancipation. In that sense, political education and quality education are inextricably connected. Writing about the woeful underachievement of African American children, Murrell (2002) explains that mainstream frameworks for improving schools "do not offer critical perspectives on power and community development, racial, and cultural identity development and meaningful education," making them inadequate. He goes on to explain: "In an increasingly racist society, connecting with contemporary problems of violence, drugs, and fear, those approaches that do not place the intellectual, social, and political life of the child at the center of pedagogical thinking will be woefully insufficient for the quality of education for African American children" (p. 9).

Although these themes have emerged in university scholarship, they resonate with the everyday experiences of ordinary members of the target group. Members may enter a Single-Group Studies program after being exposed to only a traditional curriculum, but often they very quickly experience a surge of enthusiasm for an education that finally hits home and really makes sense. However, these themes have as yet not penetrated very far, with some exceptions, in the school experience for K–12 education. There, Single-Group Studies often reproduce the themes of the dominant society, such as units featuring a string of famous people who have "made it," the implication being that society is open to anyone who tries. We urge teachers to listen carefully to what oppressed groups say about themselves and their own experience before plunging into the creation of Single-Group Studies curricula. One can learn to teach about another group very successfully but not without work.

Recommended Practices

The main goal of Single-Group Studies programs is to promote willingness and knowledge among students to work toward social change that would benefit a specific group, as stated in Table 4-1. Single-Group Studies programs have been developed most comprehensively at the university level, where courses of study lead to majors and minors at both the undergraduate and graduate levels. At the high school level, such courses have been added to the curriculum, usually within departments but sometimes across departments. At the elementary and middle school levels, one finds units or lessons about specific groups, which are usually more simplistic. Regardless of the level of schooling, however, and regardless of the group with which one is concerned, advocates recommend fairly similar practices.

Curriculum

We will sketch features common to Single-Group Studies curricula; the main commonalities are summarized in Table 4-1. First, however, we wish to caution you against creating such curricula around your own ideas of what is important about a group, without first investigating materials or scholarship produced by and about members of the groups. Your own ideas may distort how other groups see themselves and their own experience.

When trying to teach about people of color, for example, White teachers commonly draw on their own interpretation of the European ethnic experience to decide what is relevant to teach, usually without being aware of doing so. The result is a curriculum that may actually be irrelevant to what people of color see as important. Alba (1990) investigated the symbolic meaning that White Americans have attached to ethnicity today. He wondered why Euro-Americans continue to express interest in ethnicity in spite of the fact that European ethnicity in the United States—unlike racial group membership—no longer structures life chances to any significant degree. He found that Euro-Americans view ethnic identity as a matter of individual choice. They stress the commonality of ethnic immigrant histories and value expressions of ethnicity that can be shared across ethnic lines, especially food, holidays, and festivals. Many equate ethnicity with one's private family history rather than as a group's collective experience. Whites often do not connect ethnicity with social structures, such as neighborhoods, friendship groups, occupations, or political organizations.

The resulting curricula end up focusing on customs—such as food, holidays, and folk tales—brought from the old country. Another common theme is family heritage—where (what country) students' families came from and what customs the family has retained, such as recipes. Some teachers even interpret Native Americans within a European-immigrant framework, presenting Native Americans as the first wave of immigrants. By omission, such lessons imply that race no longer structures access to resources in the United States and that America's racial groups stand in equal status to one another, differentiated only by Old World customs in which anyone can participate. By focusing on an individual's achievements and ignoring her or his difficulties in attaining them, even lessons about role models can suggest that the system is open equally to anyone who will try.

Women's studies units often focus on famous women, without providing much suggestion that sexism still exists or presenting any analysis of the multiple oppressions women face. Disability-awareness lessons often describe the characteristics of people with disabilities, without critiquing the social context that reinforces barriers. The problem with such lessons is that they often do not develop ideas that group members who have studied their own history and experience consider important about themselves.

The Single-Group Studies curriculum usually contains a history of the group. For racial groups, the history might explain reasons for immigration (e.g., of Asian Americans) or enslavement (in the case of African Americans). The history might also provide information on early relationships with White settlers (e.g., in the cases of Native Americans and Mexican Americans) or, in the case of Native Americans, the history of legal settlements and conflicts with Whites. Also, the Single-Group Studies curriculum will probably contain a discussion of current problems and challenges a group is facing. Issues such as affirmative action and use of native language are discussed.

A group's great heroes and heroines, both past and present, are very often discussed in detail, as well as the group's creations in the arts, letters, and sciences. For example, the background, struggles, and achievements of noted authors, musicians, scientists, and civic workers are provided. In addition, many of the Single-Group Studies programs include selections of art, music, and other cultural expressions. Traditional and contemporary perspectives are offered to provide insight into the group's culture. For example, Mexican Americans are known to have very strong extended-family ties and certain views related to male and female behavior. One can see these concepts reflected in the art and literature of Mexican Americans. Appalachia has a rich culture that the dominant society stereotypes as "hillbilly"; studying that culture reveals the existence of great strength and creativity in mountain people. Deaf studies includes coursework in, for example, the deaf theater, and the debate over the use of technology devices to hear.

Also studied are the group's experiences with discrimination, as well as how the group has dealt with discrimination, such as the internment of Japanese Americans during World War II, the Trail of Tears that Native Americans experienced during their forced immigration in the nineteenth century, the work of Rosie the

Riveter in the defense plants during World War II, the role of labor unions in collective bargaining, and the role of community organizing for civil rights for gay communities. Many courses or programs contain information that addresses diversity within the group. For example, women's studies may address the problems and strengths arising from the fact that the group is made up of both women of color and White women. Puerto Rican studies may discuss the relationship of skin color to job opportunities. Discussions of stereotyping, myths, and cultural and institutional bias are also included.

The group's philosophical worldviews are usually studied. For example, women's studies programs often study feminist philosophy, or African American Studies may study African American political thought. Finally, contemporary issues of concern to the group are studied. For example, women's studies often address economic inequalities between the sexes, the status of gays and lesbians, and women's health care. Chicano studies may address the status of agricultural workers in the Southwest as well as the illegal alien issue. Disabilities studies may examine the implications of the Americans with Disabilities Act.

Over the past three decades, because of the burgeoning research in ethnic studies, women's studies, disability studies, postcolonial studies, and so forth, Single-Group Studies have become increasingly complex. For example, in the late 1960s and 1970s, Chicano studies programs developed mainly as courses in history and the social sciences. In the 1980s, Chicana studies were developed, and Latino critical studies were developed in the 1990s (Rodriguez, 2000). Flores (1997) explains that the framing of "Latino studies coincides with the more transnational and global character of Latino ethnic groups. In addition, the theoretical insights provided by feminists, post-colonial, and race theories, as well as lesbian and gay studies, have added a level of complexity that was not present in the early days of Chicano or Puerto Rican studies" (p. 208).

Students can complete an undergraduate major in American Indian Studies from the University of Wisconsin—Eau Claire. The major consists of 36 credits and requires three courses: Introduction to American History and Cultures, Introduction to American Indian Expressive Cultures, and Capstone, in which students complete a culminating research project. Students select 18 credits from courses such as Studies in American Indian Languages, Introduction to the Literature of the American Indian, American Indian History, and American Indian Mythology. Students may also choose nine credits from a list of elective courses.

At the K–12 level, the entire curriculum could conceivably be designed around a single group. In fact, it usually is—White Americans, mostly males. Afrocentric schools are engaged in rewriting their curricula so that they are based mainly on African American studies rather than White studies. Short of rewriting the entire curriculum, one can construct Single-Group Studies courses. More and more, however, courses are centering on multiple groups and are interdisciplinary in nature. For example, one high school in Madison, Wisconsin offers a course on the historical experiences of African Americans. Three other high schools offered courses that are multiple group and interdisciplinary in emphasis. Thus, courses still holding the traditional title, "Ethnic Studies," are metamorphizing into multicultural, multidiscipline undertakings. Although K–2 teachers can access considerable materials to construct and teach Single-Group Studies, the press to follow curriculum standards is working against such efforts. Teachers need to be creative to figure out how to teach state standards through Single-Group Studies (Sleeter, 2005).

Many school districts, teachers, and parents have been, and continue to be, wary of including gay, lesbian, and bisexual issues in the curriculum, but a growing body of literature and teaching materials are available to assist (for example, see Combs, 2000; Loutzenheiser, 1996; Macgillivray, 2004; Perrotti, 2001; Woog, 1995). Videos for classroom use are also available, such as *It's elementary* [video recording]: *Talking about gay issues in school* (1997); and *That's a family* [video recording] (2000). Organizations interested in improving the educational experiences of gay, lesbian, and bisexual students such as GLAAD, Project 10, and the Gay, Lesbian, and Straight Teachers Network have also made curriculum materials available. Books written by or for gay, lesbian, and bisexual students such as *Two Teenagers in Twenty* (Heron, 1994) or *Am I Blue? Coming Out from the Silence* (Bauer, 1994) have been useful in bringing the youth perspective into the classroom, allowing students to connect with those who are in some way "like them," and to better understand the experiences of growing up and living as gay, lesbian, or bisexual individuals.

In addition, as with other Single-Group Studies, an increasingly valued resource for curriculum development is archival material. Use of primary historical sources provides an avenue for social groups that are not traditionally represented in the curriculum to counter invisibility and establish voice and place. Increasingly, one can find such material on the Internet if one looks carefully. Transformed lessons in *Turning on Learning* (Grant & Sleeter, 2006) illustrate how to use such material in one's own curriculum.

Instructional Strategies

The curriculum has generally been a more central concern to Single-Group Studies than have instructional strategies. However, when a program teaches students who are mainly or only members of the group being studied, how one teaches may become a concern.

Murrell (2002), for example, develops a portrait of African-centered pedagogy as being situated within social rather than individual learning. He describes five elements of African-centered pedagogy: (1) practices that "promote the interest, engagement and participation of students," (2) arrangements that enable young people to explore and develop a sense of identity that is connected to their background, (3) practices that organize "the intellectual and social life of a community of learners" which incorporates African American culture and heritage, (4) teaching strategies that enable students to make meaning using intellectual tools, and (5) inquiry practices in which young people "take on and use (or sample) the phrases, signs, and images of others for use in their own expressive repertoire" (p. 53). Murrell argues that active, communal, culturally centered pedagogy has the power to engage African American students intellectually in ways that traditional pedagogy does not.

Women's studies programs have developed what is known as "feminist ped-agogy," and, in a variety of institutional settings, educators are constantly in the process of developing and reshaping a teaching environment responsive to women (Maher & Tetreault, 1994). Essentially, feminist pedagogy is a teaching approach that attempts to empower women students. The main idea is that women are socialized to accept other people's ideas. In the traditional classroom, women students read text materials that were written mainly by men, providing a male interpretation of the world. Over time, women learn not to interpret the world for themselves. In the feminist classroom, women learn to trust and develop their own insights by drawing on personal experience and using process-oriented teaching in which "control shifts from me, the teacher, the arbiter of knowing, to the interactions of students and myself with the subject matter" (Tetreault, 1989, p. 137). Hayes (2001) explains that feminist teaching arises not from the biology of women, but from the socialization that women experience. She argues that one should not overstate gender differences, but that any differences would be due to "the impact of women's socialization into gender specific roles or their relationships with parents and other caregivers" (p. 38). She then goes on to explain that, more broadly, if all learning is socially contextual, all children will tend to learn in accordance with expectations of their context, which are affected by gender, race, ethnicity, and the like."With an orientation toward personal development, educators can engage learners in identifying the gender belief systems that have affected them as learners, and in challenging those beliefs that might limit their learning" (p. 41).

Hayes' argument is important because it suggests that any pedagogical approach must take into consideration the prior socialization of students. Rather than assuming that a sociocultural group learns in a particular way because of who they are, teachers need to attend to the contexts in which students grow up, and how that context impinges on their self-confidence as intellectuals, as well as the ways in which they have learned to engage in intellectual work.

Implementation

When planning a program and designing curriculum, a teacher must make certain decisions about the relationship of that curriculum to the rest of the school program. These decisions have implications for planning and teaching. One decision is whether Single-Group Studies will be separate from the regular curriculum or integrated with it. Currently, when Single-Group Studies are implemented, the separate approach is generally used, often with superficial renderings of groups' experiences, such as a day to celebrate a particular heroine or hero, a unit during a special time (e.g., Black History Week), a festival, or ethnic cookouts. We have observed that the major implementation strategy for Single-Group Studies in the public schools is the four Fs: fairs, festivals, food, and folk tales. Usually, when a Single-Group Studies program is introduced in this manner, there is no well-thought-out reason for having it separate. There is also no in-depth study of the group itself. Perhaps it seems easier to add special activities and lessons to the existing instructional plan. However, such add-ons are usually devoid of any strategy to change the existing program substantially, even though the substantive

change of school curricula is a primary goal of serious Single-Group Studies practitioners, whether they advocate integration or separatism.

Most advocates of Single-Group Studies—especially those teaching at the
elementary and secondary levels—recommend integrating their study into the
content of the mainstream curriculum. This approach encourages including information about the group's historical and cultural experience in courses such as
social studies, government, history, literature, art, and music. Use of this strategy
moves us closer to implementing one of the approaches to multicultural education
that are examined in Chapters 5 and 6. Not to move in this direction, advocates
maintain, would make the Single-Group Studies curriculum supplementary to the
main curriculum. Banks (1997) argues, "If ethnic content is merely added to the
traditional curriculum, which in many ways is ineffective, efforts to modify the
curriculum with ethnic content are likely to lead to a dead end" (p. 83).

Integration has a flip side, however. The major problem is that "without such
centers of intellectual work and hubs for political struggle, the culture and experiences of the marginalized will be marginalized even more systematically," especially if content about the group is absorbed into courses taught by individuals
who are not trained in the study of that group (Lauter, 1991, p. 165). Single-Group
Studies need to be researched and developed as areas in their own right. Asian
Studies scholars, for example, do not necessarily advocate getting rid of Asian
Studies for the sake of curricular integration. In fact, scholars are more likely to
advocate for separate programs, departments, and centers in order to be able to
concentrate efforts collectively.

Desegregated schools still operate on a Eurocentric model, and many communities of color students experience serious alienation. Rather than continuing
to accept poor academic achievement and cultural marginality, African American
communities in several large school districts decided to try public African Ameri-
can-centered schools. The main purpose of these schools is to help students
develop a strong sense of self, high achievement, and worthy goals for the future.
Although Afrocentric schools continue to exist, the discourse surrounding Afrocentrism has shifted increasingly toward building coalitions across differences. As
such, the need for collective educational forms and political agendas that address
the knowledge and experience of multiple communities (e.g., gay men and lesbians, Native Americans) is gaining recognition. In many high schools, for example, "ethnic studies" courses, which at one time focused only on a single racial or
ethnic group, are now adopting a curriculum that addresses a range of issues and
their relationship to multiple groups. Thus, although many remain committed to
single-group-centered perspectives, discussion as well as practice reveals an evo-
lution toward the study of multiple groups, and increasingly, the importance of
teaching that is relevant to a diverse student population is being recognized.

Bilingual schools also need to plan for teaching the cultures and experiences
connected with both languages. Dual immersion schools have the greatest balance
between two languages and offer rich opportunities for constructing bicultural
curricula. In schools with small bilingual programs, we have observed the bilingual teachers teaching an ethnic studies curriculum (for instance, teaching Mexi-

can and Mexican American history), but the rest of the school teaching a far more traditional curriculum.

Another decision that must be made in implementing a Single-Group Studies program is how many disciplines will be involved and what will their relationship be to each other. The teacher has essentially three choices: using a single discipline, using a multidisciplinary approach, and using an interdisciplinary approach. The least complex, and probably the most common, approach in high schools is the single-discipline approach. This means, for example, that a history teacher develops units or an entire history course in African American history, or a literature teacher develops units or a course in Asian American literature.

The multidisciplinary approach involves teachers or professors in several disciplines, each contributing a unit or a course to a Single-Group Studies program. For example, an Indian studies program may have courses in anthropology, art, history, and religion. A women's studies program may offer courses in biology, literature, history, and psychology. The interdisciplinary approach is the most complex. It requires integrating two or more disciplines into the study of issues of concern to a group. For example, in an African American studies program using the interdisciplinary approach, teachers of history, literature, and art could develop a study of artistic expression by African American people throughout history, examining the impact of historical events on works of art and literature. Using the interdisciplinary conceptual approach is important, Banks (2002) argues, because it helps students make reflective decisions so that they can institute social change. He believes that the social science disciplines (e.g., sociology and anthropology) must be brought together and that analytical concepts within these disciplines (e.g., values and norms) must be used to help make decisions about complex societal problems such as racism or sexism. He states:

> A social studies curriculum which focuses on decision-making and the African American experience must be interdisciplinary; it should incorporate key (or organizing) concepts from all of the social sciences. Knowledge from any one discipline is insufficient to help us make decisions on complex issues such as poverty, institutionalized racism and oppression. To take effective social action on a social issue such as poverty, students must view it from the perspectives of geography, history, sociology, economics, political science, psychology, and anthropology. (p. 156)

How Single-Group Studies are taught often depends on the availability of materials and the preparation of the teachers. These factors are especially important at the elementary and high school levels, where the instructors may or may not have had the opportunity to develop the area of specialization.

Teachers must also be aware that students may be sensitive to materials and embarrassed to ask questions about groups with which they are not familiar. Woods (2002) discusses reactions many students have to being taught gay/lesbian studies by a gay instructor, for example. "Many straight students come to these courses with the conviction that the struggle for gay rights has long been won and then get upset that the course appears to be attacking heterosexuals" (p. 53). The most important ingredient for teaching Single-Group Studies, we have found, is the teacher's attitude—the awareness, commitment, and dedication of the teacher to the kind of job he or she thinks needs to be done.

The following vignette illustrates two teachers using the Single-Group Studies approach.

SEÑOR RICARDO GOMEZ AND MS. KATHY BENNETT

As Ricardo entered the school, he had mixed emotions. He was very pleased and proud that his college days were behind him and that he had his teaching certificate. He was sad and annoyed that in one week he would be 28 years old and just getting his first real job. Sometimes he counted the two years he had spent in the Navy as a real job, and other times he didn't. He felt he had really grown up in the service being a Navy seal. He had lost his two best buddies, Juan and Pedro, and had gotten banged up pretty badly himself—badly enough to remain in the hospital for six months.

The three young men had joined the Navy the day they had graduated from Lakeview High School. A number of his Latino brothers, he now thought, had lost their lives in the Middle East. Before Ricardo could allow that thought to go any further, a little kid hollered up to him, "Are you the new P.E. teacher?" Ricardo said, "No, I am the new social studies teacher."

Kennedy Junior High School was located in a suburb of a large metropolitan area. The school was in an upper-middle-class area, with a student population of 86% White, 4% African American, 2% Asian, and 8% Latino. All the students of color were bused in from the inner city.

In a short time, Ricardo established himself as one of the "good" teachers at Kennedy. He was assigned three classes in American history and one in world geography. The students liked and respected him, and the other teachers saw him as friendly and professional but also as a man in a hurry.

Ricardo had been a history buff for as long as he could remember. He was very interested in what the past teaches us about the present and future. In short order, his classroom took on an attractive and museum-like appearance, with pictures and historical artifacts everywhere.

George Glenn had been the principal of Kennedy Junior High School for six years. One of his responsibilities was evaluating all of his teachers, especially the new ones. According to district policy, he had to observe new teachers at least three times over the school year. When Mr. Glenn came to observe Ricardo, he was informed that he was to see a lesson on the fall of the Alamo. What Mr. Glenn saw was not a lesson that featured Davy Crockett and his rifle Betsy along with some Texans as fallen heroes of the Alamo. Rather, he saw a lesson that featured the Mexican general Santa Anna and his army putting down a revolt against the Mexican government. Around the room were bulletin boards, posters, and other classroom artifacts that featured aspects of the Mexican American culture.

Later, during their conference, Ricardo explained to Mr. Glenn how important he thought it was to provide his students with a broad perspective of history. He said that he believed it was his responsibility as a Mexican American to include in his teaching not only an Anglo perspective of American history, but also Latino perspectives. He asked Mr. Glenn why more attention wasn't given to Latino cultures in the daily practices of the school. He said that the school curriculum and activities were exclusively Anglo in policy and practice. Mr. Glenn was taken aback by Ricardo's comments and had difficulty responding. Ricardo continued, saying that not only were the Latinos in the school being cheated by not having their history taught, but so were the other students, especially the Anglos, many of whom displayed ethnocentric attitudes. Mr. Glenn nodded his head and concluded the conversation by saying that they should talk about this matter again soon and that he had another observation to make in five minutes.

Kathy Bennett had been vice-principal of Kennedy for 12 years. In fact, she had been Mr. Glenn's mentor teacher when he started teaching. Kathy was becoming increasingly disenchanted with her job and the school system in general. She had been passed over for a principalship so often that she now believed that receiving a promotion could never happen. The "word" on her was that she was too aggressive and would not fit in with the other administrators—most of whom were male. Kathy and her friends never would have described her as aggressive; rather, they saw her as a person who insisted on being in charge of her own life and who knew what she wanted and where she wanted to go.

Kathy did have personal and professional concerns related to the career goals of the female students at the school. Many of them, she believed, were too passive and too much into playing the role of helpless female. Their career goals were very traditional. It was as if they were living in the 1940s and early 1950s. Kathy had started an after-school club called "You Too Can Do." In the club meeting room were pictures and posters of women in both traditional and nontraditional jobs. There were books by female authors and stories of famous and not-so-famous women who had really taken charge of their lives without relying on males. "You Too Can Do" met twice monthly. During each meeting, there was usually a discussion of some work accomplished by a woman or a guest speaker who addressed some aspect of feminism.

Mr. Glenn was aware of Kathy's club and her special attention to the female half of the school's population, but he tried to ignore this activity because she was fair with the boys and it did not particularly interfere with her job. However, Mr. Glenn was not personally assertive in helping her get a principalship, as he had been with Robert Wilson, his vice-principal before Kathy.

As Mr. Glenn left Ricardo's room, he saw Kathy in the hall and asked her to come and chat with him. He said he was concerned about Ricardo's curriculum and teaching. He described what he had observed in Ricardo's room, and as he did, he became more upset. Kathy told him that although she had never seen Ricardo teach, she had heard that he was "different." However, she said, the students for the most part enjoyed his approach. She then added, "You know, I have similar feelings about the girls and feminist issues in the school." Upon hearing that comment, Mr. Glenn looked at Kathy with a facial expression that turned from puzzlement to annoyance, and he said, "I have an observation to do. We can continue this discussion later."

Ricardo and Kathy continued, each in his or her own way, to influence their students' education. Ricardo's lessons always contained both the Anglo and Latino perspectives, and Kathy's "You Too Can Do" club continued to meet and discuss feminist issues.

Mr. Glenn, meanwhile, tried to ignore the teaching behavior of these two staff members. However, he often suggested to Ricardo in a friendly manner that he would probably prefer teaching in the urban barrio.

CRITIQUE To critique Single-Group Studies is to realize that many positive statements can be made about this approach to multicultural education. The Single-Group Studies approach can be seen as a beginning because people must first understand themselves before they can hope to understand others. Banks (1997) puts it this way: "Another important goal of ethnic studies is to help individuals clarify their ethnic identities and function effectively within their own ethnic community. This must occur before individuals can relate positively to others who belong to different racial and ethnic groups" (p. 21). Single-Group Studies can also be described as a beginning because the civil rights movement of the 1960s started with one group—African Americans—demanding their social, political, and economic rights, and from that beginning, other groups also demanded their rights. Although the struggles of women and labor groups were not new, their demands to be included in the curriculum as legitimate groups for study were articulated with renewed—and, in many cases, new—vigor. Gay and lesbian studies literally help people articulate an identity and set of experiences that are usually silenced; the programs give impetus to a growing civil rights struggle based on sexual orientation. The Single-Group Studies approach has generated collective pride and a desire to discover one's roots. Congress was so swayed by this interest in ethnic heritage that in 1972 it passed legislation enacting the Ethnic Heritage Studies Program. Similarly, Title IX of the Elementary and Secondary Education Act (ESEA) and the Women's Educational Equity Act came about because women demanded equality.

For the teacher who doesn't have strong knowledge of gender issues, class issues, or race diversity, the Single-Group Studies model serves as a helpful starting place. For the teacher working with a student population that is basically Asian or Latino, for example, the Single-Group Studies approach provides a beginning point to help students develop pride in who they are and understand how their group has been victimized. Ricardo Gomez's Latino students, for example, knew little about themselves as Latino people before enrolling in his class. They learned some Latino culture informally at home, but in school they had never been taught their own history, literature, and so forth. In fact, constituting only a small fraction the student body, these students were ignored in the curriculum and treated as invisible by the school.

The Single-Group Studies approach does have certain limitations, however, although what one sees as its limitations depends on one's perspective. From the perspective of advocates of the Teaching the Culturally Different approach, the Single-Group Studies approach spends too little time on the things that subordinate groups need most and too much time on things that will not help them. This model has also been criticized for keeping students of color and White female students out of the mainstream and for promoting cultural separatism. Critics fear that minority students, for example, will fail to acquire a sufficient grasp of mainstream culture if they spend too much time studying their own culture. Knowledge of African American history, for example, will not help much on the SAT or in a traditional American history class; and the system requires success in the traditional curriculum, not in the study of oppressed groups. As Woods (2002), a professor of gay and lesbian studies, observed, opponents often preface their remarks by asking, "Where could gay studies possibly lead a student?" as if the main role of school is to prepare young people for a job (p. 47). One can argue that the requirement of preparing young people for tests and jobs vividly illustrates how the system screens out knowledge from the margins. But advocates of Teaching the Culturally Different reply that teachers must nevertheless prepare students to succeed within the system because such an approach is the most realistic course of action.

From the perspective of Human Relations advocates, Single-Group Studies can be seen as counterproductive. Human Relations advocates support studying the contributions of diverse groups, but they fear that the study of oppression will only exacerbate tension and hostility. Furthermore, they believe that studying separate groups separately will not promote unity. Rather than examining painful issues in our past, Human Relations advocates prefer to seek ways of drawing people together in the present. For example, Kathy Bennett's students will, at one time or another, experience anger toward men as they learn how women have been oppressed. Some of this anger will probably be directed toward male students, male teachers, brothers, and fathers. Similarly, Ricardo's Latino students will experience anger toward Whites and may display some hostility toward White students and teachers in the school. Human Relations advocates prefer that students learn to appreciate their similarities and their cultural differences and learn to interact as unique individuals, rather than exploring the pain and injustice of past oppression and victimization.

One further limitation that advocates of Teaching the Culturally Different and Human Relations might express is that the efforts of Single-Group Studies advocates to change the world might result in their interpreting the world in too simplistic a manner. Levin (2003), for example, criticized Afrocentrism for tending too much to reduce Africa to "an undifferentiated 'African culture'" and in the process to give too little attention not only to the diversity of African cultures but also to the diversity within any given culture (such as gender diversity and sexism) (p. 548). Similarly, Levin criticized the tendency of Single-Group Studies advocates to view one form of oppression as most fundamental, and in the process either ignore or downplay other forms. He cites the example of Marxists, who view capitalism as anchoring all other forms of oppression.

> We know that sexism, racism and homophobia were flourishing under most of the Marxist regimes before their collapse (and there was even a striking example of "classism" in the USSR, where members of the working class were prohibited from entering the best stores, which were restricted to members of the ruling class). And in the West we have seen that women, people of colour and gays were able to alter their situations significantly without having to alter the capitalist system itself—in fact, some of them are now entering and moving up in the capitalist power structure." (p. 556)

From his perspective, approaches later in this chapter address such concerns, but people who are skeptical of any approach to multicultural education often raise similar concerns.

To those who accept and support the intent of Single-Group Studies, the main limitation is that the approach leaves the regular curriculum unreformed. As Connell (1993) emphasized, "Social justice is not satisfied by curriculum ghettos. Separate-and-different curricula have some attractions, but leave the currently hegemonic curriculum in place. Social justice requires … reconstructing the mainstream" (p. 44). Of course, this result is not the fault of advocates and practitioners of the approach, for most are keenly aware of the need to reform the curriculum. It is precisely this need that prompted the development of the Single-Group Studies countercurricula. Nevertheless, as a separate program of its own, Single-Group Studies allows the rest of the education program to proceed on a "business as usual" basis. For example, Mr. Glenn had no intention of changing anything in his school and tried hard to ignore Kathy and Ricardo. As long as their activities could be compartmentalized into a separate course or an after-school activity, they were tolerable. In this and other cases, champions of the status quo can argue that students are being provided with ethnic, gender, or class-relevant experiences and that teachers such as Ricardo and Kathy are being allowed to "do their thing."

Too often, such programs exist as add-ons, supplemental to the main business of the school. As such, they tend to draw as students only members of the group being studied. For example, Filipino Studies courses ideally should be taken by everyone, and teachers within such programs see as much need for changing White attitudes toward Filipinos as for educating Filipinos about their own history and culture. However, when Single-Group Studies programs are supplemental and elective, as they almost always are, they are attended mainly by students who are members of the target group. Although some students who are members of dominant groups find such courses enlightening and worthwhile, others feel threatened, particularly when they are in the minority as class members, and so they find it more comfortable to avoid such courses. Those students who may need reeducation the most can comfortably stay away, pursuing their education in the unchanged mainstream.

Another problem is that Single-Group Studies programs do not necessarily work together. The goal of most advocates of Single-Group Studies is curriculum reform that would involve the inclusion of studies about the various groups into the curriculum. Ultimately, of course, this approach would require rewriting the curriculum because its main conceptual frameworks currently derive from studies of upper-middle-class White males. Also, at present the goal of curriculum reform is more likely to appear in the form of rhetoric than actual demonstration. Most writings about Single-Group Studies suggest including other groups, but rarely in the examples they provide has this goal been accomplished. For example, ethnic studies often focus on the males of a given ethnic group; labor studies often focus on White, working-class males; and women's studies often focus on White, middle-class, heterosexual women. Ricardo's study of Latinos, as another example, emphasized the male Latino experience; most likely Ricardo was not even aware of this narrowness of focus. Furthermore, Kathy's study of feminism centered on the concerns of White, middle-class, heterosexual females. Through not intending to exclude others, each of these teachers prioritized the concerns of one group and, in so doing, implicitly accepted other existing biases.

Teachers are often confused as to when they are really using a Single-Group Studies approach. We have observed teachers who believed they were using this approach when they taught a two- or three-week unit, for example, on Asian Americans—their main substantive attempt to teach about a group other than Whites for the entire school year. Advocates of Single-Group Studies would tell such teachers that they are not implementing Single-Group Studies but rather what we described in Chapter 1 as "business as usual." Single-Group Studies is an in-depth, comprehensive study of a group. Superficial lessons about groups do not really meet the goals and objectives of Single-Group Studies and may only promote stereotyping. Furthermore, they leave the rest of the teacher's teaching devoted as always to upper-middle-class White male studies, or business as usual. However, if such teachers taught the unit on Asian Americans and also taught similar units on other groups, then advocates of the approach would probably argue that the teacher had Single-Group Studies as part of his or her curriculum, if for no other reason than that the teacher was at least limiting the time spent on White male studies so as to have comparable time to spend on other groups. The phrase "time on task," which is very familiar to teachers, represents an important aspect of teaching any of these approaches to multicultural education.

Finally, some educators reject the idea of Single-Group Studies because they themselves have only seen it implemented as an add-on approach, usually in social studies. For example, teachers in math or music may view it as an additive approach that is not very practical because it takes too much time and is not very relevant outside social studies. However, we would argue that a mainstream curriculum in any subject area already does reflect the perspective and experiences of a group—the dominant group. As such, it is not neutral or universal. Your choice is not whether cultural groups will inform the education program but rather which groups.

REFERENCES

Afro-American Studies Department. (2000). Pamphlet. Madison: University of Wisconsin—Madison Department of Afro-American Studies.

Agbo, S. A. (2001). Enhancing success in American Indian students: Participatory research at Akwesasne as part of the development of a culturally relevant curriculum. *Journal of American Indian Education, 40(1),* 31–56.

Alba, R. D. (1990). *Ethnic identity.* New Haven, CT: Yale University Press.

Allen, P. G. (1986). *The sacred hoop.* Boston: Beacon Press.

A National Survey of Lesbian and Gay College Programs. (1990–1991). *Empathy, 2(2),* 53–56.

Apple, M. W. (1993). *Official knowledge: Democratic education in a conservative age.* New York: Routledge.

Apple, M. W. (1996). *Cultural politics and education.* New York: Teachers College Press.

Aronowitz, S. (1992). *The politics of identity.* New York: Routledge.

Asante, M. K. (1990). *Kemet, Afrocentricity, and knowledge.* Trenton, NJ: Africa World Press.

Bae, Y., Choy, S., Geddes, C., Sable, J., & Snyder, T. (2000). Trends in educational equity of girls and women. *Education Statistics Quarterly, 2(2),* 115–120,

Banks. J. A. (1997). *Multicultural education and transformative knowledge.* New York: Teachers College Press.

Banks, J. A. (2002). *Teaching strategies for ethnic studies,* 7th ed. Boston: Allyn & Bacon.

Bauer, M. D. (Ed.). (1994). *Am I blue?: Coming out from the silence.* New York: HarperCollins.

Bernal, M. (1981). *Black Athena: The Afroasiatic roots of Western civilization* (Vol. 1). New Brunswick, NJ: Rutgers University Press.

Bowles, S., & Gintis, H. (1976). *Schooling in capitalist America.* New York: Basic Books.

Byndloss, D. C. (2001). Revisiting paradigms in Black education. *Education and Urban Society, 34(1),* 84–100.

Churchill, W. (1992). *Fantasies of the master race: Literature, cinema, and the colonization of American Indians.* Monroe, ME: Common Courage Press.

Combs, B. (2000). *123: A family counseling book.* Ridley Park, PA: Two Lives Publishing.

Connell, R. W. (1993). *Schools and social justice.* Philadelphia: Temple University Press.

Cross, W. E., Jr. (1991). *Shades of black: Diversity in African-American identity.* Philadelphia: Temple University Press.

Cubberley, E. P. (1909). *Changing conceptions of education.* Boston: Houghton Mifflin.

Deyhle, D. (1995). Navajo youth and Anglo racism: Cultural integrity and resistance. *Harvard Educational Review, 65(3),* 403–444.

Dupris, J. C. (1981). The national impact of multicultural education: A renaissance of Native American Indian culture through tribal self-determination and Indian control of Indian education. In *Proceedings of the Eighth Annual International Bilingual Bicultural Conference* (pp. 69–78). Rosslyn, VA: InterAmerica Research Associates.

Flores, J. (1997, Summer). Latino studies: New context and new concept. *Harvard Educational Review, 67,* 208–221.

Freire, P. (1970). *Pedagogy of the oppressed.* New York: Seabury Press.

Gaard, G. (1992). Opening up the canon: The importance of teaching lesbian and gay literature. *Feminist Teacher, 6(2),* 30–33.

Garcia, R. L., (1982). *Teaching in a pluralistic society.* New York: Harper & Row.

Gates, H. L., & McKay, N. (Eds.). (1997). *The Norton anthology of African American literature.* New York: W. W. Norton.

Graber, B. (Ed.). (1997). Constitution of the National Women's Studies Association. *Women's Studies Newsletter, 5(1–2),* p2.

Grant, C. A., & Sleeter, C. E. (2006). *Turning on learning,* 4th ed. New York: Wiley.

Grumet, M., & Stone, L. (2000). Feminism and curriculum: Getting our act together. *Journal of Curriculum Studies, 32(2),* 183–197.

Hayes, E. R. (2001, Spring). A new look at women's learning. *New Directions for Adult and Continuing Education, 89,* 35–42.

Heller, S. (1992). Worldwide "diaspora" of peoples poses new challenges for scholars. *Chronicle of Higher Education, 38(9),* A7–9.

Helms, J. E. (Ed.). (1990). *Black and white racial identity: Theory, research and practice.* Westport, CT: Greenwood Press.

Heron A. (1994). *Two teenagers in twenty.* Boston: Alyson.

Lauter, P. (1991). *Canons and contexts.* New York: Oxford University Press.

Levin, R. (2003). Interpreting and/or changing the world, and the dream of a lost Eden. *Textual Practice, 17(3),* 543–559.

Linn, M. C., & Hyde, J. A. (1989). Gender, mathematics and science. *Educational Researcher, 18(8),* 17–27.

Linton, S. (1998). *Claiming disability.* New York: New York University Press.

Loutzenheiser, L. W. (1996). How schools play smear the queer. *Feminist Teacher, 10(2),* 59.

Maher, F., & Tetreault, M. (1994). *The feminist classroom: An inside look at how professors and students are transforming higher education for a diverse society.* New York: Basic Books.

Mazumdar, S. (1989). A woman-centered perspective on Asian American history. In Asian Women United of California (Eds.). *Making waves: An anthology of writings by and about Asian American women* (pp. 1–24). Boston: Beacon Press.

McCarty, T. L. (2002). *A place to be Navajo.* Mahwah, NJ: Erlbaum.

Macgillivray, I. K. (2004). *Sexual orientation and school policy: A practical guide for teachers, administrators, and community activists.* Lanham, MD: Rowman & Littlefield.

Mihesuah, D. A. (2003). Scholarly responsibility to indigenous communities. *American Indian Quarterly, 27(1–2),* 5–8.

Muñoz, C., Jr. (1984). The development of Chicano studies 1968–1981. In E. E. Garcia, F. A. Lomeli, & I. D. Ortiz (Eds.). *Chicano studies: A multidisciplinary approach* (pp. 5–18). New York: Teachers College Press.

Murrell. P. C., Jr. (2002). *African-centered pedagogy.* Albany, NY: SUNY Press.

National Women's Studies Association. (2005). NWSA Mission. Retrieved May 11, 2005 from http://www.nwsa.org/about.html

Pagano, J. A. (1990). *Exiles and communities: Teaching in the patriarchal wilderness.* Albany, NY: SUNY Press.

Paley, N. (1995). *Finding art's place: Experiments in contemporary education and culture.* New York: Routledge.

Palladino, G. (1997). Telling labor's story. *Labor's Heritage, 8(3),* 4–17.

Perrotti, J. (2001). *When the drama club is not enough: Lessons from the safe school program for gay and lesbian students.* Boston: Beacon Press.

Rodriguez, R. (2000). Chicano studies. *Black Issues in Higher Education, 17(16),* 26–31.

Rothschild, J. (2002). NEWSA25: In the beginning. *NWSA Journal, 14(1),* 22–28.

Sanchez, G. J. (1999). Race, nation, and culture in recent immigration studies. *Journal of American Ethnic History, 19(4),* 66.

Sears, J. T. (1992). The impact of culture and-ideology on the construction of gender and sexual identities. In J. T. Sears (Ed.). *Sexuality and the curriculum* (pp. 139–156). New York: Teachers College Press.

Sleeter, C. E., & Grant, C. A. (1991). Race, class, gender, and disability in current textbooks. In M. W. Apple & L. K. Christian-Smith (Eds.). *The politics of the textbook* (pp. 78–110). New York: Routledge.

Sleeter, C. (2005). *Un-standardizing curriculum: Multicultural teaching in standards-based classrooms.* New York: Teachers College Press.

Spring, J. (1997). *The American school: 1642–1996.* New York: McGraw-Hill.

Tatum, B. D. (1992). Teaching about race, learning about racism: The application of racial identity development in the classroom. *Harvard Educational Review, 62(1),* 1–24.

Tetreault, M. K. T. (1989). Integrating content about women and gender into the curriculum. In J. A. Banks & C. M. Banks (Eds.), *Multicultural education: Issues and perspectives* (pp. 124–144). Needham Heights, MA: Allyn & Bacon.

Thompson, C. E., & Carter, T. R. (Eds.). (1997). *Racial identity theory.* Mahwah, NJ: Erlbaum.

Tomaskovic-Devey, D., & Skaggs, C. (2002). Sex segregation, labor process organization, and gender earnings inequality. *American Journal of Sociology, 108(1),* 102–128.

Trinh, T. M. (1991). *When the moon waxes red.* New York: Routledge.

Tyack, D. (1966). Forming the national character. *Harvard Educational Review, 36,* 29–41.

Tyack, D., & Cuban, L. (1995). *Tinkering toward utopia.* Cambridge, MA: Harvard University Press.

Woods, G. (2002). Educationally queer: Teaching lesbian and gay studies in higher education. *Changing English, 9(1),* 47–58.

Woodward, J. R., & Elliott, M. (1992, May/June). What a difference a word makes! *The Disability Rag,* 14–15.

Woog, D. (1995). *School's out: The impact of gay and lesbian issues on America' schools.* Boston: Alyson.

Zinn, H. (1994). *You can't be neutral on a moving train.* Boston: Beacon Press.

Zweig, M. (2000). *The working class majority: America's best kept secret.* Ithaca, NY: Cornell University Press.

CHAPTER FIVE

Multicultural Education

How can we have a Multicultural Education approach to multicultural education? We realize that this seemingly redundant terminology may be a bit confusing, so allow us to explain. Multicultural Education is a popular term used by educators to describe education policies and practices that recognize, accept, and affirm human differences and similarities related to gender, race, disability, class, and (increasingly) sexuality. Because of the popularity of the term and what it advocates, many educators who use other approaches (e.g., Teaching the Exceptional and the Culturally Different) say they are practicing multicultural education. Thus, it is important to clarify what most advocates of the Multicultural Education approach mean when they use the term.

GOALS

According to Koppelman and Goodhart (2005), "Multicultural education is based on a commitment to pluralism; its guiding purpose is to prepare students to be active participants in a diverse, democratic society" (p. 292). Gorski (2003) explained that "[t]he underlying goal of multicultural education is to affect social change." He saw social change as incorporating three strands of transformation:

1. The transformation of self.
2. The transformation of schools and schooling.
3. The transformation of society.

Similarly, over two decades ago, Gollnick (1980) described multicultural education as having five goals:

1. Promoting the strength and value of cultural diversity.
2. Promoting human rights and respect for those who are different from oneself.
3. Promoting alternative life choices for people.
4. Promoting social justice and equal opportunity for all people.
5. Promoting equity in the distribution of power among groups.

All three conceptions of social change emphasize transformation of society and its institutions, so they support the diverse identities of diverse individuals and communities, and reflect principles of equity and justice.

Many people who use this approach deal only with race and ethnicity; in this regard Banks (1994) distinguished between multicultural and multiethnic education. Some researchers address mainly gender (often termed sex equity, nonsexist education, or gender-fair education), or, if starting with special education and inclusive education, disability. In recognition of overlapping goals, concepts, and practices that span across concerns related to race, ethnicity, gender, disability, language, and religion, this chapter will discuss multiple forms of difference and oppression as interrelated.

The Multicultural Education approach began in the late 1960s and grew energetically during the 1970s. Three forces converged during the mid-1960s to give birth to this approach: The civil rights movement matured, school textbooks were critically analyzed, and assumptions underlying the deficiency orientation (described in Chapter 2) were reassessed. The civil rights movement began as a nonviolent way of changing laws that oppressed specific racial groups. By the late 1960s, it had become an energetic movement joining all Americans of color and was directed toward self-determination and empowerment. An institution that was severely criticized at this time was the schools. As schools were desegregated, it became apparent that curricula were written solely or primarily about Whites. It also became apparent that many teachers knew little about students of color and treated cultural differences and not having English as a first language as deficiencies that needed to be remediated. As Gay (1983) described it, "the student activists, abetted by the efforts of textbook analysts and by the new thinking about cultural differences, provided the stimulus for the first multiethnic education programs" (p. 561; see also Grant & Ladson-Billings, 1997).

During the 1970s, these early ideas about school reform were tried and developed in many classrooms. Educators received encouragement and support from a variety of sources. Ethnic groups all around the United States developed expressions of their heritage and identity, and in addition, the women's movement got well under way. Support for diversity was provided by a number of court cases and federal legislation such as the *Lau* decision supporting bilingual education, the Ethnic Heritage Act funding multiethnic curriculum development, and the adoption by many states of goal statements supporting teaching for cultural pluralism.

These kinds of support diminished somewhat in the 1980s, as governmental policies became very conservative and an increasing number of critics of multicultural education became active, arguing that multicultural education was divisive and would be "disuniting" to the country. Also, lean economic conditions in the United States and a diminishing international status caused policymakers and educational administrators to argue that schools should return to the basics and put aside any curriculum that was thought to take students away from mathematics, science, reading, and writing. Beginning in the 1980s and gaining steam throughout the 1990s was a push to set national and state goals for improving student learning, by establishing content standards and then testing students over their mastery of prescribed content.

Goals 2000: the Educate America Act and the *Improve America's Schools Act*, passed in 1994, prompted efforts to establish national curriculum standards in math, science, history, English, and other disciplines. Because of philosophical disagreements over what all students should know within the disciplines, attempts to establish standards shifted from the national level to the state level. By the mid-1990s, most states had developed content standards and were designing or beginning to implement statewide systems of testing based on them. In this context, multicultural education took a back seat, with the exception of increased attention to the "achievement gap" between White, English-speaking students, and students of color or students whose home language is not English, as mandated by *No Child Left Behind* (see Chapter 1).

Nevertheless, the Multicultural Education approach has continued to develop conceptually, and most educators must profess to understand it, even if they know little or nothing about it. Next we examine the ideology of the Multicultural Education approach and theories supporting its practices.

IDEOLOGY AND MULTICULTURAL EDUCATION

In this chapter we distinguish between theory and ideology because the Multicultural Education approach, more than the others, has experienced a mixing of the two concepts that can be confusing. The large discrepancy between what ought to be and the current prevailing order in society encourages proponents of the Multicultural Education approach to argue for its implementation in school policies and practices. We define *ideology* as referring to a system of beliefs and values that define what one believes ought to be, and we define *theory* as referring to how social systems or human psychology actually work. Does equal opportunity describe a theory or an ideology? What about cultural pluralism? These are terms frequently employed by advocates of this approach. To understand and evaluate them more clearly, we first examine ideology and then theory.

Some of the earlier writings in multicultural education were based on the belief and knowledge that there is no one model American (Hunter, 1974); that the United States is a pluralistic nation, and its racial and cultural diversity needs to be recognized and prized (Stent, Hazard, & Rivlin, 1973); that women's history and point of view have been systematically ignored and omitted from the schools (Spender, 1982); and that poor people and people with disabilities have been rendered invisible. Advocates saw a need to correct the beliefs and ideas espoused by the prevailing order and to make school policies and practices affirm American diversity.

The vision of what ought to be was a major inspiration for the intellectual and emotional activities of the early advocates of this approach. The ideology of Multicultural Education is one of social change—not simply an integration into society of people who have been left out but a change in the very fabric of that society. This ideology has two main components: cultural pluralism and equal opportunity. These components are both societal goals and school goals (see Table 5-1).

Cultural Pluralism
Advocates of Multicultural Education often compare U.S. society to a tossed salad or a patchwork quilt. Both metaphors suggest the use of an array of materials and

TABLE 5-1.
Multicultural Education

Societal goals:	Promote structural equality and cultural pluralism (the United States as a "tossed salad")
School goals:	Promote equal opportunity in the schools, cultural pluralism and alternative lifestyles, respect for diverse peoples, and support for power equity among groups
Target students:	Everyone
Practices:	
Curriculum	Organize concepts around contributions and perspectives of multiple groups; teach critical thinking, analyze of diverse viewpoints, commonalities as well as differences; challenge all students academically; relate to students' experiential backgrounds; build on multiple languages
Instruction	Build on students' learning strengths; involve students actively in joint productive intellectual activity
Other aspects of classroom	Assess learning fairly, using multiple means of assessment and languages students understand; Make the classroom reflect and welcome members' pluralism, diverse lifestyles
Other schoolwide	Involve parents and community actively; reach out to low-income parents and parents of color; encourage staffing patterns to include diverse racial, gender, language, and disability groups in nontraditional roles; use decorations, special events, school menus that reflect and include diverse ethnic and religious groups; include all student groups in extracurricular activities; ensure that discipline procedures do not penalize any group unfairly; ensure that building is accessible to everyone

objects of various sizes, shapes, and colors. Each ingredient is dependent on the others, but each is still unique; together the ingredients form a collective total that is distinguished by its diversity. Although formal definitions of cultural pluralism vary, all suggest that it includes the maintenance of diversity, a respect for differences, and the right to participate actively in all aspects of society without having to give up one's unique identity.

Cultural pluralism involves balancing diverse cultures and identities within one nation, encouraging a "both-and" stance toward difference and unity. According to Koppelman and Goodhart (2005), "Advocates for pluralism believe that diversity is not a difficulty to be overcome, but a positive attribute of society. ... To pluralists, individuals have the right to maintain and be proud of their racial, cultural, ethnic, or religious heritage" (p. 155). Pluralists point to various ways in which diverse traditions serve as a strength and resource. For example, although pluralists believe that citizens of the United States should master English, they also believe that citizens' knowledge of more than one language provides an important resource, enabling the United States to communicate with peoples around the world. Rather than being a problem, linguistic diversity within the

United States is an asset and should be cultivated as such. In addition, pluralists point out that the United States is now and always has been culturally diverse.

The United States is a religiously diverse nation, and the great majority of its citizens affiliate with a religion. According to the *World Christian Encyclopedia* (2001). about 76% of U.S. citizens identify themselves as Christian (including both Catholic and a wide array of Protestant churches), 1.3% as Jewish, 0.5% as Muslim (a proportion that is growing rapidly), 0.5% as Buddhist (also growing), 0.4% as Hindu, 0.1% as New Age, and 13% as nonreligious or secular. Within any of these traditions is a wide diversity of communities and sects. The United States was established on the principle of freedom of religion and separation of church and state, enabling individuals and families to choose which religion, if any, with which to affiliate. Respect for religious pluralism brings huge debates and disagreements, such as whose holidays should be observed and how they should be observed, or how to respect diverse creation stories. Nonetheless, advocates of cultural pluralism argue that it is more important to learn to navigate disagreements than to impose one religion, thereby negating the freedom of individuals to choose.

Cultural pluralism and individual choice related to gender means that males, as well as females, should have a gender-free repertoire of roles and styles to choose from; gender should not define particular sex-role images or standards for work performance. For example, many women who enter into the corporate structure emulate the performance style of the successful male, trying to "make it in the man's world" instead of deciding what works for them in the world of work and basing their style on that. In the realm of educational administration, Bloom and Munro (1995) reveal the conflicted positions in which female school administrators find themselves as they seek to fulfill their roles successfully while not enmeshing themselves in masculinist discourses. Conflicts such as these are at the heart of why advocates of applying cultural pluralism to gender contend that both work and domestic roles should be flexible and not defined by gender, and that society's socializing practices for the young should be nonsexist. In addition they state, that neither sex should be forced into a heterosexual lifestyle; people should be able to choose a heterosexual, gay, lesbian, or bisexual lifestyle without recrimination.

Pluralists argue that identification with a community and tradition fosters healthy psychological growth in children and youth; youth, particularly youth from immigrant communities, flounder when pressures to assimilate distance them from home, family, and roots. For example, a pressing problem in the Hmong community today is that Hmong youth, feeling the need to assimilate with the dominant society in order to fit in, are finding themselves cut off from their cultural roots and their families. They are in between both but are grounded in neither. Honoring cultural pluralism means honoring the diverse cultural, linguistic, and historic traditions that exist in this country rather than promoting mainstream life as superior or most desirable.

Furthermore, pluralists view diversity as a rich resource. For example, the dominant way of life in the United States is at odds with preservation of the natural environment. In the long run, it might be necessary to human existence to learn from rather than discard bodies of human wisdom that have arisen outside the so-called Western tradition, which can give insights about living sustainably with the earth.

How much diversity and choice are possible in a society that still maintains a sense of cohesiveness? In the late 1980s, this question launched a tidal wave of attacks on Multicultural Education, which we review briefly in the critique section of this chapter. Advocates of the Multicultural Education approach maintain that U.S. society has never had either real cohesiveness or a cultural consensus because many segments of society have been locked out of decision making.

For example, White, middle-class educators sometimes look back to a supposed Golden Age of harmony and consensus during the early 1950s and wonder whether an interest in pluralism has destroyed that consensus. However, during the early 1950s, African Americans were locked out of full participation, American Indians were dealing with a U.S. policy of termination of tribal status, Mexican American children were being punished for speaking Spanish in school, and Japanese Americans were trying to deal with the fact that they had been put in concentration camps because they appeared "too different." Women were being returned to the home from the workplace and were encouraged to stay there. Gay and lesbian people usually hid in the closet because their lifestyles were even more unacceptable to heterosexual people than they are now. In other words, diversity was suppressed and discouraged, and it is still being struggled over. People who did not fit the dominant conception of how life should be lived were not supported. Advocates of Multicultural Education ask, Given the real diversity that exists in American society, how can we learn to support and respect that diversity rather than suppress and deny it?

Not only are people around the world diverse, but diverse peoples are increasingly rubbing elbows as global migration of peoples increases, owing mainly to the mobility of work, wage differences in different parts of the globe, family reunification, and political instability. About 2% of the world's population lives outside of their country of birth. The seven wealthiest countries in the world have about one-third of the world's migrants, complicating what it means to be German, Italian, Japanese, or Canadian (Surge in Global Migration, 1997). Multicultural education advocates argue that young people need to be prepared to work constructively with, communicate with, and respect diverse people of the world because this will be necessary for their adult lives.

Equal Opportunity

Equal opportunity is the other main pillar of the ideology of Multicultural Education. Equal opportunity as a legal right in education was established in 1954 in *Brown v. Board of Education*. In that decision, Chief Justice Warren wrote: "In these days it is doubtful that any child may reasonably be expected to succeed in life if he [or she] is denied the opportunity of an education. Such an opportunity, where the state has undertaken it, is a right which must be made available to all on equal terms." Acting on the right to equal educational opportunity should mean that classrooms accommodate a wide enough spectrum of human diversity so that students do not find themselves disabled by factors such as teaching processes that ignore what they know, use of a language they do not understand, or adoption of teaching strategies that do not work well for them. Nor would students feel ostracized or unwelcome because of their color, religious affiliation (including visible expressions of that), sexual orientation, or physical characteristics. Classrooms would enable all students to choose and strive for a personally fulfilling future, and develop self-respect, in a way that builds on their home culture or language. Such classrooms would prevent large numbers of students from ever being labeled as disabled and would welcome, for at least a portion of their school day, those who truly are disabled.

Since the *Brown* decision, however, exactly what school practices constitute equal opportunity has been an issue of considerable debate. The "business as usual" position is that because it is illegal to deny access to education on the basis of race, sex, language, or disability, schools that comply with equal opportunity laws and court decisions such as Title IX, the Individuals with Disabilities Education Act, and *Lau v. Nichols* are providing equal opportunity. Judging what counts as equal opportunity, however, becomes sticky when institutionalized practices that may appear neutral in fact discriminate against some groups, and when legacies of past discrimination are still felt, even when opportunities appear to be equal because students are being treated the same.

For example, if schools are segregated largely because housing is segregated, and predominantly minority schools offer students a weaker curriculum than predominantly White schools, do graduates of segregated schools have equal opportunity for college admission? Research assembled by Orfield (1998) shows that they do not, since college admission is tied directly to college preparation, which is affected by a host of race and class-related factors students experience all their lives.

Debates over affirmative action converge on what it means to provide equal opportunity in a diverse society that has a long history of discrimination. Edley (1998) points out that the legal framework for affirmative action is lodged in the Equal Protection clause of the Fourteenth Amendment to the Constitution and from the Civil Rights Act of 1964. According to these laws, institutions may not use race and ethnicity as a basis for differential treatment unless: "1) there is a compelling interest and 2) the race-conscious measure is narrowly tailored" (p. viii). Achieving the goal of equal opportunity means acting affirmatively to redress the effects of past discrimination, on the basis of a compelling national interest for offering higher education to a wide diversity of young people.

Let's take a less debated example of how equal opportunity does not always mean same treatment. In a discussion of computers in schools, Solomon (2002) noted that, "Even when students have access to the best technologies, methods, and teachers, one size doesn't fit all." For students with disabilities, tools enabling access to computers exist (such as voice-activated software), but students may not have equal opportunity unless such tools are available. English language learners, who are provided software and websites in English only, do not have opportunities equal to those of native English speakers. The existence of language translators and computer materials in languages other than English offers the possibility for equal access in the classroom, but only if these are actually used. Students from homes that lack computers lack the opportunity available to students whose homes afford time on a computer, unless steps are taken to equalize overall access to computers. Software that builds on the interests of boys may not appeal to girls. In other words, offering equal opportunity does not necessarily mean offering identical opportunities within the school, since students' backgrounds and experiences differ. Rather, it means taking differences into account.

In other words, the ideology of equal opportunity envisions taking action to equalize opportunity to learn and addressing the myriad of factors, both in and outside of school, that continue to benefit some students and not others. For example, in California two recent investigations reported similar factors that systematically reduce the learning opportunity of students who are poor, students of color, and English Language Learners (Gándara, Rumberger, Maxwell-Jolly, & Callahan, 2003; Oakes, Blasi & Rogers, 2004). These factors include reduction of bilingual education programs (which were found to produce slightly higher achievement than English-only programs) and inequitable access to the following: credentialed teachers; teachers with professional training for teaching English learners; forms of assessment that capture what language-minority students can do and that help guide classroom instruction; meaningful instructional time when students are in school; sufficient textbooks, computers, and other materials for students; materials that English learners can understand; and functional school facilities. Providing equal opportunity means addressing these barriers actively.

Therefore, advocates of the Multicultural Education approach do not see it as sufficient simply to remove legal barriers to access and participation in schooling. As long as groups do not gain equal outcomes from social institutions, those institutions are not providing equal opportunity. As long as White, middle-class children succeed and leave school with higher achievement scores than other children, as long as disproportionate numbers of boys enter mathematics and science fields and girls enter human service or domestic work after schooling, as long as children leave school seeing White male contributions as most important, schools have not provided equal opportunity.

THEORY AND MULTICULTURAL EDUCATION

If advocates of Multicultural Education champion equal opportunity, choice, and cultural pluralism, what theories inform how this vision can be realized and how schools can help realize it? First, let us define what we mean by theory. Bogdan and Biklen (1992) explain that theory is "a way of looking at the world, the assumptions people have about what is important, and what makes the world work. ... Theory helps data cohere and enables research to go beyond an aimless, unsystematic piling up of accounts" (p. 33). In other words, theory involves synthesizing data in order to explain why things work as they do, and to suggest under what conditions things might actually be changed, and how. Although advocates of Multicultural Education have written much more about what ought to be than about why things are as they are, theories from the fields of sociology, and anthropology, and applied linguistics give guidance to the Multicultural Education approach. The two main kinds of theories that support it are cultural pluralism theories and cultural transmission theories.

Theories of Cultural Pluralism

William Newman (1973) developed a comprehensive discussion of theories of cultural pluralism and their use by sociologists. We will briefly summarize his four main theories, which have been expanded on by Pieterse (1996), and will show their relevance to the Multicultural Education approach.

The first theory is *assimilation*. Newman expresses it with "the formula A + B + C = A, where A, B, and C represent different social groups and A represents the dominant group" (p. 53). The theory holds that when minority cultural groups come into contact with a majority cultural group, over time the values and lifestyles of the minority groups are replaced by those of the majority group. Pieterse (1996) connected assimilation with power and the spread of capitalism, using the term *McDonaldization* to capture Western culture being equated with modernization and then spread globally. Newman showed that although some sociological studies support the theory that dominant cultures assimilate minority culture (such as studies of second-generation immigrants), other studies do not (such as studies of third-generation immigrants or of the ethnic resurgence of the 1960s, 1970s, and 1980s). In other words, some degree of cultural assimilation usually occurs, but often it is limited and may even reverse itself after a time. Cultural assimilation is not necessarily the rule.

According to Multicultural Education advocates, much schooling has been based on the theory of assimilation and has sought to facilitate this theory. "Business as usual" has assumed that the majority culture not only should but *will* prevail. It has sought to promote, for example, one language and one dialect, one version of history, one literary tradition, one view of the relationship between people and nature, and so forth. In so doing, "business as usual" has often contradicted reality. For example, for many years, schools, especially in the Southwest, had an English-only policy in an effort to erase the Spanish language and Mexican culture. However, rather than dropping Spanish, thousands of children quit (and often were forced out of) school. Spanish has continued to be spoken throughout the Southwest. During the 1970s, bilingual education was increasingly implemented, although there have been heated debates about whether its purpose is primarily to teach English or to teach both languages (Crawford, 1999; Cummins, 2000; Fillmore & Valadez, 1985; Schirling, Contreras, & Ayala, 2000). In an ethnography of a Chinese-English bilingual program, Guthrie (1985) showed that regardless of school policy, the Chinese community has both a need and a desire to maintain the Chinese language; assimilationist school practices that deny this reality are misinformed and often place children and teachers in the middle.

Children are often the victims of assimilationist school policies, particularly when "business as usual" teaches them that their home culture or religion is inferior or un-American, when it disrupts a child's ability to function in his or her own community, or when it alienates children and causes them to reject school.

Assimilationist policies can drive a wedge between the child and his or her family, which can interfere with normal socialization. This problem is particularly troublesome when teachers tell students whose first language is not English to refrain from speaking their native language in the home in order to practice English. Not only does this practice impair communication development, but it weakens the family's power to teach its values and beliefs to the child. Assimilationist school policies are also harmful when they reinforce the mistaken idea in the minds of majority-group children that their home culture or religion is the only true American culture and that everyone else wants to or should think, behave, and speak as they do.

The second theory Newman (1973) described is *amalgamation* which he represents with the formula A + B + C = D, where "D represents an amalgam, a synthesis of these groups into a distinct new group" (p. 63). Pieterse (1996) termed this "cultural hybridization," pointing out that it always happens when people mix. Languages borrow words from other languages as people come into contact with each other; in any language, one can trace the historic roots of borrowing. For example, U.S. English has borrowed words from Spanish (such as patio), from African languages (such as goober to refer to peanuts), from Arabic (such as algebra), and from indigenous languages (such as coyote). Music is a rich terrain for cultural hybridity. For example, salsa and merengue originated in the Caribbean, drawing on blends of African rhythms, Caribbean and Latin American dances, European folk dances, rock, and jazz (Guerrero, 2004).

Newman pointed out that although many people have articulated the concept of amalgamation as the ideal of the melting pot, the theory describes very little about intergroup relations. Pieterse (1996) pointed out that hybridity often is a product of colonial relations among groups; in that context, often the dominant group simply claims the cultural creations of other peoples. For example, rock music was built partly on the work of African American musicians, but because White radio stations would not play their music, White audiences assumed rock to have originated with White musicians.

The third theory Newman describes is *classical cultural pluralism,* "expressed in the formula A + B + C = A + B + C, where A, B, and C represent different social groups that, over time, maintain their own unique identities" (p. 67). Pieterse (1996) termed this theory "clash of civilizations," pointing out that it assumes cultural group to have distinct boundaries and such deep differences that contact brings conflict rather than exchange. Newman argues that this theory does not explain all of ethnic life in the United States, but it explains enough that it needs to be taken seriously. Most U.S. cities and many suburban areas contain distinct ethnic enclaves that do not disappear over time. In fact, some ethnic groups have become stronger, and some ethnic and religious communities maintain themselves in spite of dispersed membership. For example, a Jewish family that moves to North Dakota immediately joins the only local synagogue and develops ties with the few other Jewish families in town. As another example, the African American community maintains some of its solidarity and cultural distinctiveness, in spite of dispersed membership, by developing Black radio stations, magazines, and newspapers.

Yet, as Newman points out, this theory is inadequate. It fails to account for the development of a shared American culture, for the cultural changes that groups experience over time, and for the varied experiences of different cultural groups. A fourth, and more accurate theory, is modified cultural pluralism: $A + B + C = A1 + B1 + C1$. As Newman illustrates, "An Italian in Italy is different from an Italian-American. ... A black African is different from an African-American" (p. 79). Modified cultural pluralism holds that different ethnic, religious, and racial groups will assimilate into the dominant group to some extent but that this assimilation will vary with the group, and many groups will continue to retain unique cultural characteristics. As a description of group life in America, this theory is more accurate than the preceding three.

Modified cultural pluralism and cultural hybridity are theories that support the Multicultural Education approach, which advocates that, at the very least, schools should represent cultural pluralism as it actually exists in America. To the extent that it exists, the shared culture should be recognized and taught; but equally important, the cultural diversity that actually exists should also be recognized and taught to all Americans. For example, all students should be taught that there is no single American literary tradition, nor has there ever been one. Schools that teach either implicitly or explicitly that good literature is only what White men have written or that White men have been the only authors of good literature are not teaching reality. Young Americans need to learn diverse perspectives about what constitutes good literature, as well as become familiar with the literature produced by diverse American literary traditions. When taught sensitively, this knowledge is less likely to exacerbate divisiveness among cultural groups than it is to improve relationships by fostering dialogue among groups.

This last point is worth emphasizing. Theories of cultural pluralism hold that some cultural diversity will continue to exist in a nation the size of the United States, despite attempts by the dominant group to assimilate people. People will continue to create localized shared identities, drawing on cultural resources available to them. Forced assimilation will only antagonize groups and alienate youth. If some degree of cultural diversity is natural, then it makes sense that schools embrace this diversity rather than pretend that it is not there or that it is harmful to the country.

Cultural pluralism theory has applicability to forms of difference other than race and ethnicity. For example, disability communities share a common American culture as well as distinctive subcultures. Although necessity often plays a larger role than choice in the development of disability cultural groups, the implications for Multicultural Education are similar. For example, wheelchair sports are well developed and command a fairly high level of participation. Physical education programs that fail even to alert young people to the existence of wheelchair sports are perpetuating a limited conception of American athletics. The Deaf community has a rich tradition in language, history, literature, and theater. Increasingly, language programs in schools are recognizing American Sign Language (the fourth most commonly used language in the United States) as worthy of study, and theaters are showing deaf theater productions.

Cultural transmission and social learning theories provide guidance regarding how cultural norms and roles are learned, as we now discuss.

Cultural Transmission and Social Learning Theories

The ideology of Multicultural Education highlights cultural diversity and encourages awareness and knowledge about diverse alternatives. The approach does not maintain that the world is fine as it is and that children should learn more about it. Rather, its advocates are concerned that society as it exists is unfair and oppressive to many people, and does not afford equal opportunity to all. Furthermore, people are expected to conform to restricted definitions of what is considered normal if they want to succeed. For example, people of all ethnic backgrounds are often expected to display the behavioral and linguistic style of White, middle-class Americans before they are taken seriously. Women who do not adhere to expected sex roles are labeled aggressive or masculine, whereas men who do not conform to the he-man image are often viewed as effeminate.

Multicultural Education seeks to have all young people learn knowledge, values, and behavioral patterns that support cultural diversity, flexibility, and choice. Theories of cultural transmission and social learning provide guidance by alerting teachers to how children normally acquire society's values and beliefs, and how children learn in everyday life contexts. Cultural transmission theory was developed in the field of anthropology, social learning, and modeling theory in the field of psychology, and situated learning in social psychology.

Cultural transmission refers to the wide variety of ways members of a cultural group transmit their culture to the younger generation. Culture consists of shared understandings and beliefs that may or may not overlap with ethnicity and race. As Gutiérrez and Rogoff (2003) explained, it is important not to conflate race, ethnicity, and culture because doing so leads one to make assumptions that are not necessarily true or helpful. They explain, "By cultural community we mean a coordinated group of people with some traditions and understandings in common, extending across several generations, with varied roles and practices and continual change among participants as well as transformation in the community's practices" (p. 21). Everyone participates in cultural communities, and it is through such participation that the culture of the community is transmitted. Although some transmission takes place in the school, much also takes place in the home, religious institutions, and neighborhood.

Childcare, for example, tends to be a female cultural domain, whereas automobile repair tends to be a male domain. It is not uncommon for men and women to have nonsexist intentions, but end up assuming traditional sex roles simply because, in the course of growing up, the women learned how to change diapers proficiently while the men mastered the fine art of tuning up an engine. To prepare both sexes for multiple roles, the schools would need to teach both sexes knowledge that usually tends to be learned by only one sex.

Educators need to ask which communities their students participate in, what they are learning in those communities that can be built upon in school, and how the school and classroom function as communities that transmit culture. For example, one of the authors observed the English Department in a high school that offered two courses, "Great Authors of the Past" and "Recent English and American Authors." The course "Great Authors of the Past" included only writings by White male authors and a few White female authors. The course "Recent English and American Authors" included both female authors and authors of color. This bifurcation of knowledge, presented in a seemingly unbiased manner, can teach students, among other things, the notion that great authors are only White and mostly male. Although teachers might verbally tell students that everyone's literature has value, as a cultural site the school may actually be teaching something different.

Social learning theory and modeling theory also describe principles by which individuals learn particular behavioral patterns. In Chapter 3 we described Bandura and Walters' (1963) theory of prejudice formation; their work in social learning theory also has relevance here. Social learning theorists focus on the consequences that follow behavior patterns, and modeling theorists focus on the process of imitating role models. According to social learning theory, children learn alternative behavior patterns by observing adults and then learn when to imitate this behavior through reinforcement. For example, girls learn indirect and nonaggressive speech patterns by listening to older females speak; they learn to use such speech patterns.

Cultural transmission, social learning, and modeling theories show how children are strongly molded and shaped by their environments and how the values, beliefs, and behavioral patterns that young people develop result from the constant press of their social environment. One implication of these theories is that children learn through a complex variety of messages. Often, when we think of teaching, we think of telling; both anthropologists and psychologists inform us that this way of thinking about teaching is a great oversimplification. For example, Tavris and Wade (1984) described a host of sources of information about sex roles, including how parents treat each sex, how teachers treat each sex in the classroom, toys given to each sex, messages in children's books, messages in television, sexism in language (e.g., the "use of men or mankind to refer to humanity," p. 233), and sex-different styles of speech. Thus, a teacher might tell children that males and females are equal and yet will teach children that they are different and that males are more important in a variety of unconscious ways.

A sociocultural theory of learning also draws attention to its active and social nature. As Tharp and colleagues (2000) pointed out, "knowledge is constructed through joint activity. As people (adults and children) act and talk together, minds are under constant construction, particularly for the novice and the young" (p. 44). This means that the classroom should be organized as an active context for learning in which young people engage with the teacher and with each other. Furthermore, teachers need to find out something about the context their students come from, particularly if it is different from the teacher's, and if the knowledge or language students bring into the classroom is unfamiliar. In what context does student's knowledge, ways of seeing, and language make sense, and how can it be built upon? As Gutiérrez and Rogoff (2003) put it, "Rather than pigeonholing individuals into categories and teaching to the students' 'traits' or attempting to replace those traits, the emphasis would be placed on helping students develop dexterity in using both familiar and new approaches" (p. 23).

For equal opportunity to exist, members of diverse groups need to learn to function successfully in various contexts. It is imperative that members of marginalized cultural groups learn to function successfully in mainstream cultural contexts. For example, children whose home language or dialect is not Standard English need to develop competence in Standard English, as well as the ability to know which situations require them to use Standard English. Schools that fail to teach members of marginalized groups the language, behavioral patterns, and knowledge of the dominant cultural group are not providing the means for more equal opportunities in society. At the same time, it is also valuable for everyone to learn to function successfully in cultural contexts other than the dominant one. Banks (1994) points out that it is "very difficult for Anglo-Americans to learn to respond to non-Whites positively and sensitively if they are unaware of the perceptions of their culture that are held by other ethnic groups and of the ways in which the dominant culture evolved and attained the power to shape the United States in its image" (p. 99).

RECOMMENDED PRACTICES

The Multicultural Education approach seeks to reform the entire process of schooling for all children. Unlike the Teaching the Exceptional and Culturally Different approach, this approach is not just for certain groups of students. It is for everybody, and it seeks not only to integrate people into our existing society but also to improve society for all. Unlike the Human Relations approach, the Multicultural Education approach does not stop with the improvement of attitudes but seeks also to develop skills and a strong knowledge base that will support multiculturalism. Unlike the Single-Group Studies approach, it seeks to change more about schooling than just the curriculum. We have organized our discussion of recommended practices around the following typical elements of schooling: curriculum, instruction, assessment of learning, home/community–school relationships, and other schoolwide issues. Recommended Multicultural Education practices are summarized in Table 5-1 and illustrated in the companion volume *Turning on Learning* (Grant & Sleeter, 2006).

Curriculum
Multicultural Education advocates argue that the curriculum should be reworked so that it regularly presents diverse perspectives, experiences, and contributions, particularly those that tend to be omitted or misrepresented when schools conduct "business as usual." Concepts should be developed with references to the experiences of multiple groups (Banks, 1993; Gay, 2000; Gollnick & Chinn, 2002; Grant & Sleeter, 2002; Nieto, 2001; Sadker & Sadker, 1994; Sleeter, 2005). For example, if one is teaching poetry, one should select poetry written by members of a variety of groups. Doing so enriches the concept of poetry because it enables stu-

dents to explore various poetic forms as well as study those elements that are common to diverse poems. The curriculum should reflect the contributions and perspectives that reflect how groups define themselves, showing groups as active and dynamic. To do this, a teacher must learn about various groups and gain some depth of content knowledge. For example, teachers wishing to include American Indians in the curriculum sometimes choose Sacajawea as a heroine to discuss; but from American Indian perspectives, Sequoya would be a preferable historic figure. Sacajawea served White interests by leading Lewis and Clark west, whereas Sequoya served the interests of the Cherokee by developing an alphabet for encoding the Cherokee language.

Content standards in schools today often limit teachers' ability to work with curriculum. Content standards are generally presented as consensus documents that represent agreement over what is most worth teaching and knowing within the disciplines. However, content standards are not ideologically neutral; they confer power on knowledge systems that derive from someone's point of view. For example, in an analysis of proposed national arts standards, Anderson (1996) argued that dividing the arts into four disciplines—"art, music, dance, and theater—and dividing visual art into the DBAE [disciplinary-based art education] ordered disciplines of production, criticism, art history and aesthetics is quintessentially Western in conception and structure" (p. 58). He went on to point out that in many non-Western cultures, the arts are not constructed around Western disciplines, but are integrated, and do not lend themselves to discipline-based study. It is important for teachers to look critically at content standards as a guard against teaching an ideology one does not intend. Looking critically does not necessarily mean not using them, but rather, using them reflectively.

To help think through curriculum development, Banks (1993) distinguished among five types of knowledge: personal/cultural knowledge, popular knowledge, mainstream academic knowledge, school knowledge, and transformative academic knowledge. He defined transformative knowledge as including the

> concepts, paradigms, themes, and explanations that challenge mainstream academic knowledge and that expand the historical and literary canon. … Transformative and mainstream academic knowledge is based on different epistemological assumptions about the nature of knowledge, about the influence of human interests and values on knowledge construction, and about the purpose of knowledge. (p. 9)

Transformative knowledge includes not only facts and important people who are marginalized in traditional academic knowledge, but also historical accounts and interpretations of facts that differ from and often run counter to those of the mainstream.

Diverse materials should be used to present diverse viewpoints. Students should become comfortable with the fact that often there is more than one perspective, and rather than believing only one version, they should learn to expect and seek out multiple versions. For example, New York City Public Schools (1990) published a U.S. and New York history curriculum that emphasized four themes: Culture/Diversity, Movements of People, Contributions, and Struggle for Equality (p. viii). Each unit examined a theme or time period from the perspectives of three or four different American sociocultural groups, such as Euro-Americans, Native Americans, and African Americans. Students are provided with diverse perspectives—then encouraged to analyze these perspectives and come to their own conclusions rather than a textbook author's conclusion.

Curriculum that works with transformative knowledge makes a stronger impact on students than that using a more superficial "heroes and holidays" approach, by addressing real issues that students are often aware of. Bigler (1995, 1999) found that curricula that simply label groups or group members (for example, pointing out the race, ethnicity, or gender of historical figures) draw students' attention to group markers and differences and invite stereotyping. Curricula that provide limited counterstereotypic information about members of marginalized groups that have little effect in countering stereotypes children exposed to outside school (Bigler, 1999). But curricula that provide information about racism (possibly along with successful challenges to racism) appear to affect the attitudes of *both* children of color and White children toward fairness and toward people of color (Milligan & Bigler, in press), probably because such curricula provide information about why some groups seem to fare better than others, as well as examples of steps taken to build fairness.

As much emphasis should be placed on contemporary life as on history. For example, the women included in history texts are usually White women who are involved in the suffrage movement. This is only a small fraction of what could be taught about women in social studies. African American women, too, have always actively resisted oppression. Many have become involved (both historically and today) in African American women's clubs working to improve social conditions; many have had outstanding accomplishments; and many others have been (and still are) victimized. Oversimplified bits of information can be misleading and can lead to stereotyping.

Similarly, Stearns (1988) advocates the teaching of social history in which "social historians study not only ordinary people but also the ordinary aspects of life" (p. 142). He adds,

> The basic argument here was that groups outside the mainstream of conventional history—that is, groups that were not producers of formal or higher culture or did not include individually identifiable actors on the political scene—had a past in their own right. Further, such groups were not simply acted upon by leaders of society or even by anonymous forces such as economic cycles. Though lacking an equal share of society's power and wealth, the inarticulate definitely played a role in shaping their own values and habits. (p. 142)

The curriculum should also relate to and draw on students' experiential background, or "bring the community into the schools and … bring the school to the community" (Foerster, 1982, p. 125).

In addition to helping students understand human differences and diverse points of view, a multicultural curriculum should also help students see common ground across differences. For example, Metzger (2002) points out that the academic study of religion can help students appreciate the common human condition and why people have used religious symbols, rituals, and beliefs to address human concerns. He points out that it is difficult to generate respect for people one knows little about. He suggests that one of the things people share is a desire for self-expression and freedom of belief; studying differences should be nested within this kind of shared common ground.

All these recommendations should permeate the total curriculum. In other words, all subject areas should be taught multiculturally all the time. As Nieto (2001) puts it, Multicultural Education is a process of school reform that "permeates the curriculum and instructional strategies used in schools, as well as the interactions among teachers, students and parents, and the very way that schools conceptualize the nature of teaching and learning" (p. 307).

Multicultural curricula include developing a multilingual society. One of the authors of this book was visiting a bilingual school in New York. He was sitting in the office when some African American students entered and addressed him in Spanish. They were surprised to realize that he (like most Americans) was limited to only one language. Dual-language schools structure the curriculum so that all students become proficiently bilingual. As Thomas and Collier (1999) explain,

> Well-implemented, both one-way and two-way programs accelerate all students' growth through a meaningful, bicultural, grade-level curriculum that connects to students' lives inside and outside school. These programs have achieved high levels of academic success for both native English speakers and English language learners. Instead of enduring educational isolation in remedial classes with a watered-down curriculum, students flourish in these enriched forms of bilingual education.

A dual-language curriculum is structured around two languages, teaching students a second language while teaching academic content in their first language. Usually, roughly half of the students come from English-speaking homes and the other half from homes that speak another language, such as Spanish. As students begin to develop proficiency in the second language, they receive more and more of their education together, with the language of instruction alternating between English and the other language. Dual-language schools are producing promising results. Based on a study of 20 dual-language schools, Lindholm-Leary (2001) concluded that they were "successful in promoting high levels of first-language, second-language and at least medium levels of bilingual proficiency among both language-minority and language majority students. Further, students can achieve at least as well as their peers who are not in DLE [dual-language education] classrooms" (p. 309).

Finally, all students should be afforded access to an academically rich curriculum. For example, Gollnick and Chinn (2002) recommend, "minority students, as well as white students ... make up the college preparatory and general education classes" (p. 277). The American Association of University Women Educational Foundation (1992) recommends working actively to avoid sex-segregated enrollment in courses such as upper-level mathematics, computers, and science. Programs designed specifically for low-income and minority students, such as bilingual education, sometimes reduce these students' access to the rest of the curriculum by resegregating them within the school. Recognizing this problem, Nieto (2001) posits,

> There are ways in which the needs of limited English-proficient and mainstream students can be served at the same time. Within every bilingual program, there are opportunities for integrating students for nonacademic work. Students in the bilingual program can take art, physical education, and other nonacademic classes with their English-speaking peers. In addition, bilingual programs can be integrated into the school rather than separated in a wing of the building, so that teachers from both bilingual and nonbilingual classrooms are encouraged to collaborate on projects. (p. 201)

Instruction

The Multicultural Education approach entails reworking instructional processes in the classroom so that they support high expectations, build on the strengths that diverse students bring to the classroom, and actively engage students in working with and producing knowledge. Many of the instructional processes discussed in earlier chapters are included in this approach. Here, we pull them together into a vision for reworking classroom teaching so that it supports challenging learning among a wide variety of students.

Philosophically, the Multicultural Education approach is captured in a shift within special education, from remediating learning problems outside the regular classroom to adapting the regular classroom to diverse learners. As Kohler and Rusch (1995) put it, while the concept of mainstreaming

> exemplified the notion of "fixing" students, the more contemporary regular education initiative (REI) supports the emerging focus upon individuals. Mainstreaming typically involved educating students in regular classrooms with support services provided by a "resource" teacher. Support services were focused on bringing the performance of the mainstreamed student up to the level expected of all students in the classroom. Thus, mainstreaming tended to address the deficits of students in their attempts to perform in a typical academic curriculum. (p. 115)

In contrast, inclusion, or "inclusive education," focuses on individual goals and abilities of students within regular education classrooms. Gale (2001), for example, writing with reference to learning disabilities, urges teachers to emphasize students' contributions and strengths rather than their disabilities, collaborating with students and their parents to decide on teaching processes that support students best.

The Center for Research on Education, Diversity and Excellence (CREDE) established five standards for effective pedagogy that guides instruction for Multicultural Education (Tharp et al., 2000). The first standard is facilitating learning through joint productive activity among teachers and students. This means shifting from lecture- and workbook-dominated classrooms to classrooms in which students do much of the thinking and working, with active and direct guidance from the teacher. Cooperative learning that involves students and teachers working together generally produces the richest learning environment. Bennett (1999), after reviewing research on cooperative learning, states: "research results show that student team learning improves both academic achievement and students' interpersonal relationships. All students (including high, average, and low achievers) appear to benefit" (p. 303). This is particularly true of students who are in the process of learning English and benefit from academic interaction with English-speaking peers (Arias, 1986).

The second CREDE standard is developing competence in the language and literacy of instruction across the curriculum (Tharp et al., 2000). This means that students' everyday language is linked with discipline-specific academic language, both orally and in writing, so that students develop academic linguistic fluency.

The third CREDE standard is connecting school to students' lives, and contextualizing teaching and curriculum in the experiences and skills of students' homes and communities (Tharp et al., 2000). For example, Hollins (1982) pointed out that students come to school with good conceptual schemes. Rather than replacing these with new ones, the teacher should use and build on the students' own schemes, which are reflected in the interests, knowledge, questions, and connections in students' talk in the classroom.

The fourth CREDE standard is teaching complex thinking, challenging students toward cognitive complexity (Tharp et al., 2000). Excellent teachers aim to prepare their students for college (or some other level of challenge), scaffold instruction in a way that starts where students are, and help students produce more complex work and develop cognitive tools for more complex work. Bennett (1999) argues that high expectations are a necessary prerequisite for equal education: "If teachers are to provide equal opportunities for learning, their expectations for student success must be positive and equitable" (p. 67). Teaching toward cognitive complexity also entails monitoring oneself to be sure that one is treating all students equitably. Some teachers, for example, give more attention and more academic challenge and support to boys, particularly White or Asian boys, than to girls and to students of color (American Association of University Women Educational Foundation, 1992).

Finally, the fifth CREDE standard is engaging students through dialogue, especially the Instructional Conversation. As Tharp and colleagues (2000) explain, an Instructional Conversation is an academic dialogue between teacher and student that goes beyond reciting correct answers, and it involves thinking. The teacher coaches, prompts, and models thinking and problem solving as needed, and students do much of the talking. In order to do this well, teachers need to know their students, and to know their subject matter well enough to link student thinking with academic content, in the context of conversations with students in the classroom.

Ultimately, instructional processes should help students develop positive academic self-concepts. Nieto (2001) points out that students do not simply develop poor self-concepts accidentally. Rather, poor self-concept is the result of policies and practices of schools and society that respect and affirm some groups while devaluing and rejecting others. As Bennett (1999) put it,

> When a student with low self-esteem enters a classroom, self-concept becomes one of the most challenging individual differences in how he or she will learn. Because

students with a negative self-image are not fully able to learn, school becomes an arena for failure that prevents them from achieving the success needed for high self-esteem. (p. 131)

Assessment of Learning

One cannot consider evaluation without discussing high-stakes testing. High-stakes tests are used to make significant decisions about the life of a student, such as whether the student will graduate, or a school, such as whether it experiences sanctions because students are not achieving according to Annual Yearly Progress (AYP) standards specified by *No Child Left Behind*. To some observers, high-stakes tests are a useful tool for improving student achievement and closing gaps among subgroups of students because they force educators to pay attention to how well students are learning (e.g., Fuller & Johnson, 2001; Haycock, 2001; Skrla et al., 2001).

To others, high-stakes tests are problematic partially because testing has a long history of uses for inequitable purposes. For example, intelligence testing was part of the Eugenics movement. Intelligence tests have been used to place students of color in lower tracks, classify them as retarded or in need of special education, and block entry into higher education (Kornhaber, 2004). Mensh and Mensh (1991), based on a review of the history and practices of IQ testing, concluded that "the tests are not instruments for assessing individual differences, but a means for ignoring individuality and slotting children according to prior assumptions about the races and classes they belong to," and as long as such tests continue to be used, schools will continue "to justify superior and inferior education along class and racial lines" (p. 158). Currently, school administrators are concerned that minimum-competency graduation exams, especially if imposed without additional resources, will lead students with disabilities to leave school without graduating because they identify students as failures without necessarily offering support and help (Manset-Williamson & Washburn, 2002).

Although standardized achievement tests are supposed to measure general achievement and learning, critics point out that scores on state content tests do not necessarily correlate with other established measures of student learning, such as the National Assessment of Education Progress or advanced placement testing (Amrein & Berliner, 2002; Linn, Baker, & Betebenner, 2002). Many teachers in historically underserved communities point out that "results of standardized achievement tests contradicted their first-hand classroom observations and assessments of students of color [which] revealed higher levels of student performance on targeted learning objectives" (Hood, 1998, p. 189).

For these reasons, advocates of Multicultural Education argue that tests and other means of evaluation should be based on curricula the students have actually been taught, with criterion rather than norm references, and should be used only to improve instruction. Tests to determine eligibility for special education (and especially those used to determine mental retardation) should be culturally sensitive (Townsend, 2002).

Advocates of Multicultural Education generally prefer performance assessment over standardized testing because performance assessment allows students to show what they know in varied ways. Performance assessment refers to assessing student learning through a variety of means such as "classroom observation, projects, portfolios, performance exams and essays" (Neill et al., 1995, p. 1).

Advocates argue that evaluation processes should not penalize students by requiring skills that are extraneous to what is being evaluated. For example, if a science teacher wishes to assess how well students have learned science concepts, assessment should not require students to read and write above their skill level; if a student cannot read some of the questions or write well enough to answer questions, the test should be given orally. (This is not meant to suggest that no one should be teaching reading and writing skills to the student, only that these skills should not interfere with the student's ability to display what he or she has learned about science.) Time limits should not be placed on tests (unless there is a good reason to do so) if such limits prevent those who work slowly from completing the test.

Students who are fluent in a language other than English should be assessed in their native language if their performance in English does not allow them to show what they know and can do (unless the purpose of the test is to evaluate their mastery of English). Often, such students know a good deal that is not captured in English tests, leading teachers to underestimate what they know or to make other kinds of faulty judgments about their academic abilities and skills. Furthermore, assessments of students' English language proficiency should take into account the fact that it takes substantially longer for a student to acquire the cognitively demanding English used in academic situations compared to the English proficiency required in social situations. Teachers too often judge English Language Learners as able to perform on academic assessments in English because students are able to converse in English, but ability to converse does not mean students have acquired the English academic language necessary to show mastery of academic content, even if students know the content in their first language (Cummins, 2000). Accurately assessing the language factor, in addition to the other factors already discussed, is crucial to the educational achievement of language-minority students.

Finally, educators should make sure that tests do not advantage one gender more than the other. For example, based on a study of tests, the American Association of University Women Educational Foundation (1992) reported that standardized tests still provide more male references than female and give boys an advantage by using multiple-choice formats rather than the essay formats that favor girls.

Home/Community–School Relationships

Advocates of the Multicultural Education approach encourage schools to maintain a strong relationship with the home and community. They believe that when it comes to the education of their children, parents and community members must be more than mere spectators, simply attending graduation ceremonies, open houses, or sporting events. Most school districts agree to the importance of building productive relationships between the home and school. For example, Kessler-Sklar and Baker (2000), in a survey of school district policies, found that over 90% of the school districts had a least one policy supporting parent involvement.

Based on several years' work with many schools, Epstein (1995) identified six general types of parent involvement that link them with school goals: (1) parenting, (2) communicating, (3) volunteering, (4) learning at home, (5) decision making, and (6) collaborating with the community. Schools that intentionally design activities that engage with parents in all six areas have been found to have a positive impact on students' attendance, behavior, and learning in school (e.g., Epstein & Sheldon, 2002; Sheldon & Epstein, 2002).

Although schools generally support the concept of home-school partnerships, many do not translate that support "into plans or their plans into practices" (Epstein, 1991, p. 349). One issue is that parents of color, immigrant parents, and parents in poverty communities often do not see home-school engaging with the school the same way teachers do (Lawson, 2003). For example, consider a school that holds conferences with parents of color at the beginning of the school year in order to help students of color get off to a good start. Initially, this practice may seem like a good idea, but it may be flawed if: (1) it is based on the expectations of school officials that students of color will have academic difficulty; (2) the teachers do most if not all of the talking, as we have observed at parent-teacher conferences; and (3) the purposes of the conferences are not explained to the students, who are concerned about their parents coming to school. In an actual parent-teacher conference that one of us observed, some students of color wondered why their parents had to come to school whereas the parents of their White friends were not required to do so. An advocate of such home-school involvement explained to one of the authors:

> The most productive approach to improving education for students of color has been a school-community partnership. In this partnership, the community's contribution is to help define and illuminate the interests and needs of their children. The school, representing both the dominant culture and the education profession, then contributes to problem solving abilities. The coequality of school and community can strengthen school-community relationships and can reveal problem areas which have escaped previous identification and consequently impeded progress. (Montano, 1979, p. 152)

Advocates of the Multicultural Education approach want to see the community involved in budgetary procedures, the selection of school personnel, and curriculum development. At the same time, they are concerned that schools develop involvement plans collaboratively with parents, and maintain sensitivity to the wide diversity of families that exist and to why some parents may stay away from the school. For example, Ryan and Martin (2000) point out that many educators are ignorant of and prejudiced against gay and lesbian parents. They argue that schools need to implement antibias training for teachers and policies that specifically invite both partners in sexual minority families into the school.

Advocates of this approach, like advocates of the Human Relations and the Single-Group Studies approaches, acknowledge the importance of the school in recognizing and affirming the home/community cultures of all of its students. They embrace the idea that just as there is no one model American, there is no one model home or community. Homes are as varied and diverse as the people who make up a multicultural community.

Other Schoolwide Issues

The Multicultural Education approach is concerned with additional schoolwide as well as classroom practices, including staffing, tracking, and extracurricular activities. A guide to assessing one's classroom and school for its support of pluralism and equity can be found in Chapter 5 of *Turning on Learning* (Grant & Sleeter, 2006).

Staffing patterns should reflect cultural diversity and nonsexist roles (Baker, 1994; Gollnick & Chinn, 2002). Thus, more than a token number of staff members should be of color, staff members of color should be administrators and teachers as well as aides and custodians, half of the decision makers should be female, and teachers should not be relegated to subject areas on the basis of sex stereotypes (e.g., there should be female mathematics teachers in addition to male mathematics teachers). Moreover, school leaders should facilitate relations among staff members that are collegial and cooperative. It is especially important that teachers from various programs (such as bilingual education or special education) and support services be integrated within the mainstream life of the school.

Tracking and grouping of students for instruction should not replicate patterns of discrimination and inequality. In many schools, the upper-level tracks and gifted programs are populated mainly by White or Asian students from affluent backgrounds, whereas the lower tracks and special education classes house students from low-income families, particularly students who are African American and Latino. In this way, students from privileged backgrounds are afforded access to more academically challenging (and often more interesting) instruction than students from historically underserved backgrounds. To address this problem, some schools have eliminated tracking altogether.

For example, Rockville Centre School District in New York has been "leveling up" its classes so that all students are served in heterogeneous upper-track classes. The school gradually eliminated lower-track classes, with the expectation that all students could learn to do more complex and challenging work and that teachers could learn to work effectively with their heterogeneous classes. On standardized tests of student achievement, such as the Advanced Placement calculus exam and the Regents exam, both traditionally low- and high-achievers' scores have risen, and there has been a marked closing of the racial achievement gap (Burris, Heubert, & Levin, 2004). This is an excellent example of dismantling a system that has historically been discriminatory and was serving underachievement students less effectively than many people believed.

Extracurricular activities often need attention from a multicultural perspective. For example, Baker (1994) recommended that schools make sure that athletic programs include students of color and women and that cheerleading teams include both sexes and students of color. She pointed out that female students sometimes are not actively encouraged to participate in certain sports and that students from lower socioeconomic backgrounds are often unable to participate in sports such as skiing, which requires access to facilities outside the school. Both Baker (1994) and Gollnick and Chinn (2002) recommend that clubs and organizations should not perpetuate racial or sex segregation and that one group should not dominate positions of student leadership.

Athletic opportunities opened up considerably to girls after Title IX was passed in 1972, and each year since then increasing proportions of female students have been participating in athletics. However, there is still quite a way to go in equalizing athletic opportunities. Boys still participate at a higher rate than girls, and the proportion of women coaches has decreased rather than increased. Costs of maintaining athletic programs also favor traditionally male sports such as football, which tend to bring in money (Suggs, 2001). Historically significant, however, is the establishment of the Women's National Basketball Association (WNBA)—with the first professional game played on June 21, 1997.

Many sports are still sex stereotyped, and students perceive some sports as male and others as female. For example, the American Association of University Women Educational Foundation (1992) reported, that "figure skating, gymnastics, jumping rope, and cheerleading were the only athletic activities identified as female" (p. 45). But while media often contain sex stereotypes in reporting about sports, young people do not necessarily respond favorably to such reporting. For example, in a study entitled "He's a Laker, she's a 'looker,'" Knight and Giuliano (2001) found that college students of both sexes preferred articles that focused on athletes' performance rather than their appearance.

Other schoolwide issues that can be attended to include the extent to which school lunches reflect what communities being served eat and the extent to which programs offered by the school reflect the culture of the community. The main idea is that school leaders view the entire school through the lens of diversity and equity. Asking students for their opinions is a good way to think about how the school as an organization impacts on them; students often have ideas for improving school that adults do not think of.

GETTING STARTED

John Martin, Marie Sanchez, and Ellen Foxley were returning to James Madison Junior High after spending three days at the district's in-service institute. They had been selected for attendance by their school principal, Dr. Herman Kempner, because of their interest in improving achievement and in working constructively with diversity and equity. He also chose them for their general leadership ability within the school. James Madison Junior High was a magnet school located not too far from the city's downtown area. As a magnet school, it received a richly diverse student population, which was 18% Asian, 12% Black, 10% Latino, 3% Native American, 2% Arab, and 47% White. The socioeconomic status of these students was also varied: About 55% came from families that could be considered solidly middle class, and the other 45% represented students who came from the working class. About 8% of the total student population had disabilities of one kind or another. Girls outnumbered boys by 2% this year; this percentage had fluctuated 1 or 2 percentage points in either direction over the last five years.

Kempner, or "Doc" as he was more often called by his colleagues, saw Multicultural Education as the best way to address student achievement, partly because of his recent trip to Hawaii and Japan and partly because of the mounting attention to globalization. He believed that technology and globalization create an important need for people to learn more about each other's history and culture, and to learn how to work together. He also strongly believed that students learn best when instruction relates to their strengths and identities, and he knew that too often schools treat many students from a deficiency perspective. Although his school had made its achievement targets the previous year, it had only barely done so. Clearly, improvement was needed, and Doc was convinced that academic instruction would strengthen the more teachers focused on what interested and engaged their students. Doc also argued that the school should help students accept and affirm cultural diversity as a fact of life in the United States and acknowledge that it is a valuable resource that should be preserved and cherished.

John, Marie, and Ellen had all become interested in multicultural education in different but equally fulfilling ways. John had attended an Ivy League college and had joined Teach for America. He had been assigned to an inner-city school in Los Angeles, and he had surprised himself by discovering that he really enjoyed teaching. At the completion of his assignment, he took a job at James Madison, where he has been teaching language arts for several years. Marie had grown up in a Mexican barrio in Austin, Texas. She had attended a local university in Dallas and had fallen in love with the city. She has been teaching mathematics at the junior high school for nine years. Ellen had been teaching social studies at James Madison for six years. She had come to the school after living most of her life in Alaska, where her mother was the principal in a school that had a large enrollment of Inuit students. She had worked for her mother for two years before deciding to see the "lower forty-eight." Early in her teaching career, she had become involved with the women's movement and had helped establish a local NOW chapter.

The workshop had provided two important commodities—time and material resources—to enable each of the three teachers to develop lesson plans for their classes. Also, it had encouraged and provided time for them to collaborate on developing schoolwide implementation plans. They shared these plans with Doc on their first day back.

The schoolwide plans called for each subject-area department to assess its curriculum for academic challenge afforded to all students, and for how well content was developed from multiple perspectives and inclusive of multiple sociocultural communities. Departments were to establish a procedure for improvement where needed. The plans suggested that each teacher have primary responsibility for his or her curriculum but that subject-area colleagues should worked together with an eye toward making sure the curriculum reflected subject-area standards. In addition, each teacher was to assess his or her own teaching style to determine to what extent it meshed with the different learning styles of the students and reflected the five CREDE standards. Finally, the plans recommended hiring more teachers of color for the core subject areas, because of the 35 core-area teachers, only two were Black and one was Puerto Rican.

The three teachers waited for Doc's reaction to their proposal. It was not long in coming. He said, "How do you think the teachers will respond to these area meetings and work? They have been very slow to start responding to multi-cultural education as a school goal, other than putting up a few posters here and there."

Ellen replied, "There is one thing I remember my mother saying: 'A successful instructional program requires a strong leader.' Doc, you know that unless you really get involved, most of the teachers will write this whole thing off as 'here today, gone tomorrow.' Besides, none of them wants the school to be designated as an Improvement School!"

Doc sighed and said, "I know you're right. I'll put it on the agenda for this month's staff meeting, and then we'll really get into it." He then asked, "What are each of you going to do in your own classrooms?"

John replied first, saying that he had already developed several lesson plans. He said that the first thing he did was make sure he was actually teaching toward college preparation. He realized that he had written off some of his low-achieving students as noncollege material, and as a result, was not teaching them as well as he could. One set of new lesson plans for literature required him to change not only which pieces of literature he taught but also his teaching methods. For example, he was going to include Mildred Taylor's *Roll of Thunder, Hear My Cry*, Scott O'Dell's *Carlotta*, Lawrence Yep's *Dragon Wings*, and Jean Craighead-George's *Julie of the Wolves*. He was going to involve students more in cooperative learning groups, and he also was going to have these books put on tape so that students with severe reading problems could listen and follow along.

Marie responded that she had come up with a plan to use Emma's and Paul's wheelchairs to help teach circumferences, diameters, and radii. Also, she and John were planning a lesson together that involved mathematics and essay writing. The lesson would require students to measure various dimensions of a building and then refer to those measurements in an essay discussing how architectural facilities could be redesigned to accommodate disabled individuals. She was excited as she talked, because she said that these ideas would link mathematics to thoughtful application. She commented that students tended to memorize and then forget math concepts when they couldn't see how they might be used.

Ellen said that she was changing her social studies unit on World War II to include the internment of Japanese Americans on the West Coast and the roles of African Americans, Hispanics, Asian Americans, and women in the war. She was also going to have small groups learn to use the Internet for research on these topics. Small groups would then write short papers that would be put together into a book in a Word document; small groups would also learn to present what they had learned using an LCD projector as a tool.

Doc complimented the three on their excellent ideas and asked them to share them with the staff at the next meeting. Also, he asked if they would be willing to be on call to help others get started. The meeting adjourned as the three responded yes.

CRITIQUE Some of you may be thinking that the Multicultural Education approach solves all the problems not addressed by the other approaches. Others of you may feel dissatisfied with this approach, yet perhaps you may be uncertain about what is dissatisfying to you. Although this approach has been advocated prolifically, it has also been criticized on various grounds and from various perspectives. First, we will present criticisms of the goals of the approach from the perspectives of the three approaches discussed earlier. Next, we will present criticisms that support the approach's goals but question its implementation. Finally, we will present criticisms that the approach described in Chapter 6 tries to resolve.

Advocates of the Teaching the Exceptional and the Culturally Different approach believe the Multicultural Education approach is misdirected, and so the last two decades have seen a well-financed and well-organized attack against it. The most outspoken critics implicitly accepted Teaching the Exceptional and Culturally Different but explicitly advocated assimilating everyone into a supposed national consensus and common culture. They believe that U.S. society is essentially good and just and that the worst way to deal with differences in language, culture, or learning styles is to nurture them. For example, Schlesinger (1992) complained that "ethnic ideologues" and "unscrupulous hucksters" have "imposed ethnocentric, Afrocentric, and bilingual curricula on public schools, well designed to hold minority children out of American society" (p. 130). He posited that "the national ideal had once been e pluribus unum. Are we now to belittle unum and glorify pluribus? will the center hold? or will the melting pot yield to the Tower of Babel?" (Schlesinger, 1992, p. 2).

Similarly, Hirsch (1996) argued that it is the responsibility of the school to instill in all children the knowledge they will need (e.g. traditional) to succeed economically and participate in a commonly shared culture. This is especially essential, Hirsch stressed, for those students who arrive at school with deficits and whose home culture fails to instill background knowledge relevant to their education. Critics argue that it is both undesirable and unrealistic to think that the mainstream will become pluralistic and that the best thing schools can do is to try to equip those who are poor, minority, and disabled with the skills and knowledge they will need to get a job and compete for upward mobility in the existing society. They are concerned that excessive emphasis on race and ethnicity is divisive, and will tear the United States apart much as occurred in the former Soviet Union and Yugoslavia (Barry, 2001; Ravitch, 1990). They regard the United States as "an entirely new experiment in politics" rooted in Western political thought and founded on a regard for individual rights rather than group claims (Bloom, 1989, p. 27). In spite of its imperfections, they regard the United States as having become increasingly unified for over two centuries by a common culture and by the opportunity to shed one's ethnic membership in order to speak and think as an individual American. They view attention to ethnic origin as thwarting inclusivity, commonality, and universalism; it also promotes White guilt and national self-hatred (Stotsky, 1991).

Such critics would probably fault John for teaching fewer traditional literary classics in order to include works by authors of color, Marie for taking up mathematics instruction time to discuss building accessibility for people with disabilities, and Ellen for cutting back on time spent on the political and military aspects of World War II in order to focus more on people of color and women.

These critiques were leveled against Multicultural Education very publicly, appearing, for example, in such magazines as *Time* and portraying advocates of the Multicultural Education approach as extremists. This is how many lay citizens were introduced to Multicultural Education. In contrast, educators and researchers have advanced much milder critiques of this approach.

Writing from the vantage point of disability, Kavale and Mostert (2003) argue that research on inclusive classrooms should suggest caution rather than a rush to implementing this concept. They point out that research continues to find teachers, parents, administrators, and peers to have mixed perceptions about the inclusion of special education students in general education classrooms. Research also shows that general classroom teachers are often not well-equipped or well-trained to individualize instruction for students with disabilities. Since research evidence about the impact of full inclusion is mixed, it is said that educators should be very cautious about adopting inclusive classrooms on ideological grounds.

Those criticizing the Multicultural Education approach from a Human Relations perspective raise different objections. These critics believe that U.S. society does not promote enough love and interpersonal caring for a fulfilling existence. They believe that as people learn not to stereotype others and to communicate with, share with, and care about those with whom they come into contact, eventually other social problems will be solved. They argue that the Multicultural Education approach becomes misdirected when it emphasizes cognitive knowledge about different groups over exploration of interpersonal feelings and social issues. These critics believe that the Multicultural Education approach may give students a broad knowledge base but that unless interpersonal relationships are stressed and experienced, attitudes and prejudices will not change. The objection is a question of emphasis. Human Relations advocates and Multicultural Education advocates usually do not leave each other in bitter disagreement but rather move in somewhat different directions.

Advocates of the Single-Group Studies approach usually agree with much of the vision of Multicultural Education, but they object that the approach weakens attention to the particular group they represent. Sometimes members of diverse groups initially embrace Multicultural Education's rainbow concept, but they become disenchanted when their own group continues to receive minimal attention while others receive more. For example, multicultural curriculum materials today usually give good representation to African Americans and White women, but they give barely a nod to Puerto Ricans or Hmong people. In addition, the issue of language, which is a central concern of bilingual educators, often remains peripheral to Multicultural Education. There is no theoretical reason why any particular group or issue should be left out; but the reality is that when attention is divided among a wide variety of groups, each group cannot receive in-depth and comprehensive treatment (at least, not without substantially lengthening the amount of time students spend in school).

A related objection of many Single-Group Studies advocates is that they do not see multiple forms of diversity as equally important. Many ethnic studies educators view race as the basic form of oppression, while radical feminists insist it is gender and class analysts argue that it is the economic structure. Studying multiple forms of diversity is seen as superfluous, a waste of time, and is said to weaken the study of the form of diversity that is of greatest concern. Ricardo Gomez (Chapter 4), for example, would be less than enthusiastic about Ellen's approach to teaching history because it would fail to mine the richness of Mexican American history to its fullest extent. Ellen would certainly do more than is usually done to portray Mexican Americans as active and visible contributors to American life, but Ricardo would want to focus more intensively on them.

Now let us examine some problems with implementation of the Multicultural Education approach. One problem we have observed is that educators often treat multiple forms of diversity, especially race and gender, as parallel but separate (Grant & Sleeter, 1986). For example, when teaching about African Americans and women, teachers often really teach about Black men and White women. Similarly, many teachers treat race and disability as isolated subjects, neglecting to examine how racism leads Whites to unjustly label people of color as handicapped. Moreover, many educators tend to view race, gender, and other social markers of difference as unitary, often failing to address the nonsynchronous or complex and contradictory nature of experience within groups as well as the way in which multiple characteristics intersect in shaping social life (McCarthy, 1990). The Multicultural Education approach itself does not call for such biased and essentialist treatment of diversity, but such treatment seems to occur for a number of reasons. Many educators and scholars simply become interested in one form of oppression (such as sexism) and often do not resolve their own biases related to other forms (such as racism). In addition, they often neglect to put in the increased amounts of time and effort required to learn about and integrate race, class, gender, and disability.

Another problem is that implementation requires a reeducation of the educators using the approach. The Multicultural Education approach is ambitious. For example, to teach instrumental music from a multicultural perspective, one needs to learn a wide variety of music traditions. Few of us received a multicultural education in our own schooling, so acquiring one now requires considerable commitment, time, and creativity. One cannot half-heartedly do a good job of Multicultural Education. In the vignette, the teachers were able to benefit from the time, materials, and knowledge provided at the in-service institute. They also knew that their colleagues would be unwilling to invest the necessary time and effort in the approach without the principal's strong encouragement. In addition to acquiring a broad and multicultural knowledge base in subject matter, it is also important that teachers interrogate their biographies in order to gain a deeper understanding of the way their own social positioning impacts perspective and teaching (Grant, 1991). Indeed, if multicultural education is to become a reality, teacher education will need to be more closely aligned with such initiatives. Prospective teachers, for example, will need to be immersed in community settings in order to fully appreciate the culture and history of particular groups and should be given extensive mentorship opportunities with experienced teachers (Ladson-Billings, 1994).

You have probably noticed that this chapter included only bits and pieces about sexual orientation. The dominant society currently marginalizes and suppresses gay and lesbian issues to such a degree that many multicultural educators are reluctant to mention this group. Advocates for gay, lesbian, and bisexual rights argue that teachers and communities need increased practical strategies on how gay, lesbian, and bisexual issues can be integrated into and across a multicultural K–12 curriculum. In addition, these advocates argue that educators, administrators, and parents must be encouraged to view sexual orientation as a cultural and civil rights issue that has a place within multicultural education. Although a growing number of books, articles, and curriculum materials are available to introduce gay, lesbian, and bisexual issues in the classroom (see Chapter 4 for examples), getting these materials into the schools is often still a struggle, particularly in communities that view gay and lesbian lives as immoral.

For example, in 1996, some New Hampshire teachers' jobs were threatened when they ignored a ban on the teaching of gay and lesbian issues in the classroom. In the Middleton-Cross Plains School District, Wisconsin, conflicts abounded when teachers attempted to integrate readings from *One Teenager in Ten: Writings by Gay and Lesbian Youth* into a curriculum aimed at opposing injustice. These examples of homophobia illustrate the need for education about sexual orientation as well as how conflicts related to diversity permeate society, from large, urban areas to smaller, suburban ones. Nevertheless, several multicultural scholars have begun to organize sessions at educational conferences to discuss the inclusion of sexual orientation under the multicultural umbrella. The small but steady development of educational materials (e.g., books and articles) on homophobia in education and the discussions of the influence of traditional schooling on gay and lesbian students are having some effect.

The limited attention given to social class is a serious problem associated with the Multicultural Education approach. Many educators who are very concerned about race are interested in class only to the extent that people of color are disproportionately poor; educators interested in gender are concerned about the increased pauperization of women; and Multicultural Education advocates often recommend that children have equal opportunity regardless of social class background. However, in an ideal society, if race and gender status differences are eliminated, what about class differences? Multicultural Education advocates do not come right out and say that a classless society is preferable to one stratified by class. Nor do they say that the culture of people living at or below the poverty level is just as worthy as middle-class culture in the same way they argue that the cultures of Native Americans are as worthy as that of Anglo Americans. They maintain that the people are as worthy, but they do not contend that class cultures are equally worthy and desirable. The Multicultural Education approach simply does not say very much about social class, particularly about the extent to which the ideal society should have different social classes. This lack of attention to social class was reflected in the teaching ideas proposed by John, Marie, and Ellen. The Single-Group Studies and the Social Reconstructionist approaches both offer a critique of social class; the Multicultural Education approach is relatively silent on this subject.

Disaffected Multicultural Education advocates who have moved on to the approach we will be presenting next have leveled another criticism: The Multicultural Education approach directs too much attention to cultural issues and not enough to social structural inequalities and the skills that students will need to challenge these. For example, young people in school may learn nonsexist values and roles and may learn to make choices without relationship to gender. Yet, when they leave school and enter the real world, which is still sexist, how will they respond? Sociologists often argue that they will rework their beliefs and behaviors to fit the circumstances in which they find themselves. Boys may have received as much reward in a nonsexist school for sewing as for giving orders, but out of school many will have access to rewards for more "masculine" behavior and to roles that require them to give orders, dominate, and compete. As such, Banks and Banks (1995) emphasize the need for equity pedagogy, which includes teaching students not only to question dominant cultural assumptions but also to participate in transforming the structure that supports inequality. Fraser (1997) discussed the complex relationship between demands for cultural representation with those of structural transformation and redistribution. The two camps have too frequently understood their agendas as separate when, in fact, they are closely linked.

REFERENCES

American Association of University Women Educational Foundation. (1992). *How schools shortchange girls.* Washington, DC: American Association of University Women Educational Foundation.

Amrein, A. L., & Berliner, D. C. (2002). High-stakes testing, uncertainty, and student learning. *Education Policy Analysis Archives, 10(18).* Retrieved January 15, 2003 from http://epaa.asu.edu/epaa/v10n18/.

Anderson, T. (1996). The national standards for arts education: A (multi)cultural assessment. *Studies in Art Education, 38(1),* 55–60.

Arias, M. B. (1986). The context of education for Hispanic students: An overview. *American Journal of Education, 95,* 26–57.

Baker, G. C. (1994). *Planning and organizing for multicultural instruction.* Reading, MA: Addison-Wesley.

Bandura, A., & Walters, R. H. (1963). *Social learning and personality development.* New York: Holt, Rinehart, & Winston.

Banks, C. M., & Banks, J. A. (1995). Equity pedagogy: An essential component of multicultural education. *Theory into Practice, 34(3),* 152–158.

Banks, J. A. (1993). The canon debate, knowledge construction, and multicultural education. *Educational Researcher, 22(5),* 4–14.

Banks, J. A. (1994). *Multiethnic education: Theory and practice,* 3rd ed. Boston: Allyn & Bacon.

Barry, B. (2001). *Culture and equality: An egalitarian critique of multiculturalism.* Cambridge, MA: Harvard University Press.

Bennett, C. I. (1999). *Comprehensive multicultural education,* 4th ed. Boston: Allyn & Bacon.

Bigler, R. S. (1995). The role of classification skill in moderating environmental influences on children's gender stereotyping: A study of the functional use of gender in the classroom. *Child Development, 66,* 1072–1087.

Bigler, R. S. (1999). The use of multicultural curricula and materials to counter racism in children. *Journal of Social Issues, 55,* 687–705.

Bloom, A. C. (1989). *The closing of the American mind.* New York: Simon & Schuster.

Bloom, L. R., & Munro, P. (1995). Conflicts of selves: Nonunitary subjectivity in women administrator's life history narratives. In J. A. Hatch & R. Wisniewski (Eds.). *Life history and narrative* (pp. 99–112). Washington, DC: Falmer Press.

Bogdan, R. C., & Biklen, S. K. (1992). *Qualitative research for education,* 2nd ed. Boston: Allyn & Bacon.

Brown v. Board of Education, 347 U.S. 483, 493. (1954).

Burris, C. C., Heubert, J., & Levin, H. (2004). Math acceleration for all. *Educational Leadership, 61(5),* 68–71.

Crawford, J. (1999). *Bilingual education: History, politics, theory and practice.* Trenton, NJ: Crane Publishing.

Cummins, J. (2000). *Language, power and pedagogy.* Buffalo, NY: Multilingual Matters.

Edley, C., Jr. (1998). Foreword. In G. Orfield & E. Miller (Eds.). *Chilling admissions* (pp. vii–x). Cambridge, MA: The Harvard University Civil Rights Project.

Epstein, J. L. (1991, January). Paths to partnership. *Phi Delta Kappan, 72(5),* 344–349.

Epstein, J. L. (1995). School/family/community partnerships: Caring for the children we share. *Phi Delta Kappan, 76,* 701–712.

Epstein, J. L., & Sheldon, S. B. (2002). Present and accounted for: Improving student attendance through family and community involvement. *Journal of Educational Research, 95(5),* 308–318.

Fillmore, L. W., & Valadez, C. (1985). Teaching bilingual learners. In M. C. Wittrock (Ed.). *Handbook of research on teaching* (pp. 648–685). New York: Macmillan.

Foerster, L. (1982). Moving from ethnic studies to multicultural education. *The Urban Review, 14,* 121–126.

Fraser, N. (1997). *Justice interruptus: Critical reflections on the "postsocialist" condition.* New York: Routledge.

Fuller E. J., & Johnson, J. F., Jr. (2001). Can state accountability systems drive improvements in school performance for children of color and children from low-income homes? *Education and Urban Society, 33(3),* 260–283.

Gale, T. (2001). Under what conditions? Including students with disabilities within Australian classrooms. *Journal of Moral Education, 30(3),* 261–272.

Gándara, P., Rumberger, R., Maxwell-Jolly, J. & Callahan, R., (2003, October 7). English Learners in California Schools: Unequal resources, unequal outcomes. *Education Policy Analysis Archives, 11(36).* Retrieved October 8, 2003 from http://epaa.asu.edu/epaa/v11n36/.

Gay, G. (1983). Multiethnic education: Historical developments and future prospects. *Phi Delta Kappan, 64,* 560–563.

Gay, G. (2000). *Culturally responsive teaching.* New York: Teachers College Press.

Gollnick, D. M. (1980). Multicultural education. *Viewpoints in Teaching and Learning, 56,* 1–17.

Gollnick, D. M., & Chinn, P. C. (2002). *Multicultural education in a pluralistic society,* 5th ed. Upper Saddle River, NJ: Merrill.

Gorski, P. (2003). The challenge of defining a single "multicultural education." McGraw-Hill multicultural supersite. Retrieved April 18, 2005 from http://www.mhhe.com/soc-science/education/multi/define.html.

Grant, C. A. (1991). Culture and teaching: What do teachers need to know? In M. Kennedy (Ed.). *Teaching academic subjects to diverse learners* (pp. 237–256). New York: Teachers College Press.

Grant C. A., & Ladson-Billings, G. (Eds.). (1997). *Dictionary of multicultural education.* Phoenix, AZ: Oryx Press.

Grant, C. A., & Sleeter, C. E. (1986). Race, class, and gender in education research: An argument for integrative analysis. *Review of Educational Research, 56,* 195–211.

Grant, C. A., & Sleeter, C. E. (2002). Race, class, gender exceptionality, and educational reform. In J. A. Banks & C. A. Banks (Eds.), *Multicultural education: Issues and perspectives* (pp. 49–66). Boston: Allyn & Bacon.

Grant, C. A., & Sleeter, C. E. (2006). *Turning on learning,* 4th ed. New York: Wiley.

Guerrero. J. G. (2004). Merengue and salsa: The cultural expression of the Spanish speaking Caribbean. Caribseek. Retrieved April 21, 2005 from http://kaleidoscope.caribseek.com/Articles/publish/printer_Merengue_and_S alsa.shtml.

Guthrie, G. P. (1985). *A school divided.* Hillsdale, NJ: Erlbaum.

Gutiérrez, K. D., & Rogoff, B. (2003). Cultural ways of learning: Individual traits or repertoires of practice. *Educational Researcher, 32(5),* 19–25.

Haycock, K. (2001). Closing the achievement gap. *Educational Leadership, 58(6),* 6–11.

Hirsch, E. D., Jr. (1996). *The schools we need and why we don't have them.* New York: Doubleday.

Hollins, E. R. (1982). Beyond multicultural education. *Negro Educational Review, 33,* 140–145.

Hood, S. (1998). Culturally responsive performance-based assessment: Conceptual and psychometric considerations. *Journal of Negro Education, 67(3),* 187–196.

Hunter, W. (1974). *Multicultural education through competency-based teacher education.* Washington, DC: American Association of Colleges for Teacher Education.

Kavale, K. A., & Mostert, M. P. (2003). River of ideology, islands of evidence. *Exceptionality, 11(4),* 191–208.

Kessler-Sklar, S. L., & Baker, A. J. L. (2000). School district parent involvement policies and programs. *Elementary School Journal, 101(1),* 101–118.

Knight, J. L., & Giuliano, T. A. (2001). He's a Laker; She's a "looker": The consequences of gender- stereotypical portrayals of male and female athletes by the print media. *Sex Roles: A Journal of Research, 45(3–4),* 217–229.

Kohler, P. D., & Rusch, F. R. (1995). Secondary educational programs and transition perspectives. In M. C. Wang, M. C. Reynolds, & H. J. Walberg (Eds.). *Handbook of special and remedial education, Research and practice,* 2nd ed. (pp. 107–129). Tarrytown, NY, Pergamon.

Koppelman, K. L., & Goodhart, R. L. (2005). *Understanding human differences: Multicultural education for a diverse America.* Boston: Allyn & Bacon.

Kornhaber, M. L. (2004). Assessment, standards and equity. In J. A. Banks & C. A. M. Banks (Eds.). *Handbook of Research on Multicultural Education* (pp. 91–109). San Francisco: Jossey-Bass.

Ladson-Billings, G. (1994). *The dreamkeepers: Successful teachers of African American children.* San Francisco: Jossey-Bass.

Lawson, M. A. (2003). School-family relations in context, Parent and teacher perceptions of parent involvement. *Urban Education, 38(1),* 77–133.

Lindholm-Leary, K. J. (2001). *Dual language education.* Buffalo: Multilingual Matters.

Linn, R. L., Baker, E. L., & Betebenner, D. W. (2002). Accountability systems: Implications of requirements of the No Child Left Behind Act of 2001. *Educational Researcher, 31(6),* 3–16.

Manset-Williamson, G., & Washburn, S. (2002). Administrators' perspectives of the impact of mandatory graduation qualifying examinations for students with learning disabilities. *Journal of Special Education Leadership, 15(2),* 49–59.

McCarthy, C. (1990). Race and curriculum: Social inequality and the theories and politics of difference in contemporary research on schooling. New York: Falmer Press.

Mensh, E., & Mensh, H. (1991). *The IQ mythology: Class, race, gender, and inequality.* Carbondale: Southern Illinois University Press.

Metzger, D. (2002). Finding common ground, Citizenship education in a pluralistic democracy. *American Secondary Education, 30(2),* 14–32.

Milligan, J. K., & Bigler, R. S. (2006). Addressing race and racism in the classroom. In G. Orfield & E. Frankenburg (Eds.). *Lessons in integration: Realizing the promise of racial diversity in America's schools.* Charlottesville, University of Virginia Press.

Montano, M. (1979). School and community: Boss-worker or partners? In C. A. Grant (Ed.). *Community participation in education.* Boston: Allyn & Bacon.

Neill, M., Bursh, P., Schaeffer, B., Thall, C., Yohe, M., & Zappardino, P. (1995). *Implementing performance assessments.* Cambridge, MA: FairTest.

Newman, W. N. (1973). A study of minority groups and social theory. *New York: Harper & Row.*

New York City Public Schools. (1990). *United States and New York State history: A multicultural perspective.* New York: Author.

Nieto, S. (2001). *Affirming diversity* (3rd ed.). New York: Longman.

Oakes, J., Blasi, G., & Rogers, J. (2004). Accountability for adequate and equitable opportunities to learn. In K. Sirtonik (Ed.). *Holding accountability accountable: What ought to matter in public education.* New York: Teachers College Press.

Orfield, G. (1998). Campus resegregation and its alternatives. In G. Orfield & E. Miller (Eds.). *Chilling admissions,* (pp. 1–16). Cambridge, MA: Harvard University Civil Rights Project.

Pieterse, J. N. (1996). Globalisation and culture: Three paradigms. *Economic and Political Weekly, 31(23),* 1389–1393.

Ravitch, D. (1990). Multiculturalism: E pluribus plures. *The American Scholar, 59(3),* 337–354.

Ryan, D., & Martin, A. (2000). Lesbian, gay, bisexual, and transgender parents in the school systems. *School Psychology Review, 29(2),* 207–216.

Sadker, M., & Sadker, D. (1994). *Failing at fairness: How our schools cheat girls.* New York: Simon & Schuster.

Schirling, E., Contreras, F., & Ayala, C. (2000). Population 227, Tales from the schoolhouse. *Bilingual Research Journal, 24,* 1–14.

Schlesinger, A. M., Jr. (1992). *The disuniting of America.* New York: Norton.

Sheldon, S. B., & Epstein, J. L. (2002). Improving student behavior and school discipline with family and community involvement. *Education and Urban Society, 35(1),* 4–26.

Skrla, L., Scheurich, J. J., Johnson, J. F., Jr., & Koschoreck, J. W. (2001). Accountability for equity: Can state policy leverage social justice? *International Leadership in Education, 4(3),* 237–260.

Sleeter, C. E. (2005). *Un-standardizing curriculum: Multicultural teaching in standards-based classrooms.* New York: Teachers College Press.

Solomon, G. (2002). Digital equity: It's not just about access anymore. *Technology & Learning, 22(9),* 18–20, 22–24, 26.

Spender, D. (1982). *Invisible women: The schooling scandal.* London: Writers and Readers Publishing Cooperative Society.

Stearns, P. N. (1988) Social history in the American history course: Whats, whys, and hows. In B. R. Gifford (Ed.). *History in the schools: What shall we teach?* (pp. 138–161). New York: Macmillan.

Stent, M., Hazard, W., & Rivlin, H. (1973). *Cultural pluralism in education: A mandate for change.* New York: Appleton-Century-Crofts.

Stotsky, S. (1991). Cultural politics. *American School Board Journal, 178(10),* 26–28.

Suggs, W. (2001). Female Athletes Thrive, But Budget Pressures Loom. *Chronicle of Higher Education, 47(36),* A 45.

Surge in Global Migration. (1997). *Futurist, 31(1),* 40.

Tavris, C., & Wade, C. (1984). *The longest war: Sex differences in perspective,* 2nd ed. New York: Harcourt Brace Jovanovich.

Tharp, R. G., Estrada, P., Dalton, S. S., & Yamauchi, L. (2000). *Teaching transformed.* Boulder, CO: Westview.

Thomas, W. P., & Collier, V. P. (1999). Accelerated schooling for English language learners. *Educational Leadership, 56(7),* 46.

Townsend, B. L. (2002). Testing while Black. *Remedial & Special Education, 23(4),* 222.

World Christian Encyclopedia. (2001). *A comparative survey of churches and religions in the modern world,* 2nd ed. New York: Oxford University Press.

CHAPTER SIX

Multicultural Social Justice Education

At its inception, multicultural education challenged power relations, particularly racism. However, over time, power has often become displaced by more comfortable concepts such as tolerance, which has led to apolitical versions of multicultural education. Many contemporary renderings of multicultural education examine difference without connecting it to a critical analysis of power relations. To many people, the term *multicultural* suggests starting with the idea of "many cultures." This idea fits with the idea of the United States as a nation of immigrants, in which people brought culture from diverse areas. However, it does not draw attention to institutionalized discrimination or to ways in which racism acts as a barrier of exclusion. Beginning with the premise of diversity rather than justice can lead to addressing only diversity, and ignoring justice issues. Berlak and Moyenda (2001) argued that liberal conceptions of multiculturalism support "white privilege by rendering institutional racism invisible," leading to the belief that injustices will disappear if people simply learn to get along (p. 94). "Central to critical multiculturalism," they continued, "is naming and actively challenging racism and other forms of injustice, not simply recognizing and celebrating differences and reducing prejudice" (p. 92).

Our fifth approach—Multicultural Social Justice Education—starts with the premise that equity and justice should be goals for everyone and that solidarity across differences is needed to bring about justice. The notions of equity and justice point to not just a goal of equal opportunity but also to one of equal results for diverse communities. This means that in an equitable and just society, the various institutions of society will enable diverse communities to sustain themselves, and will ensure basic human rights (including decent housing, health care, quality education, and work that pays a living wage) for all citizens.

Multicultural Social Justice Education is rooted in social reconstructionism, which Brameld (1956) noted, offers a "critique of modern culture" (p. 37). It holds that "magnificent as their services to society [may] have been in the past, the major institutions and the corresponding social, economic, and other practices that developed during the preceding centuries of the modern era are now incapable of..." (pp. 37–38), and you can end this statement by the central social issue that concerns you. To Brameld, the issues of concern were ending war and economic depression. To advocates of Multicultural Social Justice Education, the social issue of concern is the elimination of oppression of one group of people by another. Multicultural Social Justice Education, then, is not simply practice, but politically guided practice.

GOALS

Reflect on the various forms of social inequality that we discussed in Chapter 1. Multicultural Social Justice Education deals more directly than the other approaches with oppression and social structural inequality based on race, social class, gender, and disability. As noted in Table 6-1, the approach prepares future citizens to reconstruct society so that it better serves the interests of all groups of

TABLE 6-1.
Multicultural Social Justice Education

Societal goal:	Promote social structural equality and cultural pluralism
School goals:	Prepare citizens to work actively toward social structural equality; promote cultural pluralism and alternative life styles; promote equal opportunity in the school
Target students:	Everyone
Practices:	
Curriculum	Organize content around current social issues involving racism, classism, sexism, sexuality, disability; organize concepts around experiences and perspectives of several different American groups; use students' life experiences as starting point for analyzing oppression; teach critical thinking, analysis of alternative viewpoints; teach social action skills, empowerment skills
Instruction	Involve students actively in democratic decision making; build on students' learning styles; adapt to students' skill levels; use cooperative learning
Other aspects of classroom	Decorate room to reflect social action themes, cultural diversity, student interests; avoid testing and grouping procedures that designate some students as failures
Other schoolwide concerns	Involve students in democratic decision making about substantive schoolwide concerns; involve working-class and minority parents actively in the school; involve school in local community action projects; make sure that staffing patterns include diverse racial, gender, and disability groups in nontraditional roles; use decorations, special events, school menus to reflect and include diverse groups; use library materials that portray diverse groups in diverse roles; make sure that extracurricular activities include all student groups and do not reinforce stereotypes; use discipline procedures that do not penalize any one group; make sure building is accessible to everyone

people, especially those who are of color, poor, female, gay, lesbian, transsexual, disabled, or any combination of these.

This approach is visionary. Though grounded very much in the everyday world of experience, it is not trapped by this world. In fact, it is similar to the view revealed in these words by George Bernard Shaw (1921): "You see things; and you say, 'Why?' But I dream things that never were; and I say, 'Why not?'" Social reconstructionism speaks, in the words of Aronowitz and Giroux (1985), the "language of possibility. In this case, we move to the terrain of hope and agency, to the sphere of struggle and action, one steeped in a vision which chooses life and offers constructive alternatives" (p. 19).

Advocates of this approach do not loudly and clearly articulate one particular vision of the ideal society. They argue that resources should be distributed much more equally than they are now and that people should not have to adhere to one model of what is considered "normal" or "right" to enjoy their fair share of wealth, power, happiness, or respect. Nonetheless, advocates believe that it would be another form of elitism for a small group of educators to tell other people what the "right" vision of a better society is. Rather, young people, and particularly those who are members of oppressed groups, should understand the nature of oppression in modern society. Correspondingly, they should understand how their ascribed characteristics (e.g., race, class, gender) and their culture impact on that oppression, which should lead them to develop the power and skills to articulate both their own goals and a vision of social justice for all groups and to work constructively toward these ends.

This approach works toward a vision of social justice by teaching political literacy. As Freire (1985) explains:

> A political illiterate—regardless of whether she or he knows how to read and write—is one who has an ingenuous perception of humanity in its relationships with the world. This person has a naive outlook on social reality, which for this one is a given, that is, social reality is a fait accompli rather than something that's still in the making. (p. 103)

Through a process called conscientization, Freire believes that people should learn to question society, see through versions of "truth" that teach people to accept unfairness and inhumanity, and become empowered to envision, define, and work toward a more humane society.

This approach, more than the others, is called different things by different advocates. For example, one may encounter terms such as emancipatory pedagogy (Gordon, 1985), critical teaching (Shor, 1980), critical multiculturalism (Kincheloe & Steinberg, 1997; Obidah, 2000), antiracist teaching (Dei, 1996; Gillborn, 1995; Lee, 1995), anti-oppressive education (Kumashiro, 2002), culturally responsive teaching (Irvine, 2003), transformative pedagogy (Cummins, 2000), and social action (Banks, 1999). Although educators using these different terms do not advocate exactly the same things (one main difference being that some focus primarily on race, others on gender, still others on social class), their basic goals and theoretical assumptions are very similar.

This approach strives to integrate concerns related to race, social class, gender, sexuality, disability, language, and related forms of oppression such as homophobia. Most advocates do not integrate all of these very well, but most recognize the desirability of working toward it. Advocates of Multicultural Social Justice Education, regardless of the term they use for the approach, agree on several theoretical assumptions about the nature of society and the nature of learning.

ASSUMPTIONS AND THEORY

The Multicultural Social Justice Education approach reverses much commonsense thinking about the relationship between individual beliefs and behavior and the larger social order. People generally believe that if individuals become more humane, better skilled, more literate, or more civil, society as a whole will become more just. The first two approaches that were discussed rest heavily on this thinking, and the fourth approach considered contains some of this thinking. A fundamental assumption from the field of sociology, however, is that the reverse of this concept is true: Individuals shape their beliefs and behavior to fit their niche in the social structure. Similarly, one's niche in society or the social and cultural cues received from that niche influence one's performance or how the performance is viewed and accepted by others. Try to change individuals and they will quickly return to their old ways if the world they experience remains unchanged.

For example, middle-class people often wonder why housing in many low-income neighborhoods becomes so run down. Sometimes well-intentioned people try to teach the low-income residents techniques for home maintenance, assuming the condition of their housing is the product of a lack of knowledge and a lack of concern. (Even more naïve attempts to help include preaching to the residents on the value of keeping their homes up.) Often, however, the residents are contending with other factors, such as absentee landlords who own the property, charge high rents, and do not themselves maintain the property that they own. The residents may not perceive that it is worthwhile to invest their own meager earnings in maintaining property that does not belong to them or make repairs and additions that will become the property of a landlord who has demonstrated a lack of regard for the tenants, especially if they are unsure of how long they will actually remain living there. If one is really concerned about the condition of such housing, often more pertinent issues to address are landlord policies and access to purchasing affordable, low-cost housing.

The assumption is that if we change peoples' world significantly, then their attitudes, beliefs, and behavior will change accordingly. The question that arises is: Who is supposed to change society, if not individuals? Advocates of this approach argue that individuals need to learn to organize and work collectively in order to bring about social changes that are larger than individuals.

The approach actually elaborates on this idea. We will address this concept by discussing three interrelated theories on which this approach is based: critical theories, a sociological theory of culture, and theory connecting identity and democracy.

Critical Theories

Critical theories, though differing in the form of oppression from which they start, understand social behavior as being organized much more on a group basis than on an individual basis, and view much of social behavior in terms of collective conflict for power and resources. Critical theories include critical theory (which begins from an analysis of social class relations), critical race theory (which begins from an analysis of racism), multicultural feminism (e.g., Collins, 1998), critical cultural studies (e.g., Hall, 1993), critical disability studies (e.g., Linton, 1998), queer theory (e.g., Pinar, 1998), and postcolonial studies (e.g., Smith, 1999).

Critical theory, which began in Germany before World War II, connected a Marxist analysis of the social class structure with psychological theories of the unconscious to understand how oppressive class relations are produced and reproduced. In the 1980s, theorists such as Henry Giroux and Peter McLaren applied critical theory to pedagogy, creating a "pedagogy of critical theory" (Pruyn, 1994, p. 38) that conceptualizes everyday lived culture as a site of social struggle and social transformation. Critical race theory, developed initially by legal scholars of color who were concerned that critical theory gave far too little attention to race, examines "the relationship between race, racism and power" (Delgado and Stefancic, 2001, p. 2). Applying critical race theory to education, Ladson-Billings and Tate (1995) analyzed Whiteness as property. People with the best property get the best schools; in this case, race functions similarly to money. Curriculum represents a form of "intellectual property" that is connected to race. Its quality varies with the property values of the school community, taking the form of differential course offerings, classroom resources, science labs, technology, and certified and prepared teachers, distributed on the basis of both social class and race.

Whether one begins with an analysis of race, social class, gender, disability, language, or sexual orientation, "multiple forms of oppression are constantly played out in schools" (Kumashiro, 2002, p. 11). Critical theories offer intellectual tools for explaining how and why this happens and how to act in ways that probe below the superficial.

Critical theories examine how groups struggle with each other for control over resources and ideas. You can probably think of examples of these scarce resources in your own community: jobs, land, housing, political influence, perhaps even food or water. You can also think of ideas and beliefs, such as environmental issues and abortion, over which groups struggle. Groups compete because people are by nature concerned mainly with their own welfare and that of their family, and secondarily about the welfare of others whom they see as being like themselves or believing as they believe. When important resources are in scarce supply, most of us are concerned primarily about attaining these resources for people close to us. People we neither know nor identify with usually receive much less concern or sympathy—and often none at all.

The more scarce the resource, the more intense the struggle, and the more important group membership becomes. America has an ideology of individual achievement, but for the conflict theorist, this ideology masks reality. The resources with which a person starts, the opportunities open to the person, the circumstances in which the person lives, and the way others react to the person all depend to a significant extent on the groups of which that person is a member.

For example, writing about gender membership and power, Oakley (1981) stated that "power is unequally distributed in most societies, and depends not only on personal qualities of the individual but on social position. Different people occupy different social positions and men occupy a different position in society from women" (p. 281). A woman may attempt to achieve power within a community, but her individual efforts are shaped partly by her gender: As a mother, her time may be limited by domestic responsibilities; some men in the community may refuse to take orders from her; and her stand on gender-related issues may polarize would-be constituents on the basis of sex. The more influential and coveted is the position she seeks, and the more she acts as an advocate for women, the more one is likely to see sex stereotyping and denigration of women occurring to "keep her in her place."

To solidify, extend, and legitimate its control, dominant groups structure social institutions to operate in ways that will maintain or increase their own advantage. However, dominant groups try to establish and promulgate rules of society in such a way that most people will think the system is fair. For example, in a capitalist economy, people can gain wealth by investing extra money. The investor collects interest, dividends, or profits; someone else performs the labor necessary for accumulating that money. The more extra money one has, the wealthier one can become. The secretary who barely earns enough to make ends meet will have little or no capital to invest; the corporate executive will very likely have quite a bit. Yet, most people accept this system as fair because they believe that everyone has an equal opportunity to invest; it just so happens that those who need money the most rarely have any capital to invest.

The view of people with disabilities as an economic drain is another example (Linton, 1998). Abberley (1987) maintained that dominant groups oppress disabled people in an effort to control access to jobs and to convince workers of the rightness of the Protestant work ethic. People are led to believe that normal adults work full time, and people who do not work full time are viewed as abnormal, even defective. Abberley points out that most concepts of disability are purely biological in nature and that they suggest that defective people cannot be expected to want or have the same advantages as "normal" people. For example, hearing impairment is usually understood as resulting from defects in a person's auditory system, with little consideration given to the extent to which the social environment accommodates the hearing impaired. If we view disabled people as biologically defective, we tend to assume that they should be satisfied with less from life. Abberley writes: "By presenting disadvantage as the consequence of a naturalized 'impairment' it legitimizes the failure of welfare facilities and the distribution system in general to provide for social need, that is, it interprets the effects of social maldistribution as the consequence of individual deficiency" (p. 17).

Structuring institutions for the benefit of dominant groups results in institutionalized oppression. As neo-Marxist sociologists point out, the capitalist economy structures in great wealth differences and enables the class that controls production to maintain and extend its wealth. A few individuals may gain economic mobility, but the lower and working classes as a whole do not. However, because some people do become upwardly mobile, and because most people seem to act like autonomous individuals, the class system is made to seem fair. Many people do not recognize or understand how the wealthy use their wealth to control the economic and political lives of others. As Apple (1985) puts it, "We castigate a few industrialists and corporations, a small number of figures in government, a vague abstraction called technology, instead of seeing the productive and political apparatus of society as interconnected" (p. 5).

Globally, a critical perspective on large corporations, based mainly in the United States, reveals the process used to extend control over an increasing proportion of the resources and labor of the world. In 1944, the United Nations established the International Monetary Fund (IMF) and World Bank to promote economic development. Immediately following World War II, the General Agreement on Tariffs and Trade (GATT) was established to resolve international disputes related to trade policies, tariffs, and import and export quotas. These institutions have become contemporary tools of global corporate control, using processes similar to the colonization processes used by European countries and the United States during the 1600s–1800s.

In traditional economies, historically people have made what they needed and have traded for products they do not make. Using tools of the IMF and World Bank, industrial nations have pressured Third World countries to shift from producing for internal consumption to producing for export. Generally, this has been done by creating economic forecasts that predict wealth to be generated by taking on modernization projects that require World Bank loans. The economic forecasts themselves, however, deliberately overstate profits and underestimate the likelihood the country will be able to pay back its loan (Perkins, 2004). Industrial nations buy exports until they find cheaper alternatives elsewhere. As export sales decline or prices drop, which happened dramatically through the 1980s, Third World countries need to borrow more money. Money borrowed from the World Bank comes with high interest payments and strings that force a shift toward deregulation, privatization of publicly owned companies, conversion to export economies, export of natural resources, social spending cuts, and removal of foreign investment restrictions. These "adjustments" have been made to facilitate access by wealthy countries, and particularly their transnational corporations, to the resources of Third World.

The effect on Third World nations generally has been loss of autonomy, huge debt, and increased poverty among all but a wealthy elite. Between 1984 and 1990, Third World nations transferred $178 billion to Western commercial banks (Ismi, 1998) and by the early 1990s, owed $1.5 trillion to creditors in wealthy nations. At the same time, people who used to produce for local consumption were increasingly landless, unemployed, and dependent on jobs with transnational corporations. But as transnational corporations have sought the cheapest labor, Third World countries, needing to employ people, have outbid each other in order to get jobs, driving down wages. The result has been a drop in living standard for millions of Third World people, a rapidly escalating gap between rich and poor, globally, and an escalation of corporate control.

A revision of GATT in 1994 elevated corporated power over national sovereignty. It established the World Trade Organization (WTO), which has the power to set rules for unrestricted global trade. WTO rules supersede the laws of member nations. Domestic laws that restrict trade, such as environmental protection or energy conservation laws, can be overturned by challenges by one nation against another. Therefore, increasingly, national governments find themselves unable to restrict corporate demands. This shift away from national sovereignty and toward corporate control globally is not apparent to most of us primarily because we get our news mostly from the major news networks which are themselves owned by large transnational corporations. In addition, the United States has shifted strategy from that of global control via corporations to a strategy of increased military intervention.

In the face of all these oppressive circumstances, what can ordinary people do? It may appear that ordinary people are powerless. However, critical theories point toward collective resistance as an agent of liberation. The main idea behind resistance theory is that people who are oppressed should not just sit back and take it. Although it is not always obvious to people exactly how they are being oppressed, they can often act in ways that oppose their oppression.

This opposition can take many different forms. Overt behavioral opposition is visible to observers, and private, or mental, opposition is more difficult for an observer to detect. People often adapt overtly to circumstances they face while privately opposing those circumstances. Theorists such as Anyon (1983) and Apple (1985) have called this form of opposition accommodation or pragmatic acceptance. For example, many people who are bilingual accommodate English-only policies by speaking English in public, but privately they advocate bilingualism.

Overt behavioral opposition can be, on the one hand, consciously directed toward extensive and long-term social change or, on the other hand, directed toward making one's own immediate life a little better; or it can be anywhere in between. For example, protests in the 1990s and 2000s against the World Trade Organization and U.S. war policies brought together thousands of people worldwide. Although these protests have not reversed major policies, they have prompted some wealthy countries to forgive Third World debt and address global poverty. However, not all resistance to authority is consciously directed toward extensive social change. For example, some teenagers of color, especially young men, choose to join gangs partly because they see their own futures as limited because they are poor, because the adult males whom they know have been marginalized and oppressed, and because their race and culture often are not accepted as equal to those of Whites in society's marketplaces. Although society tells them to go to school to make their life circumstances equal to those of Whites, some do not accept this suggestion and therefore join gangs as a form of self-help and resistance. These teenagers' resistance to dominant social norms can be interpreted as an attempt to create more meaningful lives for themselves. In many cases as Young (2004) notes, they use the experiences in their social world to make meaning out of the complex circumstances in which they strive to succeed. Most members of their community, however, view such behavior as harmful to their group's status.

These examples illustrate quite different forms of resistance to oppression, but what they have in common is the refusal of people to accept restrictions that the social system attempts to impose on their lives and their happiness. In addition, these examples attempt to disrupt and challenge common explanations offered by teachers and other school personnel for why some poor students and students of color experience difficulties in school contexts. Rather than situating the problem facing these students in their cultural or familial environments, critical theories recognize how structural and institutional factors, such as racism, inequitable school funding, and low student expectations, impede student academic engagement.

The important point for teachers to realize is that many people are already engaged in a struggle against oppression without necessarily having been taught social theory. Many people, often as part of a group, oppose on a daily basis what they see as unfair authority or restrictions imposed by someone else. In school, this may take countless forms, such as girls resisting being viewed as sex objects, students in wheelchairs ganging up against those who tease them, or students living below the poverty line who refuse to obey middle-class teachers with low expectations of them. Furthermore, oppressed communities are often engaged in organized forms of resistance, although children may not yet be cognizant of the issues in the same way that adults in the community view those issues. For example, local chapters of the National Association for the Advancement of Colored People (NAACP), Indian rights organization such as the American Indian Movement, local gay rights or disability rights organizations, or local National Organization of Women (NOW) chapters often have organized strategies for addressing specific issues of discrimination.

These naturally occurring examples of resistance are a good place to start teaching about social issues because they are a part of real-life issues with which students can identify. In addition, organizations often produce newsletters that provide useful information about issues. After studying an issue, students may decide that their present form of resistance is not as effective as alternative forms. For example, resisting racism by refusing to learn may validate the low expectations of some White teachers. That strategy is not usually as effective as resisting racism by learning as much as possible and achieving academic success in order to gain social power, thus making certain that others do not have to endure a similar experience. Rather than dismiss or ignore students' opposition to authority, however, educators can use this opposition as a beginning point to analyze issues.

Kumashiro (2002) points out that many educators who say they want to see change for social justice resist acting, to the extent that we are comfortable with what is "commonsensical." He commented that "perhaps we resist antioppressive practices because they trouble how we think and feel about not only the Other but also ourselves" (57). For example, many critical educators who are concerned about social justice "refuse to engage with queer theory" (p. 57) because it calls attention to the role of heterosexuals as perpetrators of sexual oppression.

Sociological Theory of Culture

Chapter 5 described cultural transmission theory as anthropologists have developed it. Many anthropologists, and indeed many advocates of the Multicultural Education approach, believe that behavior is guided mainly by culturally learned ideas and that society is the way it is, largely because of our cultural beliefs and values. Change the culture, and social institutions will change. Furthermore, many cultural practices are valuable in and of themselves and can be maintained even if the life circumstances of a group change.

Advocates of Multicultural Social Justice Education see culture somewhat differently. To them, much of everyday culture is an adaptation to life's circumstances, which have been in part determined by group competition for resources. Certainly, some aspects of culture are passed down from one generation to the next. Language is a good example: Most of us simply learn and use the language developed by our ancestors, although we may make small contributions to this language during our lifetime.

At the same time, however, culture is continually created and recreated on an ongoing, everyday basis. Consider Japanese American culture in a historical context. In *Strangers from a Different Shore,* Takaki (1989) discusses how Asian Americans have continually struggled to gain acceptance in mainstream society. He writes:

> Asian newcomers encounter a prevailing vision of America as essentially a place where European immigrants would establish a homogenous white society and where nonwhites would have to remain "stranger".... But the Asian immigrants chose not to let the course of their lives be determined completely by the "necessity" of race and class in America.... Throughout their history in this country, Asians have been struggling in different ways to help America accept its diversity. (pp. 472–473)

Suzuki (1977) pointed out that many social scientists have attributed the economic and educational success of Japanese Americans to inherited cultural patterns from Japan: "strong family structure, emphasis on education, Protestant-type work ethic and high achievement motivation—values deeply rooted in the cultural milieu of Meiji-era Japan" (p. 153). Such social scientists assume that culture is an inheritance from previous generations and that Japanese American culture is a blend of Japanese culture and Anglo culture. Suzuki argues that, although Japanese Americans have retained some inherited cultural forms, what was retained and how it has been changed and redeveloped in the United States has depended strongly on the sociopolitical circumstances that Japanese Americans have encountered. Japanese Americans have had to deal with several factors: racism during World War II and the internment camps; the loss of possessions as a result of internment; quotas placed on Japanese immigration, which kept the Japanese American population very small; and the demand for technical workers immediately after the war. Suzuki described how Japanese Americans tried to reestablish themselves after the war. "It seemed prudent for them to adopt a low-profile strategy that would not attract too much attention nor elicit adverse reaction. Thus, it is understandable why the Nisei (second-generation) has been stereotyped as quiet, hardworking, non-assertive, dependable and accommodating" (p. 151).

Values and cultural patterns have provided some of the substance for interpreting and adapting to the American experience, but sociopolitical factors such as racism and economic circumstances have also been important. Japanese American culture is continually being re-created as Japanese Americans confront, interpret, and respond to social conditions. For this reason, Suzuki (1984) has warned that overemphasis on culture "has led some to pursue ethnicity almost for its own sake." Similarly, he argues that it has led others to believe that multicultural education consists merely of including ethnic content in the curriculum. With this belief, culture takes on limited meaning and comes to suggest only foods, festivals, fairs, and folk tales, as well as exotic or primitive lifestyles. Because of this overemphasis and narrow meaning, Suzuki continues, "the social realities of racism, sexism, and class inequality are often overlooked or conveniently forgotten" (p. 300). He then points out that ignoring or downplaying the importance of social structure and "the position of an ethnic group in that structure ... can lead to the mistaken and conservative view that ethnic subcultures are rooted in the past and are static and unchanging" (p. 300).

If culture involves how people make sense of the conditions of their lives, it might make more sense to attend to those conditions than to culture itself. Consider how male and female cultures in sex-segregated workplaces often take form. Those who hold secretarial jobs, usually women, are rewarded by their employers with little or no career-ladder opportunities as well as relatively low salaries. Consequently, women holding such jobs gradually learn to seek some of their rewards for working from co-workers. (Making friends with other secretaries brings satisfaction that routine word processing for a small paycheck does not.) In addition, they learn to confine work to working hours, since working overtime will not advance them in a career and may not even bring overtime pay. Such women develop a culture that nurtures relationships and cooperation and that is oriented toward completing assigned work during assigned hours only. On the other hand, the bosses for whom they work, usually men, often have access to a career ladder with increased pay and power. Getting the work done and spending time outside normal work hours on work-related matters pays off more than developing relationships with co-workers. The men, therefore, develop a culture that is somewhat impersonal, intense, and competitive. Since culture emerges as an adaptation to conditions and access to resources, which are based in part on membership in unequal groups, at issue are conditions and access that, if changed, will lead to changes in behavior.

As these examples illustrate, culture represents a group's attempt to interpret, give meaning to, and function within shared circumstances. McCarthy (1998) noted that too often "culture, identity, and community are narrowly read as the final property of particular groups based on ethnic origins" (p. 148). Teachers commonly conflate ethnicity and culture, seeing them as synonymous and culture as a thing rather than as a process.

If culture is viewed as an ongoing creation of everyday life, however, culture is not only a reflection of conditions in which communities live, but also a site of power. Popular culture includes the movies, music, 'zines, video games, fashions, and graffiti that young people consume and produce. As a site of power, it serves as a context in which young people make meaning and can exercise some control. As Giroux (2000) pointed out, for kids, popular culture "is one of the few places where they can speak for themselves, produce alternative public spheres, and represent their own interests" (p. 13). Through popular cultural forms such as music or graffiti art, youth talk back at the various forms of control over their lives, and they imagine public spaces where ordinary people have the power to speak and create. Some teachers draw on popular culture, for example, by teaching literacy skills through music videos or poetry slams. When popular culture is viewed politically, it means developing youth's ability to use popular cultural forms to generate the power to act.

Taking a critical perspective toward culture also entails questioning dominant cultures. For example, many teachers who work with multicultural education study "other" cultures (i.e., cultures within communities of color and nations outside the United States) but do not look critically at mainstream White American culture. One might ask, what is it about White American culture that has led to a history of people of European descent claiming superiority over other peoples of the world? As another example, disability scholars question the taken-for-grantedness conceptions of "normal." As Titchkosky (2000) points out, "normalcy is the unmarked viewpoint from which deviance is observed" (p. 207). But if one views "normal" from the standpoint of having been marked as "deviant," one begins to see ways in which so-called normal society has defined others in a way that upholds socially constructed notions about normalcy that benefit some people at the expense of others. In this way, disability is a place from which to see, a standpoint from which to interpret the dominant culture. Similarly, "of color" serves as a place from which to critically analyze White culture, and female serves as a place from which to critically analyze patriarchal culture.

Essentially, then, one should study culture not just to appreciate and admire it, but also to understand the sociopolitical circumstances that helped give rise to it. One should recognize that members of a given group struggle to change their sociopolitical circumstances, which in turn will result in some cultural change.

Identity and Democracy
Multicultural Social Justice educators view learning as active, social, and inextricably entwined with identity development. Like Multicultural Education advocates, they see learning as a process of constructing knowledge through the interaction of mind and experience. Knowledge always has a concrete basis, and young people need concrete experience in order to develop knowledge by interacting mentally and to some extent physically with people and objects around them. Knowledge that is poured into a passive mind is quickly forgotten. As Dewey (1938) remarked, "The educator cannot start with knowledge already organized and proceed to ladle it out in doses" (p. 82). In addition, Vygotsky's

(1986) social cognitive theory points up the importance of culture and language to facilitate learning. He believes that language is a social and cultural phenomenon that is central to the development of thinking and that cognitive development is greatly influenced by one's cultural and social environment. The knowledge that children remember and use relates to their interests and social and cultural milieu, comes in a language that they understand, is constructed by the children (often with guidance from a teacher, parent, or another child), and includes their active involvement.

Claiming intellectual power entails learning to see oneself as capable of producing and using knowledge and connecting this view of self with one's ethnic, racial, and gender identity. Generally speaking, White heterosexual male students, particularly those from middle or affluent backgrounds, have no difficulty seeing people like themselves as producers of knowledge, even if they don't see themselves personally in that way. (You can test this claim by asking children to draw a picture of a scientist. Regardless of who the children are, their pictures usually depict someone who is White, male, and wearing a lab coat.)

Murrell (2002, pp. 52–54) developed a framework for learning that places students and their developing identities at the center. The framework has five components of learning:

- Self-definition, in which young people explore themselves and try on different roles.
- Self-mobilization, in which young people learn to use their interests as a basis for sustained effort, commitment, and engagement in learning.
- Recursive appropriation of signs, in which young people learn to use symbol systems and various academic cultural forms as tools for interpretation and meaning-making.
- Inventive reappropriation of signs, in which young people use symbols and other forms of representation created by others to express their own meanings.
- Belonging, in which young people develop identities that connect them with an intellectual community of learners.

Notice the connections among identity exploration, learning to see oneself as a knowledge creator, and developing identity in a community context or in relationship to others.

To advocates of Multicultural Social Justice Education, connecting one's sense of self with the authority to create and use knowledge for one's own purposes and the good of one's community is empowering. Consider a class of urban high school students of color who, through the use of research, learned to identify specifically how their neighborhood was denied basic city services. They learned to formulate questions and gather data, and at the same time read sophisticated analyses of institutional racism and institutionalized poverty. School suddenly became relevant to them in ways that it had not been before. As school knowledge spoke to the realities of their lives, and as they were helped to learn to use research tools to examine those realities more closely, they began to take on the identity of scholar activist. Some of those students are now juniors and seniors in the university where one of us teaches. The students credit a team of teachers who engaged them as described here with helping urban youth learn to claim education as a tool for themselves and their communities.

RECOMMENDED PRACTICES

Multicultural Social Justice Education has much in common with the Multicultural Education approach, and it also borrows from the other three approaches. However, it is distinctly different from the other approaches. First, we will describe and discuss four practices that are unique to it, and then we will briefly discuss practices drawn from previously discussed approaches. Table 6-1 summarizes recommended practices that are specific to this approach, as well as practices it shares with other approaches. Readers will find practical illustrations of these recommended practices in *Turning on Learning* (Grant & Sleeter, 2006).

Practicing Democracy

U.S. citizens believe in the ideals of democracy, which are written into documents such as the Constitution, the Bill of Rights, and the Declaration of Independence. However, advocates of Multicultural Social Justice Education point out that most schools do not actively encourage democracy. There, the practice of democracy often does not go beyond reading the Constitution and learning about the three branches of government in a social studies class.

Advocates of Multicultural Social Justice Education point out that practicing democracy also means learning to articulate one's interests, to openly debate issues with one's peers, to organize and work collectively with others, to acquire power, to exercise power, and so forth. Schools are one of the institutions in which democracy can be cultivated. Dewey (1938) believed that democracy requires citizens who are capable of critical thought and collective social action. These skills are not developed by telling people to think or by explaining the principles of democracy, but rather by practicing critical thought and social decision making in school. Dewey saw schools as ideal laboratories for developing an informed and active citizenry because schools are social institutions inhabited by groups of future citizens. The raw material is there. He wrote: "Most children are naturally 'sociable.' Isolation is even more irksome to them than to adults. A genuine community life has its ground in this natural sociability. But community life does not organize itself in an enduring way purely spontaneously. It requires thought and planning ahead" (1938, p. 56). It is not enough just to know that the Constitution exists or that the law says that Americans are equal: Citizens need to learn to make these ideas work for them. As Banks (2004) emphasized, "Students must attain democratic values in school if we ever hope to change the political, social, and economic structures of stratified societies and nation-states because they are the future citizens and leaders" (p. 10).

Parker (2003) explained that teaching for democracy should mean preparing young people for enlightened political engagement: "the action or participatory domain of citizenship" (p. 33), such as voting, contacting officials, deliberating, and engaging in boycotts, based on enlightenment, or the "knowledge, norms, values, and principles that shape this engagement" (p. 34). These norms, values, and knowledge include literacy, knowledge about issues and the political process, tolerance of diverse communities and diverse points of view, and commitment to liberty. They also include being able to judge the relative value and veracity of conflicting knowledge claims in order to ascertain the best courses of action that balance individual liberties with the common good. To Freire (1985), this practice would produce women and "men who organize themselves reflectively for action rather than [women and] men who are organized for passivity" (p. 82).

Shor (1980) discusses helping students become subjects rather than objects in the classroom. According to this view, students should learn to direct much of their learning and to do so responsibly rather than always being directed by someone else. This is not to say that teachers should abdicate and simply let students do whatever they want. Such a response can result in chaos or "trivial pursuit." Rather, teachers should guide and direct so that students can grow and develop a sense of responsibility in the way they make decisions. McPhie (1988) argues that students should have the opportunity to debate issues and make decisions that affect their immediate lives, both directly and through representation, as long as those decisions abide by the principle of hierarchical authority. He points out that educators have allowed student-government elections to become too much of a popularity contest, with a carnival atmosphere, and that little is done to teach students how to effectively lobby to promote change (p. 152).

Many observers argue that empowering students is the most effective, not to mention the most ethical, way of dealing with discipline. By learning to obey others, young people may learn discipline but not responsibility because obedience does not require examining situations, thinking through alternative courses of action, or forecasting the consequences of various courses of action.

Consider the example of a junior high social studies teacher who has built into his curriculum opportunities for student decision making and student exercise of power, specifically so that his students, who are working class and racially diverse, can practice affecting an institution. After teaching students about various forms of government, he has the class select a form to use to govern the class (the usual selection being representative democracy). Under his guidance, the class then practices that form for a period of time. He also has the class run school-wide elections: They organize balloting, make campaign posters, plan campaign strategies, and so forth. He provides opportunities for them to select topics to research in small groups and to plan their research strategies. Again, he guides their thinking so that their decisions are usually workable; when their decisions are not workable, the students understand why not and what might work better next time.

Practicing democracy also has implications for how teachers interact with the communities they serve. A teacher or a school committed to democracy makes a point of involving parents in deciding on the goals and educational practices of the school. The parents and the community are viewed both as partners and as valuable resources. The community actively works to connect with the school and to extend the programs and experiences begun during the school day. For example, the community library staff and the school teaching staff work together in preparation for students to visit their capitol. Parents are accepted as valuable members of their son's or daughter's educational team. They are seen as able to contribute much more than telling their children to go to school, to listen to the teacher, and to behave. The utter centrality of providing students with the opportunity to develop and participate in the democratic life of schools and involving teachers, parents, and community members in collaborative, educational efforts is illustrated quite compellingly in a recent publication highlighting schools engaged in attempts to democratize education (Apple & Beane, 1995).

Analyzing the Circumstances of One's Own Life

Earlier, we discussed the concept of resistance; here we develop its implications. Anyon (1981) explains that people have a practical consciousness that coexists with a theoretical consciousness. Practical consciousness refers to one's common-sense understanding of one's own life, of how the system works, and of "everyday attempts to resolve the class, race, gender and other contradictions one faces" (p. 126). Theoretical consciousness refers to dominant social ideologies, explanations that one learns from how the world works that purport that the world is fair and just as it is. These two sets of consciousness do not always mesh; most of us learn to believe a mixture of them. For example, children are taught that America is the golden land of opportunity and that anyone can get ahead by working hard. Yet poor children whose parents work hard for low wages know that this teaching does not necessarily apply to their own families; children of color learn firsthand that racism often thwarts their opportunities. Nevertheless, schools proclaim the dominant ideology, rarely giving much attention to insights that run counter to it that may develop in everyday life.

Advocates of Multicultural Social Justice Education recommend that schooling help students analyze their own lives in order to develop their practical consciousness about real injustices in society and to develop constructive responses. Freire (1985) long used this approach to help South American peasants learn to read, having them learn words that would help them examine the limitations placed on their own lives, such as vastly unequal land distribution. Most reading texts bear no relationship to their lives, teaching only the dominant group's version of reality. Freire either does not use these texts or teaches students to question them. He viewed empowering pedagogy as a dialogical process in which the teacher acts as a partner with students, helping them to examine the world critically, using a problem-posing process that begins with their own experience and historical location.

The published literature offers more guidance on how to work with adult students in analyzing power relations in their own lives (e.g., Ada, 1988; Curtis & Rasool, 1997; Mayo, 1999; Simon, 1992; Solorzano, 1989) than in doing the same with K–12 level students (Bigelow, 1990; Goldstein, 1995; Peterson, 2000/2001). Following Freire, a teacher starts with students' lived experience and involves students in analysis of that experience, treating students as active agents of knowledge creation and classrooms as democratic public spheres. Class materials are used as tools for expanding students' analyses rather than as content that is simply deposited into the students. For example, Shor (1980) had his students examine hamburgers for nutritional value and then determine who benefits economically when we eat junk food rather than food that is good for us. Kobrin (1992) implemented a collaborative project with four public school teachers in which students were taught to become historians and learned to use history to understand and shape the problems of their own lives.

Salas (2003), an elementary teacher, became concerned about the health issues of her students, particularly asthma and (as she gradually discovered) lead poisoning. So, she integrated into the teaching of health and science a series of investigations into these two health issues. She began by having students locate available material on symptoms, causes, and responses to asthma. Students generated questions they had about it, and also generated lists of ways to prevent it, as well as constructive responses to asthmatic attacks. Salas then, with her class, investigated asthma and lead poisoning as health issues that affect impoverished communities much more than affluent communities. After gathering background information about these issues, students designed science projects that looked into children's health. Their projects involved creating a hypothesis, gathering data, and formulating conclusions. Salas's work illustrates how teachers can engage young people in examining conditions that affect them personally, connect personal experiences with broader power relations, and do so within curricular subject areas.

Similarly, one could help Latino students analyze the impact of current immigration legislation on themselves and their communities, examining its effect on undocumented workers as well as on those who have been citizens for years. Students could survey their neighborhoods for patterns of employment among adults and also for ties, if any, with relatives in Puerto Rico, Mexico, Cuba, and so forth. Tate (1995) encourages math teachers to adopt culturally relevant teaching methods. He gives an example of a teacher and her students who used math to analyze community problems (e.g., tax incentives that supported the location of liquor stores near the school) and to influence change through the production and public sharing of quantitative data (e.g., maps and graphs presented to the city council).

Members of historically privileged groups can also learn from their own lives how their privileged position allows them advantages that others cannot afford or gain access to. For example, middle-class White students can analyze housing patterns in their community to determine where the various racial, ethnic, and social class groups live. To look into the basis of housing patterns, they can interview someone from Fair Housing or some realtors; they can also investigate how zoning laws are made and by whom. To examine the effects of housing patterns, they can compare two different neighborhoods in terms of access to schools, to public transportation, or to bank loans. It is imperative, in fact, that students reflect on the ways "whiteness" bestows on them particular privileges. In this way, students may come to recognize their own complicity in forms of oppression, the destructive impact it has on their own humanity, and the need for them to contest injustice in all its forms (Frankenberg, 1993; Sleeter, 1994; Tatum,1994).

Students should analyze not only their own lives but also their responses to life circumstances. For example, many children who live at or below the poverty level, many gay and lesbian students, and many students of color give up and drop out, recognizing that society and the school are strongly biased against them. Although their interpretation of society may be quite correct, their response is not constructive. They are not, according to Hale (1982), seeing school as a place to gain an education for struggle and survival. Dropping out, having babies, taking drugs, joining a gang, and other behaviors may be active forms of opposition, but these forms do not empower the young to change the circumstances that they are facing. Criticizing aspects of the student revolt of the 1960s, Aronowitz and Giroux (1985) argued that "if students are to be empowered by school experiences, one of the key elements of their education must be that they acquire mastery of language as well as the capacity to think conceptually and critically" (p. 158). What these authors are stressing is the need for young people to recognize those responses that will empower them, probably requiring them to use school to develop the skills needed to work for social change and to better their own lives. Writer bell hooks (1994) envisions schooling as a means for liberation, advocating a pedagogy that empowers both teachers and students to actively oppose dominance inside the classroom as well as outside.

Developing Social Action Skills

Developing social action skills brings democratic political skills to bear on issues involving race, class, and gender inequalities in the students' everyday world. Bennett (2002) defines social action skills as "the knowledge, attitudes, and skills needed to help bring about political, social, and economic changes" (p. 210). She argues that ignoring the fact that some groups "are unable to gain, maintain, and effectively use political power, to ignore this goal, is to make a sham out of the rest of multicultural education" (p. 210).

Advocates of Multicultural Social Justice Education do not expect children to reconstruct the world. Rather, advocates view schools as connected with other institutions in society, either working with most institutions to reinforce inequality or working with opposition movements to institute change. Suzuki (1984) argued that "the schools cannot avoid transmitting values. ... The only honest position educators can take is to impart values they believe reflect their vision of the highest achievable human ideals"; educators should recognize that "while the schools cannot operate independent of the prevalent culture, they can still play a significant role in the process of social change" (pp. 303–304).

Advocates of this approach view the school as a laboratory or training ground for preparing a socially active citizenry. Bennett (2002) argues that this preparation should begin at the kindergarten level in classrooms operating democratically, as described earlier. Thus, students learn to begin seeing themselves as powerful agents within a social institution. Primary-grade teachers often ask if their age group of students can participate in social action. The answer is that they can and actually do participate in social action, for example, when they lobby to get home and school rules changed to meet their interests and needs. For example, several students in a first-grade class, who were tired of drinking white milk each day, wondered why they could not have chocolate milk sometimes—at least one or two days a week. These students joined with the rest of their classmates and approached their teacher with this idea. Their teacher told them that the school did not order chocolate milk. The students asked, "Why couldn't the school order it sometimes?" They argued that the same brand of milk they received at school was available in the store as both white milk and chocolate milk. Some students said their parents bought them chocolate milk. Their teacher then informed them that the lunchroom manager had to decide this matter. The students asked if they could write the manager a letter and explain how they felt. They did, and in short, the students are now receiving chocolate milk twice a week.

Older students can engage in more sophisticated social action projects. Banks (1994) recommended a variety of projects:

> Conducting a survey to determine the kinds of jobs which most minorities have in local hotels, restaurants, and firms, and if necessary, urging local businesses to hire more minorities in top level positions.
>
> Conducting boycotts of businesses that refuse to hire minorities in top level positions.... Conducting a survey to determine what local laws exist (and how they are enforced) regarding open housing, discrimination in public accommodations, etc., and if necessary, developing recommendations regarding changes which should be made in the laws or in the ways in which they should be implemented. Presenting these recommendations to appropriate public officials and pressuring them to act on the recommendations. (p. 123–124)

The purpose of such projects is to politicize students' resistance—to help students turn resistance activity into constructive political activity.

For example, Reed and Davis (1999) described a project in which a teacher helped urban high school students to consider changes they would like to see in their lives. The students decided that they would like to begin by making their environment brighter and more inviting. They identified organizing a school cleanup campaign as something they could actually do. Over the year, the students took charge of organizing peers and people in their neighborhood in order to improve the school physically. In the process, students developed a sense of efficacy. Reed and Davis noted that by the end of the year, school attendance and grades had improved, and students felt empowered and able to make a difference in their lives.

A number of curriculum guides, such as *Open Minds to Equality* (Schniedewind & Davidson, 1998), are available to help teachers teach students social action skills. *Open Minds to Equality* provides first a step-by-step series of activities to build group cooperation, then collective skills in analysis of local issues and taking action. *Rethinking Globalization* (Bigelow & Peterson, 2002) provides a wealth of resources teachers can use to help children and youth understand how power plays out in current global economic restructuring, how

ordinary people are affected, and what ordinary people can do. A role play entitled "The People v. Global Sweatshops" helps students learn to distinguish
between systems and individual people. It has five characters: multinational corporations, poor country ruling elite, poor country workers, U.S. consumers, and
system of profit. "System of profit" is introduced by explaining: "This gets complicated. You are not a person or even a group of people, but a system. We like to
blame crimes on people. But in this case, the real criminal is not human. The fact
that you are invisible is part of your strength" (p. 185). The directions then point
out that people often consider profit seeking to be a part of human nature rather
than something that could be otherwise, which gives the system a huge amount of
power. By making the system visible, the role play tries to help students question
and change it. *Rethinking Globalization* shows various strategies young people use
to take action. For instance, Canadian labor activist Craig Kielburger was only 13
years old when he became active. In a speech before the American Federation of
Teachers in 1996, he called on teachers to believe in young people, challenge them
to play a greater role in society, and not underestimate their power.

Coalescing

One of the main differences between the Multicultural Social Justice Education
approach and the Single-Group Studies approach is that the former promotes the
formation of coalitions across race, class, and gender lines. There are some very
good reasons for learning to form coalitions. One reason is that race, social class,
and gender often should not be treated as separate issues. Not only do these forms
of difference involve common concerns of oppression, but everyone's identity
includes multiple forms of difference such as gender, language, religion, race or
ethnicity, and social class; separating the issues is often somewhat artificial.

   Coalitions are also more powerful than individual groups. For example,
although the poor may be economically weak as a power base, they gain strength
when joined by middle-class people of color and additional strength if joined by
White women. Advocates have noted that disenfranchised groups sometimes find
themselves fighting over crumbs, whereas if they worked together, they might all
be able to make substantial gains.

   Furthermore, coalescing guards against a kind of chauvinism that can result
when issues of race, class, and gender are dealt with separately, and helps avoid
the limitations of taking on an "ism" at a superficial level. For example, hooks
(1994) criticized "lifestyle-based feminism" (p. 70), which she saw as involving
adopting symbols of feminism without becoming involved in the real-world
issues that women from diverse backgrounds face. She wrote, "In this capitalist
culture, feminism and feminist theory are fast becoming a commodity that only
the privileged can afford" (p. 71). By linking feminist causes with the concerns of
women of color and women in poverty, White women would be able to participate in making substantive progress toward justice. By failing to make such a link-
age, economically privileged White women would enhance their own lives but at
the same time remain perpetrators of other people's oppression.

   Forming coalitions is not easy. Throughout our nation's history, groups have
attempted to coalesce, often fragmenting as a result of internal competition. For

example, Roediger (1991) explored the dynamics underlying the formation of the White working class during the post-Revolutionary period, ultimately revealing how the tendencies of White laborers to define themselves against and forge an identity in relationship to an enslaved Black class inhibited them from recognizing the economic system accountable for the exploitation of both. Advocates warn that people need to recognize and struggle against all forms of oppression, keeping in mind that the common goal is eliminating oppression rather than simply furthering one's own interests. This awareness involves learning how to handle compromise and how to cooperate with members of diverse groups. It also involves continually examining one's own biases and recognizing the sources of one's own advantages.

For example, African Americans, Latinos, and Asians find themselves divided along gender and class lines to the extent that middle-class males of all colors fail to take seriously the concerns of women and working-class members of their racial groups. African Americans and Latinos at times find themselves on opposite sides of the fence with regard to bilingual education. Whereas bilingual Latinos argue that language is inseparable from identity and bilingualism supports a bicultural identity, many African Americans who are not bilingual see attention to language as draining resources and energy from the education of monolingual African American children.

One promising approach to coalition building is using the school as a base for local social action projects that draw together diverse groups to accomplish something for the community. The school can serve as a coalescing point if community input is regarded seriously and not just as a rubber-stamp PTA. For example, Carter and Chatfield (1986) described a school that included students who were White middle class, Mexican migrant, Filipino, and Southeast Asian. The school became involved with helping a senior citizens' community nearby, and this action helped the school develop cohesion and identification with a common community.

Commonalities with Previous Approaches

Multicultural Social Justice Education shares with Single-Group Studies an emphasis on social issues, a concern with representing the interests of oppressed groups, and its desire to mobilize young people to work actively for social justice. It shares with the Human Relations approach an interest in developing cooperation among students and a concern for developing student self-concept. And it too, desires to eliminate stereotyping, but it does not view as particularly effective the use of lessons about stereotyping or attempts to deal with stereotyping without changing the social sources of stereotypes. As is true of Teaching the Exceptional and Culturally Different, this approach agrees that teaching should start where students are, should relate to their experiential background, build on the language and learning style they bring from home, and develop more effectively students' mastery of basic skills. But it diverges from that approach in its long-term purpose.

Multicultural Social Justice Education embraces the recommended practices of the Multicultural Education approach, especially the idea that the school and the classroom should reflect and celebrate diversity. For both approaches, the curriculum—including materials, visual displays, films, guest speakers, and content taught orally—should represent the experiences, perspectives, and contributions of diverse groups and should do so in a comprehensive rather than in a fragmented way. The curriculum should be thus formulated all the time, in all subject areas. Gender-inclusive language should be used, and bilingualism or multilingualism should be endorsed. The curriculum should be equally accessible to all student groups; grouping practices or teaching procedures that enable only certain groups of students access to high-status knowledge or better teaching should be avoided. Teachers should build on students' learning styles and cultural assets rather than assume that everyone learns best in the same way, and they should maintain high expectations for all students. Cooperative learning should be used to develop skills and attitudes of cooperation.

Teachers should cultivate behavior that affirms and includes a wide diversity of students, and should work to develop positive self-concepts in all students. (Incidentally, educators warn that White male students often find the approach discussed in this chapter threatening to their own self-concepts, and they strongly suggest that teachers work to affirm these students as individuals and include them as valued partners in social action efforts.) Biased forms of evaluation of learning should be avoided; evaluation should be used for improving instruction, not for sorting and ranking students. Home/community-school relationships should be developed, and efforts to invite and include parents should be active, particularly as relating to parents who are at or below the poverty level and/or minority. Staffing patterns should reflect diversity and offer a variety of role models for males and females of different race and class backgrounds.

PUTTING IT INTO ACTION

Elizabeth Harvey was having mixed emotions about her upcoming fortieth birthday. She was happy and also unhappy to be celebrating the big "four-O," but she also felt special because her best friend from college, Beth, was flying in to celebrate the day with her. College, she thought to herself, seems so long ago; but with Beth, they would relive the good memories. Liz had been a campus activist. She was one of the student leaders who fought to give the students a choice of a non-Western Civilization course. The faces of the students who had worked with her to make the non-Western course happen were mentally passing before her, when a distant bell interrupted the reminiscing. The ringing of the bell signaled her that her ninth-grade U.S. history class would convene in three minutes. She quickly washed and stored her coffee cup, gathered up her papers, and headed out of the teachers' lounge and up the stairs to greet her class.

The class was composed of 28 students: 13 were White, 8 were African Americans, 6 were Latino (3 Mexican Americans, 2 Puerto Ricans, and 1 Guatemalan refugee), and 1 was a Native American (Winnebago tribe). The socioeconomic status of the students ranged from working class to below the poverty line. The students were typical of those found in many classrooms. Their achievement levels and reading scores spanned a wide range: 10 of the students were reading on or above grade level, 12 were reading between one and two grades below grade level, and 6 were reading at the sixth-grade level. This class was typical of the classes Liz had taught at O'Henry High School during her seven years of teaching there.

Directly across the hall from Liz, Erick Cosby taught general science. He and Liz were the same age and often joked about their big four-O birthdays. Erick had grown up in Nashville, Tennessee, and had come to Central City after spending four years in the army before he was honorably discharged because of a service-related accident. The student composition of Erick's class was very similar to that of Liz's class, except that two of his students were in wheelchairs and two were Hmong.

Next door to Liz's room was Ross Wisser's room. Ross had been teaching English at O'Henry for the last 20 years. He was divorced, lived alone, and was a sports enthusiast. He spent most of his free time following Central City's four major sports teams. He often team-taught with Liz and Erick because he liked their style and enjoyed teaming up on some units or assignments.

Because Liz, Ross, and Erick taught the same classes of students, they often worked together to plan activities and assignments that would combine English, social studies, and science. Presently, Erick's classes were studying health, Liz's classes were studying city government and local agencies, and Ross's classes were studying general composition. The philosophy and style of teaching of all three teachers were geared to challenge and involve the students as much as possible in curriculum planning and instructional processes and to include activities and experiences that would take into account the students' home background and place in the economic structure, as well as any so-called learning or physical disabilities. All three also believed that if their students were going to succeed in life, the students needed to know how the system worked and develop the skills and knowledge necessary to take charge of their own lives.

Earlier that day, during their planning period, Erick had persuaded Liz and Ross to use County Hospital as their theme of study. He argued that the recent controversy about closing the facility was receiving a good deal of media coverage. The mayor's office and city council were locked in dispute over whether to close the hospital and have its services picked up by the other hospitals in the area, renovate it so that the community could keep its own hospital, or build a new hospital at a site closer to the center of town. He maintained that this lively debate would be excellent for Liz's unit. The students could learn not only about the different branches of city government and the way laws are passed but also how the members of the council, the mayor, and the different factions within the council bargain and compromise to get their way. The students could also study how people often vote along racial lines and how the benefits and rewards that a councilperson's district will receive often give direction to the way he or she votes.

Erick added, "You know, there is considerable debate as to which companies will get the contract for either the renovation or new construction, and one aspect of the debate centers upon the minority representation of the companies bidding for the contract." He suggested that Ross have the students write letters to the newspaper expressing their views on the subject as well as interview people in the neighborhood. He also suggested that the students publish their own newspaper about the topic. Ross added that he could borrow a TV mini-camera so that the students could learn to do real, live TV interviews.

Erick said that he would ask the students to contact doctors and other health personnel to get their views on the role of science in this decision-making process, investigating any medical factors that emerged as for or against the proposed plans. He added, "Results of the students' work could be printed in the newspaper they will publish. What the students learn from this process may not influence the way things at City Hall go on this issue, but it may influence what goes on in City Hall and in the students' lives regarding future issues."

Liz and Ross quickly agreed, telling Erick it was a super idea and now they should begin to get down to details. Ross pointed out that they would need to map this idea against the state content standards they were expected to follow. As Liz groaned, Ross said, "Be a little creative. For instance, a big piece of my curriculum is teaching expository writing. I can teach students to write about anything, and you can't deny that expository writing is important." Erick said that he would be able to identify the science standards that this unit would address, and Liz conceded that she would be able to figure out how to connect the project to her social studies standards. She commented, "But I still think citizenship is a more important goal of education than test score production!"

Liz then suggested that they reserve the little theater for the following Monday, bring all three classes together to see what the students thought of the idea, and if students liked the idea, begin to organize around the three subjects. She said, "We can explain what each student's requirements are, as well as give students the opportunity to work in areas of their own interest."

"One requirement," said Ross, "is to get the students to work together in groups and to make certain that they are integrated across the lines of race, gender, and class. Also, we don't usually have a problem with the kids with disabilities fitting in, but let's make certain they are really a part of the groups."

Liz said, "I believe it is important that we guide the class in a way that students learn how the system works and how they can make it work for them. And something to that effect is in the social studies standards I'm supposed to be following."

Erick said, "Anywhere you go in this world, there are people making decisions that will affect your life. You need to know and understand this fact and learn to become a part of the process. Otherwise, those decision makers will make many of your life decisions for you."

The final bell sounded, and it was time for Liz to start her U.S. history class. She completed greeting her class, and as she moved to close the door to her room, she guardedly called out to Erick, who was doing the same thing across the hall, "Happy four-oh, ol' friend!" Erick pushed the button on his wheelchair, turning himself into direct view of Liz, and said, "The same to you, ol' friend. Let's go and see what they think about the new unit and get ready for our joint meeting tomorrow."

CRITIQUE We opened this chapter by noting that this approach is called different things by different people. This observation points to a difficulty that the approach currently faces and will reflect how we critique it.

In a review of the literature on multicultural education, we found fewer works on this approach than on any other (Grant, Elsbree, & Fondrie, 2004; Sleeter & Grant, 1987). Actually, advocates have come to this approach from a variety of camps. Some have come from the Multicultural Education approach; some from Black studies, women's studies, Asian American studies, or some other Single-Group Studies approach; some from bilingual education after rejecting the remedial/compensatory model that many programs follow; some, disaffected neo-Marxists, after seeing social class critiques as too limited; and some, social reconstructionists, who have only begun to apply this philosophy to race, class, and gender (and who perhaps had applied it mainly to peace education, world hunger, or ecology). As a result, the literature developing the approach is rather scattered, and advocates often do not recognize or dialogue with each other. Earlier we noted that coalition building is difficult; it is also not automatic among advocates of Multicultural Social Justice education.

As a result, the educator who wants to learn about the approach may become frustrated attempting to do so, partly because material is housed under different titles and partly because it is not abundant. In addition, there is relatively little material giving teachers specific guidance in what to do. We located some well-developed theoretical material and a few very specific teaching guides (e.g., Schniedewind & Davidson, 1998; Bigelow, Christensen, Karp, Miner, & Peterson, 1994; Bigelow & Peterson, 2002). Relatively little connects theory with practice in an open-ended fashion that would guide a teacher in developing his or her own plan of action. Having said this, however, teachers will consistently find rich discussions and practical ways of working with this approach in monthly issues of *Rethinking Schools* (available online at http://rethinkingschools.org).

There are few explicit critiques of this approach, although criticisms of multicultural education in general as being too radical perhaps apply more to this approach than to others. We suspect that those who view it as too radical more often ignore it. Next we raise four general problems with the approach and then examine objections from the vantage point of each of the other four approaches.

One problem is with the role of the school in building a "new social order" (Counts, 1982). George Counts, who has written rather extensively about social reconstructionism, asked if the school would dare take such action. Skeptics ask if it can, and there is good reason to question whether it can. Schools are instruments of society, charged with the mission of preparing the young to take their place in society. As Chapter 1 explained, schools go a good job of reproducing the existing society. The standards movement, which by the late 1990s was in full swing, has aimed mainly to make sure that schools ground students in traditional knowledge. This movement expects schools to reproduce society well, not necessarily to change it. Expecting schools to change society may be unrealistic.

Advocates of Multicultural Social Justice Education usually counter that schools alone cannot change society. However, they can collaborate with other institutions in doing so, and because teachers cannot avoid taking a stance toward society, the issue is what stance a teacher will take. We think it is an open question as to how much impact schools can have on social change: This approach or variations of it have not been implemented frequently enough for anyone to know what results can be expected.

A second problem involves the contradiction between having students think for themselves and persuading them to think like the teacher. Multicultural Social Justice Education advocates taking seriously what students think, but students often do not recognize as problems what the teacher sees as problems, nor do students always agree with the teacher's interpretations or solutions. This situation is due in large part to students' lack of experience, background, or exposure, as well as to teachers who do not fully understand how to proceed or who protect vested interests they may have in the status quo. In the vignette, Erick, Liz, and Ross will have to face this issue if some of their students decide that the Country Hospital should be closed and that the people it now serves should make do with other medical facilities. Without necessarily stating it to their students, the three teachers believe that closing the hospital will hurt low-income people, that this action is unfair, and that taxpayers should be willing to make certain that all communities that make up the city have equal access to comparable medical facilities. In setting up the unit, the three will need to decide how much coverage to give to arguments in favor of closing the hospital and how to respond to students who agree with those arguments.

The problem of tension between freedom of thought and taking a multicultural social justice political analysis plays out in debates about "political correctness." For example, Closson (1992) charged that multicultural education removes "the freedom of speech from students who fail to conform to the correct position on a broad spectrum of topics." Even disallowing speech that some communities find offensive, in his view, discriminates against some students by restricting freedom of speech. Walking the tension between freedom of thought and one's own political analysis is difficult to do but very important to attend to.

A third problem lies in implementation more than in conceptualization of the approach itself. Some who believe in the ideals of the approach still teach in very traditional lecture-based ways (Pruyn, 1999). But learning to engage students actively through Multicultural Social Justice Education requires far more than learning steps or seeing lesson plans, since doing so directly opens up very difficult and painful issues in the classroom (Ellsworth, 1989; Obidah, 2000). It is quite possible for an educator to sensitize students to social issues and then leave the students hanging—feeling frustrated and hopeless about what they can do about these issues—or angry. Shor (1980) noted that critical teaching can blow up in a teacher's face if the teacher has not thought carefully about how students may be feeling and has not planned for the constructive release of energy. For example, if students recognize the problems inherent in capitalism, they will not necessarily see what can be done short of tearing down our whole economic structure (which a class of students is powerless to do and for which they probably do not have a full-blown alternative system and a strategy for getting that system instituted). There are constructive actions one can take toward much more circumscribed problems, such as dealing with the provision of medical care for the poor in one's own community, but the teacher needs to be ready to deal with this issue and with the emotions surrounding it.

A fourth problem is that the approach can be implemented in simplistic ways that "fail to address the tremendous inequities that exist in our schools" (Nieto, 2003, p. 7). Nieto points out that, although she advocates and works for multicultural education that is oriented toward social justice, too often she has seen it implemented as a program designed to make children feel good about themselves. We have also seen it take the form of teaching about social issues, in the absence of supporting students' academic achievement or confronting inequity that is structured into schools. Nieto writes: "although educators may call attention to the fact that the curriculum in U.S. schools is becoming more multicultural (an overblown claim in any event), they may neglect to note that the achievement gap between white students and students of color is growing," (p. 7). She argues that who is in the curriculum must be dealt with alongside, rather than instead of, challenging inequitable access to a college-preparation curriculum. Teachers who themselves have not been involved in social movements or social protests, or who are not members of social action organizations, often are the ones least likely to see these larger issues.

With regard to criticisms from the vantage point of the other approaches, the main objections raised by advocates of Teaching the Exceptional and the Culturally Different are that this approach is ideologically-driven, seeks too much (and too unrealistic) change, and diverts students who live at or below the poverty line and students of color from what they really need. Many educators do not see society as fundamentally flawed, and they view the role of education as preparing young people to take part in society, particularly to be employable. They believe that Multicultural Social Justice Education exaggerates problems such as racism, and diverts attention from strong academic teaching. They, as well as others who agree with the magnitude of society's problems, argue that this approach gets students away from mastery of the skills and knowledge they will need to "make it." As Cummins (2000) put it, being critical of "an obsession with test scores and the extremely narrow concept of 'achievement'" comes across as disinterest in academic achievement (p. 247). A principal of an urban high school, for example, told us how important he thought it was that his students acquire the skills to get a job or go to college in order to have a productive role in a society stacked against them. He cautioned that educational approaches such as the one described in this chapter would take time away from that preparatory work, as well as encourage students to expect social changes that will not be forthcoming.

Human Relations educators fear that this approach will aggravate conflict and tension among people, escalating rather than reducing problems. Even though the approach values cooperation, Human Relations educators are concerned that too much open discussion of past and present injustices will fuel the fires of hate and distrust and that social action projects will promote confrontation. They fear that acts performed in the name of social justice will promote anarchy rather than fashion a better society.

Advocates of the Teaching the Exceptional and the Culturally Different approach as well as of the Human Relations approach take issue with a fundamental premise of Multicultural Social Justice Education: that the mainstream of society needs serious restructuring in order to be minimally fair to everyone. Single-Group Studies and Multicultural Education advocates agree with that premise; their objections center around strategy rather than goal. Advocates of Single-Group Studies feel that the approach discussed in this chapter bogs down in building coalitions across groups, making efforts toward change ineffective. For example, although bilingual educators share some similar concerns with sex-equity advocates, there are also major differences of priority between the two groups. Joining forces might make for a stronger front, but hashing out a mutually agreeable common agenda can consume much of the energy of both groups. Historically, coalitions, if they are formed at all, have been fragile. Thus, groups with partially overlapping concerns may wish each other well but choose not to try to work together.

Finally, Multicultural Education advocates generally embrace the intent of this approach but view its feasibility with skepticism. To advocates of Multicultural Social Justice Education, the Multicultural Education approach is too limited and usually not assertive enough. However, to many business-as-usual educators, the Multicultural Education approach is too radical. Multicultural Education advocates know that it is hard to get teachers and administrators seriously interested in implementing their approach, particularly in the context of standards and testing. Multicultural Social Justice Education would be even harder to sell, more controversial, and more different from business as usual. We have also observed a certain amount of elitism among some social reconstructionists who see themselves as "correct" and Multicultural Education advocates as too accommodating. This attitude of elitism fosters distrust between the two approaches, which compounds disputes over goals, assumptions, and strategies.

Our last chapter explains which approach we favor and why. Most of the objections raised about the different approaches center on differences in priorities, assumptions, and perspectives. It cannot be proved that one approach is right and the rest are wrong. Our choice results from our own study of society, our own interactions with people, and our own convictions about which actions will go the farthest toward improving society. If you disagree with us or with your colleagues, we encourage open dialogue, since this is an excellent stimulus to further learning and growth.

REFERENCES

Abberley, P. (1987). The concept of oppression and the development of a social theory of disability. *Disability, Handicap, and Society, 2,* 5–20.

Ada, A. F. (1988). The Pajaro Valley experience. In T. Skutnabb-Kangas & J. Cummins (Eds.). *Minority education: From shame to struggle* (pp. 223–238). Philadelphia: Multilingual Matters.

Anyon, J. (1981). Elementary schooling and distinctions of social class. *Interchange, 12,* 118–132.

Anyon, J. (1983). Intersections of gender and class: Accommodation and resistance by working class and affluent females to contradictory sex-role ideologies. In S. Walker & L. Barton (Eds.). *Gender, class and education* (pp. 19–38). Barcombe, England: Falmer Press.

Apple, M. W. (1985). *Education and power* (Ark ed.). Boston: Routledge & Kegan Paul.

Apple, M. W., & Beane, J. A. (1995). *Democratic schools.* Alexandria, VA: Association for Supervision and Curriculum Development.

Aronowitz, S., & Giroux, H. A. (1985). *Education under siege.* South Hadley, MA: Bergin & Garvey.

Banks, J. A. (1994). *Multiethnic education: Theory and practice,* 3rd ed. Boston: Allyn & Bacon.

Banks, J. A. (1999). *An introduction to multicultural education,* 2nd ed. Boston: Allyn & Bacon.

Banks, J. A. (2004). Introduction: Democratic citizenship in multicultural societies. In J. A. Banks (Ed.). *Diversity and citizenship education* (pp. 1–16). San Francisco: Jossey-Bass.

Bennett, C. I. (2002). *Comprehensive multicultural education,* 5th ed. Boston: Allyn & Bacon.

Berlak, A., & Moyenda, S. (2001). *Taking it personally.* Philadelphia: Temple University Press.

Bigelow, B., Christensen, L., Karp, S., Miner, B., and Peterson B. (1994). *Rethinking our classrooms: Teaching for equality and justice.* Milwaukee Rethinking School.

Bigelow, B., & Peterson, B., Eds. (2002). *Rethinking globalization.* Milwaukee, WI: Rethinking Schools Press.

Bigelow, W. (1990). Inside the classroom: Social vision and critical pedagogy. *Teachers College Record, 91(3),* 437–448.

Brameld, T. (1956). *Toward a reconstructed philosophy of education.* New York: Holt, Rinehart, & Winston.

Carter, T. P., & Chatfield, M. L. (1986). Effective bilingual schools: Implications for policy and practice. *American Journal of Education, 95,* 26–57.

Closson, D. (1992). Politically correct education. Probe Ministries International. Retrieved on May 10, 2005 from http://www.leaderu.com/orgs/probe/docs/pc-educ.html.

Collins, P. H. (1998). *Fighting words.* Minneapolis: University of Minnesota Press.

Counts, G. (1982). *Dare the school build a new social order?* New York: John Day.

Cummins, J. (2000). *Language, power and pedagogy.* Buffalo, NY: Multilingual Matters.

Curtis, A. C., & Rasool, J. A. (1997). Motivating future educators through empowerment: A special case. *Educational Forum, 61(4),* 307–313.

Dei, G. J. S. (1996). *Anti-racism education.* Halifax, Nova Scotia: Fernwood Publishing.

Delgado, R., & Stefancic, J. (2001). *Critical race theory; An introduction.* New York: New York University Press.

Dewey, J. (1938). *Experience and education.* New York: Macmillan.

Ellsworth, E. (1989). Why doesn't this feel empowering? Working through the repressive myths of critical pedagogy. *Harvard Educational Review, 59(3),* 297–324.

Frankenberg, R. (1993). *The social construction of whiteness: White women, race matters.* Minneapolis: University of Minnesota Press.

Freire, P. (1985). *The politics of education: Culture, power, and liberation* (D. Macedo, Trans.). South Hadley, MA: Bergin & Garvey.

Gillborn, D. (1995). *Racism and anti-racism in real schools.* Buckingham, England: Open University Press.

Giroux, H. A. (2000). *Stealing innocence.* New York: St. Martin's Press.

Goldstein, B. S. C. (1995). Critical pedagogy in a bilingual special education classroom. *Journal of Learning Disabilities, 28(8),* 463, 7 charts

Gordon, B. M. (1985). Toward emancipation in citizenship education: The case of African-American cultural knowledge. *Theory and Research in Social Education, 12,* 1–23.

Grant, C. A., Elsbree, A. R., & Fondrie, S. (2004). A decade of research on the changing terrain of multicultural education research. In J. A. Banks & C. M. Banks (Eds.), *Handbook of Research on Multicultural Education,* 2nd ed., pp. 184–210. San Francisco: Jossey Bass.

Grant, C. A., & Sleeter, C. E. (2006). *Turning on learning,* 4th ed. New York: Wiley.

Hale, J. E. (1982). *Black children, their roots, culture, and learning styles.* Provo, UT: Brigham Young University.

Hall, S. (1993). What is this "black" in black popular culture? *Social Justice, 20(1–2),* 104–115.

hooks, b. (1994). *Teaching to transgress: Education as the practice of freedom.* New York: Routledge.

Irvine, J. J. (2003). *Educating teachers for diversity: Seeing with a cultural eye.* New York: Teachers College Press.

Ismi, A. (1998). World Bank: Plunder with a human face. *Z Magazine, 11(2),* 9–11.

Kincheloe, J. L., & Steinberg, S. R. (1997). *Changing multiculturalism.* Buckingham, England: Open University Press.

Kobrin, D. (1992). My country, too: A proposal for a student historian's history of the United States. *Teachers College Record, 94(2),* 329–342.

Kumashiro, K. (2002). *Troubling education: Queer activism and antioppressive pedagogy.* New York: RoutledgeFalmer.

Ladson-Billings, G., & Tate, W. (1995). Toward a critical race theory of education. *Teachers College Record, 97,* 47–68.

Lee, E. (1995). Taking multicultural, antiracist education seriously. In Levine, D. P., et al (Eds.). *Rethinking schools: An agenda for change* (pp. 10–16). New York: New Press, distributed by W.W. Norton.

Linton, S. (1998). *Claiming disability.* New York: New York University Press.

Mayo, P. (1999). *Gramsci, Freire and adult education: Possibilities for transformative action.* London: Zed Books.

McCarthy, C. (1998). *The uses of culture.* New York: Routledge.

McPhie, W. E. (1988). Teaching American democracy in American public schools. *Social Education, 52(2),* 152.

Murrell. P. C., Jr. (2002). *African-centered pedagogy.* Albany, NY: SUNY Press.

Nieto, S. M. (2003). Profoundly multicultural questions. *Educational Leadership, 60(4),* 6–10.

Oakley, A. (1981). *Subject women.* New York: Pantheon.

Obidah, J. E. (2000). Mediating boundaries of race, class, and professional authority as a critical multiculturalist. *Teachers College Record, 102(6),* 1035–1060.

Parker, W. C. (2003). *Teaching democracy.* New York: Teachers College Press.

Perkins, J. (2004). *Confessions of an economic hit man.* San Francisco: Berrett-Koehler Publisher.

Peterson, B. (2000/01). Planting the seeds of solidarity. *Rethinking Schools, 15(2).* Retrieved on September 10, 2003 from http://www.rethinkingschools.org/archive/

Pinar, W. F. (Ed.) (1998). *Queer theory in education.* Mahwah, NJ: Erlbaum.

Pruyn, M. (1994). Becoming subjects through critical practice: How students in one elementary classroom critically read and wrote their world. International *Journal of Educational Reform, 3(1),* 37–50.

Pruyn, M. (1999). *Discourse wars in Gotham West.* Boulder, Co: Westview.

Reed, D. F., & Davis, M. D. (1999). Social reconstructionism for urban students. *Clearinghouse, 72(5)*, 291–294.

Roediger, D. R. (1991). *The wages of whiteness: Race and the making of the American working class.* New York: Verso.

Salas, K. D. (2003). Teaching about toxins. *Rethinking Schools, 18(2).* Retrieved May 15, 2005 from http://www.rethingschools.org/archive/

Schniedewind, N., & Davidson, E. (1998). *Open minds to equality.* 2nd ed. Needham Heights, MA: Allyn & Bacon.

Shaw, G. B. (1921). *Back to Methuselah*, Pt. 1, Act I.

Shor, I. (1980). *Critical teaching and everyday life.* Boston: South End Press.

Simon, R. I. (1992). *Teaching against the grain: Texts for a pedagogy of possibility.* New York: Bergin & Garvey.

Sleeter, C. E. (1994, Spring). White racism. *Multicultural Education, 1(4)*, 5–9.

Sleeter, C. E., & Grant, C. A. (1987). An analysis of multicultural education in the U.S.A. *Harvard Educational Review, 57*, 421–444.

Smith, L. T. (1999). *Decolonizing methodologies.* London: Zed Books, Ltd.

Solorzano, D. G. (1989). Teaching and social change: Reflections on a Freirean approach in a college classroom. *Teaching Sociology, 17*, 218–225.

Suzuki, B. H. (1977). The Japanese-American experience. In M. J. Gold, C. A. Grant, & H. N. Rivlin (Eds.). *In praise of diversity: A resource book for multicultural education* (pp. 139–162). Washington, DC: Teacher Corps.

Suzuki, B. H. (1984). Curriculum transformation for multicultural education. *Education and Urban Society, 16*, 294–322.

Takaki, R. (1989). *Strangers from a different shore.* Boston: Little, Brown.

Tate, W. F. (1995). Returning to the root: A culturally relevant approach to mathematics pedagogy. *Theory into Practice, 34(3)*, 166–173.

Tatum, B. D. (1994). Teaching white students about racism: The search for white allies and the restoration of hope. *Teachers College Record, 95(4)*, 462–476.

Titchkosky, T. (2000). Disability studies: The old and the new. *Canadian Journal of Sociology, 25(2)*, 197–224.

Vygotsky, L. S. (1986). *Thought and language.* E. Hamsman & G. Vankan (Eds. and Trans.). Cambridge, MA: MIT Press.

Young, A. A. Jr. (2004). *The minds of marginalized black men: Making sense of mobility, opportunity, and future life chances.* Princeton, NJ: Princeton University Press.

CHAPTER SEVEN

Our Choice: Multicultural Social Justice Education

By now, you probably have a sense of which approach to multicultural education you prefer. We have tried to present and critique the approaches thoroughly and objectively enough to help you make your own choices. At the same time, we cannot remain neutral and detached. We have a strong sense of which approach we believe goes the furthest toward providing better schooling as well as creating a better society. Furthermore, based on our own experience in schools, our research on schools, and our long-standing study of multicultural education, we feel we have an obligation to share our thinking.

Our thinking is based largely on social conditions that persist and that limit and often damage or destroy the lives of many people. A significant segment of U.S. society has always been poor, and the size of this group in recent years has been growing rather than diminishing. Globally, poverty and hunger are more the norm than is the wealth many of us take for granted. Racism in the United States is as intact now as it was decades ago, even if it has shifted in form somewhat; and as the population of color in the United States grows, one can predict increased competition among racial groups. The family structure in the United States continues to change as more women enter the workforce, but family role changes and cooperative networks are not emerging on a large scale. For example, rather than involving husbands and the extended family more actively in childcare, many families simply reduce the time spent on childcare when the mother takes on additional roles. These are some of the trends and the persistent problems that concern us.

People tend to live in small, rather insulated worlds with others who share their advantages or disadvantages. Consequently, the educator who is experiencing a relatively comfortable and privileged life may have difficulty fully appreciating and understanding the very real problems faced, for example, by the Mexican American father searching desperately for work, the single mother wondering how to make ends meet, or the laid-off worker who feels powerless as the local factories close down. The educator who has had a difficult life may be able to empathize with others with similar experience, but may also assume that every individual can transcend difficulties in the same way that so many have managed to do. Nevertheless, problems and injustices exist, and they are part of the very fabric of U.S. society. There may be periodic improvements (often cosmetic more than fundamental) and these may be widely publicized, but the character and magnitude of the problems have not changed much in the past two or three decades.

The revolt in Los Angeles following the April 1992 acquittal of the police who brutalized Rodney King, the verbal debates between Blacks and Whites after the O. J. Simpson verdict in 1996, the mistreatment and racial profiling of Arab Americans after 9/11, and battles between "red" and "blue" states in 2004 reveal the depth of social divisions that exist in the United States. Although many believe that divisions no longer exist and that the nation has realized its democratic aspirations, the evidence reveals otherwise. Many Americans, including many of our students, viewed these events as isolated and unfortunate but also as unpredictable as a hurricane. Now that the revolt is past, the trial has concluded, the profiling has decreased, and the election is behind us, such "incidents" have been moved to the recesses of the public mind.

We believe that the kinds of events epitomized why Multicultural Social Justice Education must be taken seriously. For example, about a year before the 1992 revolt in Los Angeles, some educators in Southern California told one of us that the rest of the nation has time to address its injustices and to take its diversity more seriously than California has done. The poverty, joblessness, retrenchment, and despair that spawned the outbreak were long in the making, and they were visible to people who lived or worked in inner-city areas every day. In fact, we use the term *revolt* deliberately. The term *riot* suggests a disorganized overreaction to an immediate event, whereas the term *revolt* suggests an uprising against a long-standing system of deprivation.

People who were surprised by the revolt and who viewed its main solution as tighter law enforcement were not looking closely at the systematic impoverishment of large parts of the U.S. population. Across the nation, growing segments of the population, particularly youth in impoverished areas, are feeling locked out, powerless to change their lives, robbed of dignity, and silenced. We believe that it is essential to the survival of the nation that social justice issues be taken seriously. The last approach to multicultural education presented in this book is most explicit in its serious treatment of social justice issues.

The importance of a position that champions both multicultural education and social justice is illustrated, we think, by reactions to President Clinton's 1997 initiation of an agenda aimed at bettering race relations. Forming an advisory panel on race, Clinton hoped to steer the nation in a direction that would be more accepting of diversity. Yet many criticized his efforts, complaining that his agenda aspired to change public attitudes while lacking any substantive goals, such as enacting policies, allocating funds, or developing social programs for, say, housing, education, or jobs. Roger Wilkins, a professor of history at George Mason University, states, "I don't believe that exhortation—when you are dealing with the poorest people in this society and the historical forces that created their desperation—is going to do it" (Mitchell, 1997). President Clinton's efforts dissipated and his political agenda fell short. This happened because in order to promote a harmonious multiracial society, it is necessary both to recognize diversity with concrete proposals and to promote social action centered on socially reconstructing the system that unjustly disadvantages many of its citizens.

Globally, we are witnessing a similar inability to link violence with people's frustrations about equity and justice. For instance, in the Middle East, most U.S. citizens have little awareness of the United States' control of Iraqi oil. The British initially built British Petroleum (BP) on Iraqi oil prior to World War I, and the British created Iraq itself in 1921, even giving the country its name. British policies at the time were designed to keep Iraq weak and under British control. In 1919, Standard Oil (of the United States) became involved. By the 1920s, the United States was competing with the British for power over Iraq; it and Britain subsequently divided up control of Middle Eastern oil between themselves, the French, and the Dutch. From then onward, U.S. policies have been aimed toward controlling oil in that region. Everest (2004), who has documented this history, points out that the main reason the United States embarked on "regime change" in Iraq was not to bring freedom and democracy, but rather to oust a leader who refused to bow to U.S. dictates.

We offer this example because it contradicts what one commonly hears in the U.S. media but matches what one commonly hears outside the United States. If Iraqis are resisting the United States, is it because they hate freedom, as we are told here, or because they strongly resent being controlled by the United States? Rather than offering young people one position on these questions, we believe that it makes sense to help them unearth multiple positions, learn to evaluate and think through information from diverse perspectives, and then learn to take action on their own analysis rather than on analyses given to them.

Let us return to the hypothetical class of students with whom we opened the first chapter. How should they be taught? Before proceeding with business-as-usual techniques or with any of the approaches to multicultural education, the teacher should consider these students in relationship to the society in which they live today and will live as adults. As they grow up, what is in store for these students? Which approach to education might make a genuine difference?

Half of the students are girls, half are boys. If present trends continue, virtually all of them will attempt to join the labor force as adults. The girls may be only dimly aware of it, but most will wind up with two careers: child raising and housekeeping, as well as holding down a job, which will very likely pay at or near minimum wage. Many of the girls will be heads of households fighting to stay above the poverty line; the African American girls who find themselves as heads of households will have a better than 50–50 chance of living in poverty. Many of the boys, though economically better off, will find themselves psychologically alienated or living apart from their children, in some cases even feared by their children. Many will find themselves forced to make a decision about becoming involved in a gang and living up to the responsibility that gang membership entails. Many will find themselves trapped in jobs they dislike but must keep for the sake of their role as breadwinner. Some will become angry and resentful of their wives and beat them. Some of the girls will have babies at a young age and find themselves without a partner to share in the raising of the child. Some girls can look forward to being battered wives. Many of the students already know these things because their parents experience them. To try to adhere to the feminine image that is being sold to them, some of the girls are already beginning to starve themselves or surgically remake their bodies. Nevertheless, at this point, most of the students believe that adulthood holds a happy marriage with clearly divided responsibilities and a comfortable income (Sidel, 1988).

The first approach discussed in this book—Teaching the Exceptional and the Culturally Different—which is an improvement over business as usual, would address one of the current problems by equipping girls better to compete with boys in male-dominated areas, especially in fields requiring mathematics, science, and computers. This strategy will help some girls, maybe 1 or 2 out of 15. However, it does not address the dual career that most women must take on, which causes many not to consider entering full-time, demanding professions that conflict with domestic responsibilities. It also does not help homemakers to receive a full reward for their work. Nor does it address the low wages paid for jobs that women dominate. Moving women out of secretarial work into the sciences, for example, does nothing to raise the pay of secretaries; it only increases the competition for more lucrative jobs. Furthermore, it ignores backlash attempts to control women.

The second approach examined in this book—Human Relations—would help build better cross-sex understanding, which one hopes would lead to better communication and more respect between the sexes. Again, however, economic problems and role responsibilities would tend to remain intact, probably disrupting relationships among men and women. Although this approach fosters attempts to get along, it does not develop discussion and action on economic and political inequalities that often lead to not getting along.

Women's studies (part of the third approach discussed, that of Single-Group Studies) would help students examine sexism and mobilize them (mainly the girls) to challenge it. Although this approach has greater potential than the approaches previously discussed (and certainly greater potential than business as usual) for preparing students to recognize and struggle against institutional sexism, it is limited. Women's studies focuses on a single form of human diversity and does not necessarily attend to issues such as poverty (which is also a very important problem) or racism (which the girls of color will face). It also often excludes men, unintentionally presenting sexism as a problem only for women.

The fourth approach examined in this book—Multicultural Education—would address sexism by promoting nonsexist role and job choice and by giving as much attention to the female experience as to the male experience in the curriculum. It would also include the experiences of women of color as well as those of White women, the experiences of poor women as well as those of middle-class women. It would attempt to eliminate a sexist division of labor in the home and encourage the young to choose careers without reference to masculine versus feminine roles. Still, this approach has limitations—the biggest one being that it does not prepare students to take steps to change the rules of the game that incorporate sexism into society. We will illustrate this point with three structures that help perpetuate sexism.

First, many careers, particularly those with the greatest pay, do not lend themselves well to maintaining an active role in parenting. The very existence of careers that greatly reduce available hours for parenting is one structure that helps maintain sexism because such careers automatically exclude their holders from active parenting and because women are assumed to have primary responsibility for childcare. Men greatly outnumber women in such careers, and their wives end up with most of the parenting responsibility.

A second structural rule of the game that reinforces sexism is the nuclear family in which the woman's primary role is child caretaker and the man's is breadwinner. Even if young people start married life believing they will share roles, later they often divide roles by sex as the result of a lack of alternatives. For example, when children are young, either one parent stays home part of the day or the family pays for day care, which can cost as much as or more than many women make at work. Thus, the woman usually stays home. The extended family, familiar to many people of color, can provide more alternatives because more adults are in the home who can share roles, lessening the need to shift all of the domestic work to one adult. Although the extended family is growing in popularity, the nuclear family is offered as the norm and is legitimated in the structure of houses and in the tax structure. To encourage and support greater role flexibility as well as foster attitudes that support role sharing, one would want to legitimate the extended family as well as the nuclear family.

A third structural problem is the institution of domestic help. Many career-oriented people who can afford it hire domestic help to do the jobs for which the husband and wife do not have time, or they make use of services such as day care. In and of themselves, these are viable options, but these jobs pay very poorly and are usually filled by women, often women of color. Furthermore, jobs such as "cleaning lady" rarely provide benefits such as health insurance or retirement pay. These are more rules of the game that society accepts and plays by that continue to trap many women.

The approach discussed last—Multicultural Social Justice Education—would help students examine these sorts of issues and begin to think about what they believe needs to be challenged or reworked. In so doing, the approach offers several advantages. First, it speaks to issues that currently impact on many of the students and eventually will impact on all of them. For example, students who may see little relevance in studying economics see considerable relevance when economics is used to help them understand changes in the availability of jobs locally or the reduced availability of government loans for college. Second, it encourages students to take an active stance—to take charge of their lives. It helps them connect what they are doing now with their future lives as adults but in a way that does not fit them into the status quo with all its problems; rather, it teaches them to challenge the status quo. Finally, this approach helps them learn to work collectively to speak out, be heard, and effect change, if that is what they wish to do. Furthermore, unlike Single-Group Studies, this approach attempts to join the White girls with the girls and boys of color and the middle-class students with those of the lower class as they examine common or related concerns.

Four of the students in our hypothetical class are Latino. If present trends continue, and especially if schools continue with business as usual, one and possibly two of the four will not graduate from high school. They will leave mainly to help take care of their families but also because many will experience alienation in school. Culturally, the school will connect only partially with their own life experience, and most, if not all, of the teachers and authority figures will be White. As teenagers, all four may have to look for jobs, but at least one will not find a job. Unable to find a job and alienated from school, one of these students may choose to join a gang because gangs can offer a source of identity, an underground economy, a source of income, and a means of controlling something, even if it is only a city block. As adults, the family income of these four Latino students will average only about 75% of the family income of their White peers. One of the students will probably live in poverty, and the other three will live in the lower middle class. All four will continually feel caught in a cultural tug of war that will probably intensify. As the Latino population has become the largest American racial/ethnic minority group, Mexican culture is gaining a firmer foothold. Anglos will probably continue to respond by asserting the primacy of English and the legitimacy of Anglo-American culture. Almost 7 million American students speak Spanish at home (Pearson Education, 2005), and language policy will increasingly be a source of tension. The Latino students will feel, for example, somewhat alienated from mainstream media, which render Latinos almost invisible except in advertisements for Mexican food or gang characters in movies. Lack of representation will be a problem in many other areas as well, although Latinos are experiencing some gains in political decision making. Moreover, the Latino students as adults may find themselves competing with their African American former classmates or with recent immigrants for control over elective inner-city offices.

Teaching the Culturally Different deals with these issues mainly by trying to get Latinos through school, helping them to learn English, and preparing them to compete for jobs. These steps are all highly important, but they are also limited. This approach does not deal with the cultural tug of war, except by acknowledging that it is okay to be Latino as long as one can also function effectively in an Anglo world. It ignores racism entirely; in fact, it denies it. The Human Relations approach helps all the students learn not to stereotype Latinos, and it develops more positive attitudes about Latino culture. However, it does not deal with poverty and political powerlessness; it only teaches that these problems will be resolved if people communicate better and appreciate each other more.

Chicano studies and Puerto Rican studies would offer Latino students a chance to develop group solidarity with other Latinos. It would provide a source of identification with school and a counter to cultural alienation because Chicano studies and Puerto Rican studies embrace Latino culture and concerns and offer a forum for examining the life circumstances and needs of Latinos. However, the

Single-Group Studies approach could subordinate and ignore Latino women, would not encourage Latinos to work with other oppressed groups, and might even aggravate cross-group conflict. Furthermore, the concerns of the many Latinos who are not Chicano or Puerto Rican might be completely ignored.

The Multicultural Education approach would make Latino cultures and concerns an integral part of the curriculum, along with the cultures and concerns of other groups. It would help Latino students succeed in school by building on their learning styles and experiential backgrounds. It would offer all the students role models of successful Latino men and women and would encourage bilingualism as a norm. A good Multicultural Education curriculum would accurately represent the diversity among Latino groups. However, it would not offer a plan for attacking poverty and unemployment, nor would it necessarily help build the political skills and group solidarity that Latinos need.

Multicultural Social Justice Education offers a more direct response to these concerns in addition to other benefits of the Multicultural Education approach. For example, Latinos have a pressing need to improve representation in decision-making roles at many institutions. Although Latinos are developing more political clout at the local level in areas where the Latino population is large, they are still virtually powerless in most states and at the national level. Two issues directly affecting Latinos are periodically debated and voted on at the national level: language policy and immigration policy. As the Latino population in the United States grows, as the Mexican economy continues to suffer, and as Central America continues to be a hotbed of political unrest, these two issues will probably take on greater urgency. The Free Trade Agreement with Mexico, for example, can be viewed as an Anglo attempt to divide Third World people from Americans of Mexican decent in a competition over jobs. As Anner (1991) put it, "The worst irony is that, economically speaking, low-income workers in the U.S. will be pitted against their counterparts in Mexico in competition for the same jobs" (p. 4). The approach we discussed last does not teach a certain stance on these issues so much as it encourages young people, including (and in this case especially) Latinos, to learn how to research the issues, to mobilize, to articulate a stand, to gain access to the media, to use the legal system, and to perform other activities.

A final example relates to the issue of unemployment. It is not enough to equip people better to compete for jobs when there are not enough jobs to go around and when existing jobs are not amply available in minority neighborhoods. Youth of color should learn to seek jobs more effectively, to interview skillfully, to complete school, and to perform other job-search activities. However, future citizens should also begin to examine the job structure itself and consider improvements. For example, students could research the availability of jobs in African American, Latino, and White neighborhoods, and on Indian reservations. They could find out why businesses tend not to locate in lower-class neighborhoods, and they could study ways of attracting business. Students could find out how to assess hiring discrimination and how to fight it effectively. The students could analyze wage structure in relationship to the cost of living in order to understand the extent to which local employers tacitly support near-poverty existence by keeping wages low, and then they could find out how to change this situation.

It may appear that we are writing a social studies curriculum, but we are not. The topics we have suggested lend themselves to reading (one can learn reading skills by reading about virtually any topic), writing, mathematics skills, science methods and some science topics, art, and music (here we are referring to the content of song lyrics), as well as social studies.

We could continue with examples from the hypothetical class, but we suspect that our point has been made. However, there is one group whose presence and probable discomfort we would like to acknowledge: that of White, middle-class or upper-class males. This group would be comprised of about eight members of our hypothetical class and a sizable portion of the readers of this book. We could catalog the problems members of this group will face after schooling—indeed, there are problems. Over the last couple of decades, as jobs have been outsourced, many members of this group have found themselves and their families downwardly mobile. Yet, the group composed of White, heterosexual, middle-class males will tend to have greater access to resources and more power than any other group.

How does the Multicultural Social Justice Education approach regard White, middle- or upper-class males? It regards the group mainly as a necessary potential ally. There are and always have been White males who have joined the struggle against oppression and who have worked with (rather than dominated) members of subordinate groups. Their presence and help are necessary partly because of, rather than in spite of, their membership in dominant race, class, and gender groups. At the classroom level, White male students are often willing to join with others as long as they feel valued and a genuine ethos of cooperation is fostered. As they become adults, they will be offered advantages not available to their classmates; they will need to decide whether to use their privileged status for their own benefit or for the benefit of others.

Before concluding, we issue a caution to enthusiastic readers. In our experience, readers often declare that they agree with us that Multicultural Social Justice Education is the best—without having thought through the issues for themselves. If this is your first attempt to grapple with social justice and multicultural issues, recognize that you have taken the first step in a long process of learning. These are very complex issues. Often those who agree with us on our choice of approaches do so at a rhetorical level only: They adopt our words, but they have yet to think through the implications of these words for living and teaching. Learning any of the approaches well means learning to teach differently—and in most cases very differently—from business as usual.

Which approach is the best one is a value decision that the individual educator must make. This book has outlined the goals, assumptions, underlying values, and practices of five ways of approaching diversity in the classroom. One cannot choose not to choose because to accept the status quo is also to make a choice. We hope that this book helps the educator in making a decision that is best for him or her.

REFERENCES

Anner, J. (1991, Summer). Trading away labor rights. *The Minority Trendsletter, 4,* 3–5, 14–15.

Everest, L. (2004). *Oil, power and empire.* Monroe, ME: Common Courage Press.

Mitchell, A. (1997, June 16). Clinton feels sure-footed on the tightrope of race. *The New York Times,* p. A12.

Pearson Education. (2005). Education facts at a glance. Fact monster. Retrieved May 27, 2005 from http://www.factmonster.com/spot/schoolfacts1.html.

Sidel, R. (1988). *On her own: Growing up in the shadow of the American dream.* New York: Penguin.

Name Index

Subject Index

Note: Page numbers followed by f indicate figures; those followed by t indicate tables.